MONSTERS IN PRINT

A Collection of Curious Creatures
Known Mostly from Newspapers.

Researched and Compiled by

Adam Benedict

ISBN: 9781691242535

Imprint: Independently published

Written in Janesville, WI - 2019

Front and back cover design by Adam Benedict.

Printed by Amazon.com, Inc. in the United States of America.

First Printing: September 2019.

Researcher website: www.pinebarrensinstitute.com

Note: All newspapers published within the United States of America prior
to 1924 are part of the public domain in their entirety. Papers published
between 1924 and 1977 without a copyright notice are considered part of
the public domain due to failure to comply with required formalities.

All stories within this book were found via research through the digital
newspaper archive maintained by The Library of Congress. It is assumed
by the L.O.C. that all newspapers within its archives are within the public
domain and have no known copyright restrictions.

For more information as to the above statement, please refer to:
chroniclingamerica.loc.gov

FOR MY WIFE.
The one who's making sure four real monsters grow into four decent humans.

"What would an ocean be without a monster lurking in the dark? It would be like sleep without dreams."
— **Werner Herzog**

Table of contents

Preface

Over the course of many months during 2019, I took on the personal project of gathering a unique collection of obscure and often overlooked monster stories in which to share with the masses. Many of these stories, which were written and presented as fact well over two centuries ago, were collected from the historical newspaper archive maintained by both *The Library of Congress* and the *National Endowment for the Humanities*. These stories cover everything from the widely known Sea Serpents and Wild Men, to the somewhat lesser-known Giant Eagles, Phantom Animals, and Mermen. There are even a few stories which feature truly bizarre "creatures" that are unable to be categorized or accurately described at all. The writing styles of these select stories range from the truthful and informative, to the doubtful and condescending; while some can be described as humorous and lighthearted, others come across as warnings of danger to all readers and nearby citizens.

While working on this project, I gave myself two personal main goals. These acted as a sort of unofficial guideline that helped the overall project continue forward. One of the main goals was to present all found articles in their pure form; this means unedited and unfiltered. To meet this goal, it meant that all spelling, grammatical, and formatting errors had to be knowingly left within the stories and kept true to their original printing. This was done specifically to present these articles to you, the reader, as they would have been presented and seen on their original publishing date. While some may question this choice, I personally feel it preserves the history and time period in which the story falls within. As you progress through each year of stories, you begin to see the writing styles change, the odd-looking spellings begin to evolve into what we are more used to seeing today, and specific word choices no longer get used to describe specific people, locations, or cultures.

Now, that last sentence above may come across as a bit of a shock to some readers; yes, there are certain words or phrases within some of these stories that some may personally find disrespectful and/or not politically correct by today's standards. Again, these were left in by choice in order to present the stories in their pure unedited form, but I must say, this was not an easy choice to make. There were a few instances where the decision to edit a story was highly considered, but that decision was ultimately scrapped after realizing once you edit a piece of history to fit modern social guidelines, then the ability to truly learn from that history becomes non-existent. While I do not condone some of the descriptive terms and word choices used by a few of the original authors within this book, I also do not condemn them for being products of their times (remember, some are from nearly 200 years ago). While they, and most of the country at the time, didn't know any better, we as a society today currently do. Remember, we can only continue to get better if we actively recognize the issues from our history, but instead of altering them to better suit us now, we learn from them to better influence the future moving forward.

The second goal I had for this project was to present these stories without any trace of spin or bias. You see, a large majority of books of this nature are typically released with an underlying tone which attempts to sway the reader into believing the author's personal opinions on the presented subject matter. While that may work for some people, it does not work for me. I am rooted firmly in the camp that people should always be given just the facts, and from there they can decide for themselves what to believe. It is because of this personal belief that you will find no short summaries following each story in which I attempt to explain what may or may not have been seen. There are no sections where I try to link these past occurrences with modern-day Fortean events. There are zero instances in this book where I make any attempt to get you to think a certain way or believe a specific thing. What you are getting here is exactly what you would have gotten if you were to have read these stories the day of their release. You are getting just the facts. Nothing more, nothing less.

Finally, one last thing before you start your read, I would like to personally say thank you. By deciding to pick up this book and read these stories, you are helping to support a resurgence within the modern-day cryptozoological/paranormal/Fortean fields. So, whether you truly believe in monsters, or you just like to keep an open mind, your support is greatly appreciated. And if this book just so happens to open the door for wanting more monsters in your world, well, to that I say, welcome to the club.

Adam Benedict
August 2019

Introduction

Monsters. What is it about strange and unusual monsters that fascinate us so much? They've never really been proven to exist, and the "real" ones that were once considered "terrible" and "horrific" have long since been added to the scientific catalog and given proper names, studied extensively and documented to the fullest. But it seems that as soon as one monster goes the way of the dodo, another one shows up to take its place. Why is that? Why do we as a modern and advanced people, a collective group that has mastered space travel, split the atom, and completely eradicated once terrible diseases through the wonders of science, still feel the need to search for unbelievable and legendary monsters? Well, I can tell you why, it's because they're cool.

You might have been expecting some deep, in-depth answer to the question with supporting cultural evidence, statistics, and all that other jazz. Well, sorry to have to break it to you, but that's not how I do things. I like honesty, facts, and telling it how it is. And I am telling you right here and now, that monsters of myth and legend are just plain cool. If people didn't think they were, they wouldn't have been the subjects of countless legends since humans first learned to talk. They wouldn't have been both heroes and villains in numerous stories strewn across multiple continents for thousands of years. And they wouldn't have managed to get top billing in both classic and modern-day shows and films.

Seriously, who doesn't love a good monster movie? We all love them in some way. Sure, you can call them low brow entertainment if you wish, hell, you can even call them B-grade if you want to give them a better sounding title, it doesn't really matter. You can call them whatever you want, but if I were to ask you right now what/who your favorite movie monster was, I bet you wouldn't have a problem answering. You could probably even give a top-five ranking without much thought if you truly felt like it! And you know what else? I bet you would rank them based upon how cool they were overall. Know how I know? Because that's how nearly everyone ranks their favorite monsters.

It makes no difference if we are seeing them on a screen, reading about them in a book, or hearing stories about them while sitting around a campfire, monsters are something we as a people seem to need in our lives in one way or another. It doesn't matter how far we have come as a species either, we are still compelled to search for them in our own ways. These searches could lead us between dusty old library stacks, deep within pages of obscure websites, or physically out into the world in search of their supposed haunts. The creatures themselves can even be seen as representations of the dangers we had gotten away from so long ago, yet still quietly desire in order to liven up our daily routines. The embodiments of fear, comedy, tragedy, and adventure all rolled into one. The symbols of the childhoods we never truly grew out of and the fantasies we refuse to stop daydreaming about.

They can represent many things to many different people, and there is nothing wrong with any of those representations. Monsters are whatever you want them to be and it doesn't matter if they are scientifically considered real or not. There is no rule that says you must believe monsters actually exist to believe in them. Just like there is no rule says you must view them as nothing but fantasy. Remember, monsters don't have to follow the rules, because they're monsters.

So, whether your favorite monsters are feathered, hairy or slimy; whether they come from the depths of the ocean or from deep within the forests, remember this one simple thing: Your monsters are cool, and they know it.

Everything you are about to read is real.
Real in the sense that it was really written, but still unknown if
what was written, really happened that way for real.

The decision to believe is yours.

STORIES FROM THE:

1820's

THE SEA SERPENT.

Alexandria Gazette & Daily Advertiser – January 3, 1820 – Virginia

The Gazette de France contains an extract of a letter from a Dutch Merchant, who recently went to America, giving some account of the famous Sea-Serpent which has appeared on the shores of the United States. He says –

"We were sailing with a light wind, the land being about six miles distant, when all at once we felt a shock which made us think we had struck upon a rock. We, however, were soon undeceived by seeing above the waves, the head of the greatest monster I ever beheld. He raised himself about fifteen feet over the surface of the water, and coming towards us, he glided across the stern of the vessel in such a manner as almost to upset us. A cabin boy who was near the bowsprit, was overwhelmed by the enormous mass. A sailor then advanced courageously and fired at the Serpent with a carbine, but the ball rebounded from his scales, and appeared not to make the least impression upon him. The animal turning quickly, seized the sailor round the middle, and plunged with him under water. Our tackle was broken, and our bowsprit almost unshipped. While we were occupied in repairing the damage we had sustained, we again saw the monster lying on the surface of the water, but we saw our unfortunate sailor no more."

SEA MONSTER.

The Monticello Gazette – June 28, 1823 – Mississippi

The Douglass sailed from this port on the 2d of April, and on the 6th, at 3 P.M. lat. 35 W long, 58 40, discovered as they supposed, a vessel bottom upwards, three points on the weather bow. The Douglass braced sharp, and came within forty feet of her, or rather of a Sea Serpent, or a sea monster of some sort.

The height out of water was about 10 or 12 feet; length 25 to 30 feet; breadth 12 feet with flippers like a turtle on each side, one third of the way from the tail. Length of the flippers from 12 to 15 feet, one on each side near the tail, 5 or 6 feet in length, with a tail from 20 to 25 feet long. The head appeared doubled round by the tail, and the monster had a huge lions face with large and terrible saucer eyes. – At least 30 or 40 rods distance, the shell of the monster looked like a clinkerbuilt vessel, of 25 to 30 tons, bottom upwards – the seams or laps newly paid. There were large barnacles on the body, and his velocity was about 1 1-2 mile per hour. The last the Douglass saw of this Son of Neptune, he was apparently bearing away for Bermuda.

– N.P. Spec.

A MONSTER OF THE DEEP.

Phenix Gazette – October 22, 1827 – Virginia

Frederic Chase, who tends the light on Gull Island, gave us, a day or two since, the following brief but very extraordinary description of a sea monster which he saw a few days before, near the Island on which he resides. He and another person, Mr. Edward Conklin, were in a small boat in the Sound, a short distance from land, when they suddenly discovered, within a few yards of the boat, a monster of very uncommon size and appearance. Its head was raised at least five feet above the water, was as large, and much resembled in shape, the one half of a hogshead when cut directly in two longitudinally, the protuberant part being upwards. Its body, he judged, was 15 or 16 feet in width, across the back; and he could plainly see about 30 feet in length of the body, which was, however, farther below the surface of the water as the distance increased from the head, so that he could not see the extreme part, but thinks it must have been of much greater length, as the body, so far as he could see it, appeared to be of about the same width. The colour of its body was black, and its head brown. He could distinctly see the eyes of this monster, as its head was within a few feet of the boat and remained above water two or three minutes. Its motion was neither slow nor very rapid, but seemed to stem a pretty strong current which was setting at that time.

Mr. Chase is a man of veracity, and his testimony may be relied on.

– Sag Harbour Eagle.

STORIES FROM THE:

1830's

THE SEA SERPENT AT TOWNSEND HARBOR.

Phenix Gazette – July 2, 1830 – Virginia

From the Portland Courier, June 28

We are informed, from unquestionable authority, that one of these monsters of the deep, [for they are seen so often, there must probably be more than one.] about a week since, paid a social visit at Boothbay harbor. He passed the afternoon rather lazily in the neighborhood of Burnt Island on which the light house stands, sometimes approaching within two or three rods of the shore, and anon booming off straight as a mill-log, and then turning, cutting a circle through the water as broad and graceful as that of a seventy-four. He was distinctly seen by Mr. Chandler, who keeps the light house, and his family, and several other persons. He did not raise himself much out of the water, though Mr. Chandler judged that the part which he saw of him at one time was a hundred feet in length. He is described as having the usual appearance of "bunches" or undulations upon his back, which all of his family are represented to have. From some of his sudden & quick movements it appeared as though his excellency was now and then nabbing a fish.

A row-boat which was coming to the island, loaded with potatoes, approached rather near him; and whether his snakeship smelt the potatoes, and thought he should like a mess to go with his fish, is not known, but from some cause or other he turned himself very leisurely towards the boat. And the boatmen, with a courage like that of Putnam's men at the battle of Bunker Hill, let the enemy approach so near they might have seen the white of his eyes, if he had only lifted his head out of water, and then they began to pelt him with potatoes. The Mogul of the waters, however, paid no more attention to them than if they had been but a few light drops of rain. He appeared to be on the whole very peaceable; quarreled with no body about politics; and so far from electioneering, he did not even give any indication whether he was a Huntonite or a Smithite. In short no rational account of the object of his visit could be assigned, unless he might be an agent of the general government sent along the coast to see that the light houses were kept in good order and properly lighted.

A NORTH AMERICAN MONSTER.

Burlington Free Press – May 31, 1839 – Vermont

In a file of the "New York Mercury," published in 1761, we find the following advertisement of a monster, the like of which we have never heard or read of. It beats all modern monstrosities, animal or human. The advertisement reads as follows:

"Whereas a surprising Monster was caught in the woods of Canada, near the River St. Lawrence, and has with great difficulty been tamed and brought to the House of James Elliott at Corlaer's Hook. This is to inform the Public, that it will be exhibited at the said house till the curious are satisfied.

"This Monster is larger than an elephant, of a very uncommon shape, having three heads, eight legs, three fundaments. It is of various colors, very beautiful, and makes a noise like the conjunction of two or three voices. It is held unlawful to kill it, and is said to live to a great age. The Canadians could not give it a name, till a very old Indian said he remembered to have seen one when he was a boy, and his father called it a Gormagent."

A subsequent advertisement states that this monster was removed to Jamaica, L.I. for exhibition at "Mr. Coom's."

STORIES FROM THE:
1840's

WILD MAN OF THE WOODS.

Salt River Journal – February 15, 1840 – Missouri

From the Boston Times.

Robert Lincoln, Esq., agent of the New York Lumber Company, has just returned from St. Peter's river, near the head of Steamboat navigation, on the Upper Mississippi, bringing with him a living wild Man of the Woods, with two small cubs, supposed to be three months old.

Mr. Lincoln went out to the North West as agent of the New York Lumber Company in July last, with a view to establish mills on the pine lands near the Falls of St. Anthony; & he has given us a detail of the operations of the company, and the circumstances which led to the capture of the extraordinary creature mentioned above.

The company set out on their expedition in July last. The workmen and laborers with the principal of the machinery went by the way of New Orleans, and at that city they chartered a steamboat and proceeded up the Mississippi. The whole business was under the direction of Mr. Lincoln. They had on board all the necessary tools and saws, together with the apparatus for a gristmill horses, cows, a good stock of provisions, arms, ammunition, &c. &c. – These passed directly up the river, & reached St. Peters in safety.

During the winter, Mr. Lincoln, and several of his workmen made frequent excursions, in pursuit of game, which was very abundant, and their camp one continued scene of festivity. The Indians brought in large quantities of furs, which Mr. Lincoln purchased for a mere trifle, and lined his cabin throughout, which rendered his rude hut very warm and comfortable.

About the fourth of January, two or three of the carpenters who had been out in pursuit of a gang of wolves, that had proved very troublesome, came into the camp and reported that they had seen a huge monster in the forest, on a branch of the Mississippi, having the form of a man but much taller and stouter, covered with long hair and of a frightful aspect. They stated that when seen he was on a log, looking directly at them, and the moment they raised their muskets, he darted into the thicket and disappeared. They saw him again in about half an hour, apparently watching them, and when they turned towards him, he again disappeared. Mr. Lincoln was first disposed to think lightly of the matter, believing that the men might be mistaken about the size and height of the object, or supposing it might have been a trick of the Indians to frighten them. He was informed however by some of the natives that such beings had often been seen on the St. Peters, and near the falls on the Mississippi; and they proposed to guide a party of workmen to a bluff where it was thought they might be found. – The men were all ready for the adventure, & arming themselves with rifles & hunting knives, they started in pursuit under the direction of Mr. Lincoln and the Indian guides. On the way they were joined by several of the natives, and the whole party numbered twenty-three.

They arrived at the bluff in the afternoon, on the 21st day of January, and encamped in a cave or grotto at the foot of the hill. – Early next morning, two of the Indians who were sent out to reconnoiter, in about an hour returned, and said that they had seen the Wild Man on the other side of the hill. The whole party immediately prepared for the pursuit. Mr. Lincoln gave positive orders to the men not to fire on him unless it should be necessary in self defense as he wished to take him alive. The Indians stated that although a powerful creature, he was believed to be perfectly harmless as he always fled at the approach of man. – While Mr. Lincoln was giving his men their instructions the Wild Man appeared in sight. He ordered them to remain perfectly quiet, and taking out his pocket glass surveyed him minutely. He appeared to be eight or nine feet high, very athletic and more like a beast standing erect than a man. The Indians had provided themselves with ropes prepared to catch wild horses, with which they hoped to ensnare and bind the creature, without maiming him.

The instant the company moved towards him, he sprang forward with a horrid and frightful yell which made the forest ring. – The Indians followed close upon him, and Lincoln and his men brought up the rear. The pursuit was continued nearly an hour, now gaining upon the object of their chase, and now losing sight of him. He finally darted into a thicket, and they were unable to find him.

They then began to retrace their steps towards the place of encampment, and when within about a mile of the cavern the Wild Man crossed their path within twenty rods. They immediately gave chase again and accidentally drove the creature from the forest to an open prairie. At length he suddenly stopped and turned upon his pursuers. Mr. Lincoln was then in the advance. Fearing that he might attack them or return to the woods and escape, he fired upon him and lodged a charge of buck shot in the calf of his leg. He fell immediately, and the Indians sprang forward and threw their ropes over his head, arms and legs, and with much effort succeeded in binding him fast. He struggled however most desperately gnashed his teeth and howled in a frightful manner. They then formed a sort of litter of branches and limbs of threes and placing him on it they carried him to the encampment. A watch was then placed over him and every effort made that could be devised to keep him quiet but the continued to howl piteously all night. Towards morning two small cubs about three feet high and very similar to the larger monster came into the camp, & were taken without resistance.

As soon as the monster saw them he became furious – gnashing his teeth and howled, and thrashed about until he burst his cord and came very near effecting his escape. But he was bound anew and after that was kept more carefully watched and guarded. Next day he was placed on his litter and carried down to the mills on the St. Peters.

For two or three days Mr. Lincoln says he refused to eat or drink, or take any kind of food, but continued to howl at intervals an hour at a time; at length however he began to eat but from that time his howl ceased and he remained sullen and stupid ever since. The cubs took food very rapidly, and became quiet and playful.

Mr. Lincoln is a native of Boston and some of the workmen engaged in his mills are from this city. He arrived here on Sunday afternoon in the Brig St. Charles, Stewart, master from New Orleans; with the Wild Man and two cubs, and they were all removed from the vessel that evening. By an invitation of Lincoln, who is an old acquaintance, we went down to his rooms to examine the monster. He is a horrid looking creature, and reminds us very strongly of the fabled satyrs as we have pictured them to our own mind. He is about eight feet three inches high when standing erect, & his frame is of a giant proportion in every part. His legs are not straight but like those of any other four footed animal and his whole body is covered with a hide very much like that of the cow.

His arms are very large and long and ill proportioned. It does not appear from his manner that he ever walked on all fours. − The fingers and toes are mere branches armed with stout claws. His head is covered with thick coarse black hair, like the main of a horse. The appearance of his countenance, if such it may be called, is very disgusting − nay, almost horrible. It is covered with a thinner and lighter coat than the rest of the body − there is no appearance of eyebrows or nose, the mouth is very large and wide, & similar to that of the baboon. His eyes are quite dull and heavy and there is no indication of cunning or activity about them. Mr. Lincoln says he is beyond doubt carnivorous, as he universally rejects bread and vegetables and eats flesh with great avidity. He thinks he is of the ourang outang species; but from what we have seen, we are inclined to consider him a wild animal somewhat resembling a man. He is, to say the least one of the most extraordinary creatures ever brought before the public from any part of the earth, or water under the earth, and we believe will prove a difficult puzzle to the scientific. He lies down like a brute and does not appear to possess more instinct than common domestic animals. He is now quite tame and quiet, and is confined with a stout chain attached to his legs.

It is Mr. Lincoln's intention to submit these animals to the inspection of the scientific for a few days in order to ascertain what they are; and after that to dispose of them to some person for exhibition. Mr. Lincoln himself, will return to the St. Peters in the course of three weeks.

A MOST SINGULAR SEA SERPENT.

Jeffersonian Republican – May 1, 1845 – Pennsylvania

The following description of an anomalous Sea Monster is received from an old resident at Cape Island, Cape May. The writer is a man of the most undoubted veracity, and his account is worthy of implicit credence.

Extract of a letter from a resident at Cape May, to a gentleman in this city.

Cape May, April 13, 1845

Respected Friend: - In consequence of the many events, not of an every character, that have occurred here since the 1st of March, I have taken the liberty of writing you, knowing that in one you would take an interest, inasmuch as it is to us a great curiosity. Indeed it is so much so, that at any time, when the object is in sight, you may see twenty or thirty persons at a time watching its maneuvers, and almost every one differs in opinion respecting this monster of the deep. What it is I do not pretend to say, but that it is not a whale I am quite certain. I will give you the best description of it that I am able, and you can draw your own conclusions. It appears to be about sixty or seventy feet long and not more than eight feet wide at the widest part, which is about one third of the way from the head; from this point it gradually tapers to the tail. It cannot be very thick, as we had an opportunity of viewing it yesterday, as it lay, apparently lifeless, on the top of the water in not more than ten feet of water for fifteen minutes at a time; it would then sink out of sight, then come up again in the same place and blow, but its blowing is not like the blowing of a whale, since the jet of water appears to proceed from very near the widest part of it. After blowing, it will rear its head on high, (say at least 6 feet) look around, and then lay quietly down. The water caused by the blowing does not rise higher than ten feet, and the column is not larger than your cane, (3 to 4 feet) and does not keep in a body, but flies about in every direction. After it (the animal) has gone one half the height to which it raises, the head is about as large as a hogs head, and appears to be flat on the top, as some say who have been along side of him, a hooked beak, like a loggerhead turtle.

The person who gave me this information respecting the appearance of the head is a man whom I can depend upon; the animal passed within ten feet from him whilst he lay to an anchor in one of the pilot boats, and he thus had a fair opportunity of seeing him. The monster is perfectly black and is covered with a kind of black muscle or barnacle. As regards its movements I find it difficult to convey an idea of them to you – sometimes its appears to have fins, or flappers along his sides, which make a great foam and wake in the water – at another time he will appear to be rigged out with one of the most powerful propellers, after the fashion of the Princeton, and he goes faster than any steamboat, but does not make any wake – again he will go tumbling along like an old bay porpoise. His favorite resort appears to be from Cold Spring Inlet to around in the Bay, say two or three miles above the steamboat landing, and almost always so near the shore that you can see him without the aid of a spy glass; at times, when it is smooth, he is observed to be just outside of the breakers.

It was first seen on the 18th of March by a great many persons at once; these spectators were principally strangers, twenty-five of whom were down here at work at McMakin's house. It is not seen every day – sometimes it will not be seen for three or four days at a time.

We have made up our minds to take him at every hazard – we have four good whale boats and every thing which may be requisite for the enterprise, except that we are still wanting the proper number of men necessary for the undertaking.

Yours, &c.

P.S. – If you could only see our rig to catch this strange bird, you would have a hearty laugh. I am furnished with a search warrant in the shape of a harpoon.

– Philad. Morning Post.

STORIES FROM THE:
1850's

THE WILD WOMAN OF THE NAVIDAD.

The Athens Post – February 22, 1850 – Tennessee

About a year since an account was published in the Victoria Advocate respecting a strange creature, whose tracks had been discovered on the banks of the Navidad, near Texana. The foot marks of this creature resembled those of a woman and a report was circulated to the effect that a wild-woman had made her retreat in the forest of the Navidad. Within a few weeks several attempts have been made to capture this singular being. Mr. Glascock pursued it for several days with dogs, and at one time approached so near it as to cast a lasso upon its shoulders. It however, with great adroitness eluded the snare, and fled to a dense thicket, where it could not be traced. Mr. Glascock states that he was near a small prairie enclosed by the border forests of the river, when the creature emerged from the woods, and ran across the prairie in full view. It was about five feet high, resembling a human being, but covered with hair of a reddish brown color. In its hand it held a stick about six feet long, which it flourished from side to side, as if to regulate its motions, and aid it when running at full speed. Its head and neck are covered with very long hair, which streamed backward in the wind. It ran with the speed of a deer, and was soon out of sight. The dogs pursued it, and came so close upon it at a small creek, that it was compelled to drop its stick, which was taken by its pursuers.

This stick is about six feet long, straight and smooth as if polished with glass. Several other persons have repeatedly seen the creature, and they all concur in representing it as a human being, but so covered with shaggy hair as to resemble an ourang outang. It has frequently approached the houses of the settlers in that neighborhood during the night, and stole various articles – among other things it carried off a quantity of towels, one or two books, and has also taken several pigs. One of its nests were found in the forest, in which were several napkins, folded up just as they were taken from the house, and a Bible marked J.J. Wright. A bill for washing also enclosed in the Bible. The foot-marks of this strange being have been traced to the bottom of the Navidad, but it has eluded all attempts to capture it. The old settlers in that section say that these foot-marks have been noticed for ten or twelve years, and that several years ago there were other foot-marks, indicating that three of these creatures were in company. Within the last year the foot-marks of only one have been noticed.

Mr. Glascock intends to collect a pack of good hounds and resume the pursuit, and he is confident that he will succeed in capturing it. He has incurred considerable expense, and has exposed to great hardships and danger to secure it, thus evincing his full belief in the identity of this mysterious being. It is not improbable that during the war of Revolution when the people of that section were driven from their homes by the victorious army of Urrea, some children might have been secreted in the woods or left there, and their relations never returning, have become like the wild beasts, clothed with hair, and feeding upon herbs and such small animals as they can capture or pilfer from settlers.

– Houston (Texas) Telegraph.

THE MONSTER SNAKE TAKEN.

Carroll Free Press – August 30, 1855 – Ohio

Correspondence of the Buffalo Daily Republic
Perry Village, N.Y., Aug. 13, 1855.

This part of the country is wild with excitement. The immense snake, with various descriptions of which the papers have been crowded for two weeks back, is at length captured. You have undoubtedly heard all the particulars of his appearance, the many doubts and sneers as to the existence of a 'lusus naturae' of this character in a lake but four miles long and not quite three-quarters of a mile in width. At any rate it has been doubted. Daniel Smith, an old whaleman, came here about two weeks since, after hearing of the appearance of the creature, and while here had the good fortune to see him. He immediately sent to New York for an old shipmate of his and his 'irons,' and on Friday last both arrived with harpoons, cordage and everything necessary to catch a monster. Many strangers who are stopping at the Walker House in this city, attracted to this part of the country by the excitement in regard to the monster, and who had obtained no glimpse of him, laughed at them for their pains; but they kept on with their preparations in spite of the sneers and jeers. Boats have been stationed all over the lake for upward of eight days, and the two whalemen had a sharp lookout kept all the time beside watching themselves.

This lake has several outlets, the largest of which runs through the village and finally empties or becomes Genesee River. In the vicinity of this outlet he was seen first, and on Sunday he came to the surface, displaying about 30 feet of his long, sinuous body, remaining, however, but a very few moments. The boats were on watch all Sunday night. The whalemen had 1,200 feet of strong whaleline in their boat, the end of which run ashore and fastened to a tree. On Monday morning everything was on the alert. The shores were lined with town's people and strangers, and everybody seemed very much excited.

About 9 o'clock the animal made his appearance between the whalemen's boat and shore, revealing twenty or thirty feet of his length. He lay quiescent upon the surface, when the whalemen's boat moved slowly toward him – Mr. Smith of Covington poising a Lilly-iron in the air, (a Lilly-iron is a patent harpoon, a heavy cutting knife being attached by the middle to the end of the iron by a rivet. As soon as the knife enters the body of an animal this moveable blade turns at right angles to the wound, and being entirely blunt and flat on one side it is impossible to extricate it except by cutting out.) When they had got about ten feet from the animal the iron whistled thro' the air and went deep into his body, in a moment the whole length of the monster was lashing in the air, at a bound revealing his whole enormous length, and then making the water boil in every direction, he described rapid, foaming circles and acres of circles, with such a swiftness the eye could scarcely follow him. Then he darted off in another direction toward the upper part of the lake, the suddenness of his movement almost dragging the boat under water. Line was gradually given him, and after the space of half an hour, it was plain that his strength was almost exhausted. The whalemen then came ashore and gradually hauled the line in. The body was within fifty feet of the shore, when renewed life appeared to have been given him, and with one dart he carried nearly all the line out.

This was his last great effort. He was slowly dragged ashore, amid the wildest excitement and tumult ever known in the vicinity of Silver Lake. Four or five ladies fainted upon seeing the monster, who although ashore was lashing his body into tremendous folds, and then straightening himself out in his agony, with a noise and power that made the very earth tremble around him. The harpoon had gone entirely through a thick muscular part of him about eight feet from his head.

The snake, or animal, is fifty-nine feet five inches in length, and is a most disgusting looking creature. A thick slime covers his hideous length, a quarter of an inch thick, which, after being removed, is almost instantly replaced by exudation. The body of this creature is variable in size. The head is about the size of a full grown calf's; within eight feet of the head the neck swells up to the thickness of a foot in diameter, which continues for fifteen inches, and then tapers down the other way, constantly increasing in size, however, as it recedes from the head, until the body of the monster has a diameter of over two feet in the center, giving a girth of over six feet. It then tapers off toward the tail, which ends in a fin which can be expanded in the shape of a fan until it is three feet across, or closed in a sheath. Along the belly, from the head to the tail, are double rows of fins, a foot in length – not opposite each other, but alternately placed. The head is a most singular affair. The eyes are very large, white, staring and terrific. Attached to the edge of the upper and lower lids, which are like those of a human being, a transparent film, or membrane is seen, which, while it protects the eye of the animal, does not interfere with its vision. He has no nostrils or gills, apparently. The mouth of this serpent, or whatever it may be, is underneath – is almost a counterpart of the mouth of the fish called a sucker, possessing the same valvular power, pursed up – but it can be stretched so as to take in a body of the diameter of a foot or a foot and a half. No teeth can be discovered. A hard bony substance extends in two parallel lines around the upper and lower part of the head. His color is a dusky brown on the sides and back, but underneath the belly it is of a dirty white. It is sinuous like a snake, but has along its back, and on each side, a row of hard substance, knob-like in shape – the largest raised four inches from the surface of the body, extending from head to tail.

The news of his capture spread like wildfire, and before night hundreds and hundreds of people from this neighboring towns and villages had collected to see this wonder. The animal still has the harpoon in him. It passed thro' the muscular portion of the back and touched no mortal part. He lies in the water, an ingenious contrivance of ropes having been placed on him while he was on shore, keeping his body in a curve, preventing him from getting away or proving dangerous. He can use but his head and tail, with which he occasionally stirs up the water all about him for rods. He keeps his head under water except when he rears it up as if looking around, and presents a most fearful aspect. When rearing he expands his mouth and exhibits a cavity bloodred, most terrible to look upon. As he does this air rushes forth with a heavy, short puff. I have no more time to write you. The hotel is full, and people have a great difficulty in getting a meal in the village. Some of them go up to Castile to get their meals. The whalemen contemplate keeping the monster in his present position until an agent of Mr. Barnum arrives, who has been telegraphed. He is expected here to-night.

Very truly your friend and a subscriber,

– O.M.E.

A MONSTER REPTILE.
Orleans Independent Standard – September 18, 1857 – Vermont

A correspondent of the Abington Democrat, writing from Walnut Hill, Lee county, Va., who is, as the Democrat assures its readers, "a gentleman in whom implicit confidence can be placed, gives the following account of the killing of a monster reptile in Harlan county, Ky.

He says: -

"About three weeks ago five men went to gather whortleberries in the mountainous part of Harlan county, Kentucky, and in their travels came to a small branch at the foot of a steep ridge where they discovered a smooth beaten path, or rather slide, that led from the branch up the ridge. Curiosity tempting them to know the meaning, they followed the trail to the top of the ridge, where, to their astonishment, they found about an acre of ground perfectly smooth and destitute of vegetation, near the centre of which they discovered a small sink or cave, large enough to admit a salt barrel.

They concluded to drop in a few stones and presently their ears were saluted with a loud, rumbling sound, accompanied with a rattling noise; and an enormous serpent made his appearance, blowing and spreading his head, and his forked tongue protruded. The men were struck with wonder and affright, and suddenly the atmosphere was fillen with a smell so nauseating that three of the five men were taken very sick; the other two, discovering the condition of their companions, dragged them away from the abode of death. About ten feet of the snake had, to their judgement, made its appearance, when they hurried home and told what they had seen to their neighbors.

The next day were mounted some ten of the hardy mountaineers, armed with rifles, determined to destroy the monster. On approaching within one hundred yards of the dwelling of his snakeship, their horses became restive, and neither kindness nor force could make them go any nearer. The men dismounted, and hitching their horses, proceeded on foot with rifles cocked, to the mouth of the cave. They hurled in three or four large stones, and fell back some fifteen steps, when the same noise was heard as before, and out came the dreaded reptile, ready, as his looks indicated, to crush the intruders.

About the same length of snake had appeared from the hole, when eight or ten bullets went through his head, and, as the monster died, he kept crawling out until twenty feet of that huge boa lay motionless on the ground. It was a rattle snake of twenty-eight rattles – the first was four inches in diameter, the rest decreasing in size to the last. With difficulty the men dragged him home, and his skin can now be seen by the curious in Harlan county."

MONSTER LUSUS NATUA.

West-Jersey Pioneer – October 15, 1859 – New Jersey

From an authentic source, which forbids us to doubt the truth of the story, the following facts have been received: One day week before last, the passengers on board a ferry boat, near Quebec, were attracted by the singular appearance of a woman who occupied a rather secluded position, and who seemed to be under the care of some persons who acted as if anxious to shield her from observation. Her arms were bandaged, but not so closely as to prevent a constant and very unusual motion; and her head, which was completely covered and hidden from sight, was observed to sway incessantly backward and forward beneath the folds of cloth. As soon as the ferry boat reached the shore, the figure was conveyed to the train of cars in waiting, and seated therein; but at this moment a sort of struggle and tumult again attracted the notice of the bystanders, and the car was filled with eager inquiries. Those who entered, however, hastily returned, their faces pallid with horror.

Among them was the conductor of the train, who begged that no one would approach, for the bandage had been thrown off, and it had been discovered that the creature was a monster possessing the form of a woman, except the head and arms, which were those of a pig. No mere human resemblance, but the absolute fact. This would seem incredible, were it the only case of this kind. It is known, however, that there lived in Albany, N.Y., a few years ago, a similar creature, having a woman's body and a pig's head; in this instance the arms were human. This being was always kept in close confinement, and never suffered to leave a certain room in the house, where those who had charge of her resided, excepting when no visitors were about. She could talk imperfectly, and was capable of some degree of mechanical labor, for her sewing was said to be very beautiful. Her head was in every respect that of a pig, no particular was wanting – ears, bristles, even tusks, all were there. This creature died at the age of thirty five years, after having been for some time destitute of the little reason she once had.

STORIES FROM THE:

1860's

A CUMBERLAND RIVER MONSTER.

Nashville Union and Dispatch – April 12, 1868 – Tennessee

The Great Sea Serpent Supposed to Have Reached Nashville.

Thrilling Adventure of a Party of Fishermen.

They Fire Upon the Monster and Narrowly Escape.

Wondrous things have been recorded of Nashville and the mud dyed Cumberland, but the latest sensation gets beyond anything we remember to have ever heard or read of this mysterious region. The story is certainly marvelous, and we tell it as 'twas told to us, without undertaking to vouch for a thing so strange which we ourselves have never seen.

For some six months past, a gentleman living not far from the bank of the river, and about a mile below this city, where a little island lifts itself above the surface of the rapid stream, has been the loser of considerable stock, the cause of the mysterious disappearance of which he until recently has never known. Many a promising pig loosed from the sheltering sty has gone forth for the last time, and all search for its whereabouts proved unavailing. The owner attempted to account for his loss in various ways, and finally concluded that his valuable swine, like those of Holy Writ, had been seized of devils and plunged beneath the sweeping tide near by.

A day or two since, however, the mystery was cleared away. A party of fishermen were out in a boat, taking in a trotline that extended from bank to bank, when they discovered only a short distance from them, an object moving upon the water which they took to be the head of some domestic animal which had taken a notion to swim the river. Their curiosity being somewhat aroused, they approached a little nearer, when to their horror and astonishment a scaly monster, the like of which they had never before seen, slowly raised itself from the water, which fell in a sparkling shower from its body as it rose full six feet above the surface. It appeared to have ears resembling those of a human being, but the head and body were like those of a mammoth serpent.

The party in the boat at once gave chase, and one of them fired several revolver shots at the strange object, but before they could come upon it, they observed a ruffling of the water at a distance of what seemed to their excited imagination to be thirty or forty feet from the body of the monster, and almost instantly a loud splash followed, and a sharp tail like that of a huge snake appeared above the surface, and began thrashing the water furiously as if the wrath of its possessor had been suddenly kindled. The men dropped their oars in blank amazement, but quickly picked them up again as the enraged monster slowly threw its great head and body in the direction of the boat and commenced moving slowly toward them. In the inexpressibly short space of time that a twinkling is supposed to occupy, the boat was partially reversed, and shot out to the shore, where the party landed in safety and put themselves beyond the reach of their terrible pursuer, which, seeing no danger threatened, quietly drew its scaly body beneath the water, and as the ruffled surface became smooth again, the men who stood upon the bank began to doubt the evidence of their senses, so strange was the sight they had so unexpectedly witnessed.

Exactly what sort of a creature the ungainly monster could have been, we have little idea. The persons who saw it state that it had some of the characteristics of and a slight resemblance to the whale. Its resemblance to a serpent would indicate its relation to the great sea serpent, about which so much was said and written a number of years ago, and, for aught we know, it is the veritable old "snake" who created such a sensation at the time. "If this be he," he must have come up from the Caribbean sea after a detour of the West Indies, and getting into the Gulf of Mexico, entered the delta of the Mississippi. Thence ascending the Father of Waters to the junction of the Ohio, he must have visited Cincinnati and Louisville, and struck the Cumberland at Paducah, probably following up some steamer with a case of small-pox aboard, in hope of making a lunch from the unfortunate victim, should the victim be heaved over the side.

Since his appearance the other day, he has not again been seen, and it is surmised that he has now gone on toward the Upper Cumberland, and only got above water here to take a first look at the new country he had reached and to prospect upon his chances of making a living in a fresh water region. The disappearance of porkers and other stock in the vicinity where he was seen, would indicate that he has been near Nashville for some time. If any of our up-river readers get a look at him when he visits them, we trust they will immediately forward us an accurate description of this wonderful denizen of the deep, that the excited public may be set at rest as to his identity.

THE WILD MAN ON THE MANITOUS.

The Daily Phoenix – October 1, 1868 – South Carolina

A correspondent of the Cleveland (Ohio) Plaindealer gives this interest account of the pursuit and probably death of a wild man on one of the Manitou Islands in Lake Michigan:

Our party consisted of six men and two boys, with several dogs that we proposed to use in case a chase was necessary. On reaching the island, we divided into three parties of two each, the boys going by themselves. Signals were agreed upon in case we came across the strange monster, and we all started with a firm determination to thoroughly explore the island and capture the creature if possible. It must have been 2 o'clock in the afternoon, when the report of a gun from one of the exploring parties gave us notice that the unknown had been discovered, and we all at once hastened to the spot. I was so fortunate as to be within a short distance of the scene of the discovery, and was soon upon the spot, and found two of our party parleying with something or somebody that they had chased into a tall beech tree. His description tallied exactly with that given in my former letter. It was a form that had the appearance of a man, at least eight feet tall, entirely naked, with his body covered with hair. His face had the appearance of intellectuality, his brow being quite high, his beard descending nearly to his stomach, and his hair was disheveled and coarse. Though I am of the opinion that he could not have been over six feet high, my companions differ from me. His language was perfectly unintelligible, sounding more like the growl of a bear than that of a human being. When we pointed our guns at him, he would howl, gnash his teeth, and run like a monkey higher up the tree. After holding a consultation of war, we concluded to adopt peaceful measures, and sending for our basket of provisions, and laying aside our guns, we, after an hour or more spent in conversing, induced the stranger to descend the tree. He had no sooner struck the ground, than one of our dogs started for him, and, evidently frightened, he started upon a run, we all following him closely. He gained rapidly upon us, but the dog overtaking him, he turned, and, grasping the animal by the throat, literally tore him to pieces. Throwing the dog's carcass upon the ground with evident disgust, he again started towards the lake, where, as he arrived on the edge of the island, we saw him throw himself fearlessly into the blue waters of Lake Michigan. For a time he swam out boldly and gracefully, but while some of our party went out in quest of our boat, those who remained to watch him saw him rise several times in the water as though in agony, and then beheld him sink to rise no more. He was gone. Who he was, what he was, or where he came from, no one will ever probably know. Some person may be able to trace out all the facts of this strange creature's life. I have merely endeavored to give you the facts just as they occurred, and just as they are.

A MONSTER.

Nashville Union and American – March 14, 1869 – Tennessee

A Frog Weighing 93 Pounds Captured in a Cave Four Miles South of Columbia – Great Excitement.

From the Columbia Herald.

We received the following letter late yesterday evening, at the hands of Mr. Lem. Matthews, who vouches for every word in the letter, and from his well-known integrity, and that of this brother, we feel not the least hesitancy in saying that it is just as they represent:

Near Indian Camp Spring, Wednesday, March 10, 1869. – Mr. Horsley – Having a large cave with in a short distance of my house – and it having excited the curiosity of my two little boys, aged respectively eleven and thirteen years, they ventured this morning to explore its hidden wonders. With torches in hand they proceeded to the distance of about one hundred yards from the entrance, when they were terribly startled by the appearance of a monster frog, as large as a hogshead, as they said, when they came running up to me at my house.

Having seen so much in imagination, when young, and possessing a considerable degree of curiosity – I was determined to see for myself what it was. I went to the residence of Mr. W.D. Matthews to get assistance in exploring, and found several neighbors, J.W.B. Thomas, Richard McCanless, Geo. Dixon, John Due, and Sol. Porter there, who were eager to go right away, as their curiosity seemed as great or greater than mine. In a short time we fixed up three torches, procured some candles, and a lantern, we proceeded on our voyage of discovery.

Having arrived at the mouth of the cave, the torches were soon lighted, but some hesitancy seemed to be shown by all as to who should go first. Mr. Thomas led the van into the damp cavern, whose gloominess produced a chilling melancholy, (and one of the party was extremely anxious that they should retrace their steps,) but the indomitable Thomas and daring Mathews and Porter prevented, by telling the party that *"we can whip out all the frogs in creation."*

We wended our way slowly to the place my sons saw the frog, and sir, I do say to you, without exaggeration, that the frog was not near as large as when my children saw it, but it is undoubtedly the largest specimen I have ever seen or heard of before in this or any other State.

We advanced to within about twenty feet and halted. It was then sitting with its side to us, and when all of the torches were brought up it turned slowly around facing us – and such a hideous sight! I never before beheld. Its eyes, as they glistened in the torch light, made such an impression upon me, and in fact upon the whole party, that we trembled as if in the presence of a real demon, for in all my imaginations of the appearance of a demon, I must acknowledge that I never conceived of anything that would be calculated to fill the mind with such a horror as this.

We stood in the position we had first taken for some time. Mr. Matthews threw a small stone towards the frog, it rolled and struck him lightly. It bowed or ducked its head twice towards the ground in succession and made a leap towards us; and if I tell you he leaped ten feet I do not believe that I would miss it six inches. As soon as it struck the ground an instant retreat was simultaneously agreed upon, *without* consultation. The torches were thrown to the ground and in an instant Egyptian darkness reigned and a struggle was made to gain the entrance. The noise and excitement was intense amongst the little boys who attended us, and above the din of confusion the voice of Dick McCanless could be heard: *"Is a frog bite poisonous?"*

Mr. Porter having some matches the candles were soon lighted, and with the light came back the courage of the little boys. An advance of a few steps brought us in sight of the monster again. A plan for its capture was soon determined upon. Mr. Matthews sent to his house for a large goods box, which soon after arrived. The box was dragged in and the top removed. The box was pushed by Messrs. Dixon and Due towards the frog; Mr. Mathews using the top as a shield, succeeded in getting behind the frog, and by throwing stones at it for some little time, made it change its position to a place near the wall. The box was then pushed slowly up and covered it; the top was slipped down, the box was turned over and secured by a few nails, and the prize was ours. Right glad did we all feel at our success, and with high hearts we commenced the work of dragging the box out of the cave, which we accomplished after much labor; and we lifted it into a cart and started for the residence of Mr. W.D. Mathews, to have it weighed, as I had no balances that would draw enough at my house. A rope was tied around the box and the frog and box were weighed together. The frog was then turned out into a chicken coop and the box weighed and showed that the frog weighed exactly *ninety-three pounds*.

I will be willing to make an affidavit of this fact before any justice of the peace in Maury county. Those present and saw the weighing can attest to this. It is, I dare say, as rare a curiosity as was ever found in our county before. Mr. Mathews measured it while it was in a sitting posture and its height was exactly *three* feet four inches. Its eyes, as near as we could guess, were two and one-half inches in diameter. The color of the breast or belly was a dark yellow, while its back was a dark green, and apparently mossy, around its neck are two distinct red and one dark stripe. From the center of the head, or rather commencing from the top center of the nose there are apparently a thousand small light stripes springing out from a common center like rays of light. Its feet are of large proportions and are perfectly black.

I laid claim to it, as my boys were first to discover it, which claim was not objected to by any of the party who went with me. If nothing happens to it, I will bring it to Columbia next week and give your town people an opportunity of seeing something worth seeing. I will probably come to town on Tuesday and it will remain at Mr. W.D. Mathews' until that time. I would like very much for you to see this frog before its moved.

— A.P.N Mathews.

THE INEXPLICABLE SEA MONSTER.

The Pacific Commercial Advertiser – July 31, 1869 – Hawaii

"Part Beast and Part Fish."

In one of the *Harpers' Weeklies* appeared a detailed description, with an illustrative engraving, of what we are compelled to call an indescribable sea monster, "part beast and part fish," which had just been captured, under circumstances of great excitement, near Eastport, Me. The size of the monster, its strange form, and the peculiar way in which it was caught, aroused the incredulity of a portion of the community to such an extent, for a time, the reputation of the Harpers – the greatest publishers on the continent, and as noted for their integrity as for their business sagacity – was shaken! We give here the descriptive article from *Harper's Weekly*, taken from page 648 of the volume:

A WONDERFUL FISH.

This curiosity of natural history, caught "down East," near Eastport, Maine, a few weeks ago, has attracted so much attention and excited so much wonder, even among naturalists, that we give a representation of it in the accompanying illustration. The Bangor *Daily Whig* gives the following detailed description of this fish:

"The strange animal recently captured near Eastport, meagre reports of which had reached us, arrived in this city a few days ago, and has been on exhibition during which it has been visited by our citizens, all of whom have expressed their wonder as well at the remarkable size of the monster as at its anomalous character. This animal, part beast and part fish, is over thirty feet in length, and girths twenty-one feet. It has one enormous dorsal fin, two side belly fins, and a broad shark-like tail. About one-third of its length from its tail, in connection with small fins, it has two huge legs, terminating in web feet. Its mouth makes a line five or six feet in length, the whole extent of which is set with innumerable small teeth, very much resembling in size and shape the kernel of a species of sharp pointed pop-corn. It has a series of gills which overlap each other like the flounces once the style in ladies' dresses. Its immense body, which was estimated to have weighed when captured about 11 tons, had no frame-work of bones, its most solid portions consisting of cartilage, incapable of preservation. Its skin is dark and tough, like that of the elephant and rhinoceros.

"There is no record of his species, and to none is it a greater wonder than to naturalists, whose attention is being drawn to it. Among others who have had the opportunity of seeing it is Professor Baird, of the Smithsonian Institution at Washington, who is as yet unable to place it in the known lists of the animal kingdom. It is indeed a veritable wonder calculated to excite popular curiosity, and to invite the researches of the scientific.

"At various times during the past fifteen years a strange monster, believed to be a huge serpent, has been reported seen in Lake Utopia, in New Brunswick, just across the State line; but as these reports in each instance rested upon the testimony of but one or two individuals, they were generally discredited. Latterly however, the reports and the number of witnesses had so increased as to take the story out of the realm of fiction. On Sunday, August 3, the monster was discovered near the shore on the west side of Eastport Island, where Passamaquoddy Bay is connected with Lake Utopia by a marsh a quarter of a mile long. – Being attacked by musketry, it struck for the marsh, and probably for the lake, which was undoubtedly its home, and before being rendered incapable of locomotion, it had worked its way with its fins and legs a number of rods. – The report of its presence at once spread to the town, attracting a large number to the spot to aid in its destruction. It received some seventy musket balls, and although attacked in the forenoon, it exhibited signs of life the following day.

"Thus the northeastern point of our State, with the assistance of New Brunswick, has the honor of producing the nearest approach to a veritable sea-serpent, which is destined to make a popular sensation wherever exhibited. It is to be at Portland during the forthcoming State Fair, and is thence bound for Boston, New York, and other principal cities."

The discovery of a monster of such marvelous peculiarities, and unknown to science, at once attracted the attention of scientific men – among these, Professor Baird, of Washington; Professor Hamlin, of Waterville, and Professor Stanley, of Bates College. These gentlemen confess that the monster is too much for them – they do not know what it is, where to classify it, or what name to give it! It is simply one of Nature's biggest freaks. Perhaps it is the sea-serpent. Of course, the Down-Easters have been in a state of bewilderment. That a monster so long that it could not be laid across Nassau street unless head and tail went into the show windows; of such circumference that, were the framework strong enough, its skin could be used for a lifeboat, and with a mouth in which a few children could find shelter – that our Maine friends should have a call from such a stranger is reason enough for "sensation."

The article in the Bangor paper, which *Harpers Weekly* copies, omits to state that the monster, whose hide had resisted 70 bullets, was at last "brought to" by a broadside of spikes from a cannon!

If the Messrs. Harpers or the eminent Professors still find the public incredulous, it may comfort them to know that Mr. Wood has placed the monster on exhibition for a short time in his Museum, corner of Broadway and Thirtieth street.

THE SEA SERPENT AGAIN.

The Charleston Daily News – December 6, 1869 –
South Carolina

THE MONSTER IN THE GULF STREAM WITH A RECRUIT.

A New York Skipper Encounters the Serpent off the Delaware Bay – A Young Serpent in Company – The Captain's Account – Superstitious Horror of the Sailors.

The sea serpent still lives and has an heir for the protection of his race. Captain Allen, of the ship Scottish Bride, which arrived at New York on Sunday, brings the latest intelligence from his marine snakeship, the captain having encountered the monster on the 23d instant, in latitude 38.16, longitude 74.08. The remarkable feature of the meeting was that the old, familiar serpent, fifteen or twenty feet long, and as big around as a hogshead, was accompanied by a juvenile monster of the same species, only about five feet in length.

This meeting, as will be seen by reference to the charts, was on the edge of the Gulf Stream, about two hundred miles off Delaware Bay. But as Captain Allen is a credible witness, well known by the shipping merchants of New York, and everywhere conceded to be an intelligent man, his own narrative of the singular meeting will be read with greater interest than any more studied account:

CAPTAIN ALLEN

Is a through type of an American skipper – sharp, shrewd, bluff and honest – and has followed the ocean from boyhood, rising by his own energy and merit from a cabin boy to the command of one of the finest clipper ships sailing from New York.

FIRST VIEW OF HIS SNAKESHIP

Captain Allen says that on the 23d of this month, he descended to his cabin after a fruitless effort to get a meridian observation, the sky being too much overcast. He was just about eating his dinner when his second mate descended the cabin stairs, and, in an excited manner, told him his presence was required on deck.

Thinking the ship had sprung a leak or that some other dire mishap had befallen them, he dropped the tempting morsel before him and rushed up. When he arrived on deck, he found the crew assembled on the starboard side of the vessel, looking with awe-stricken countenances into the water. Not knowing the meaning of their strange conduct, he also went to the ship's side, and a sight met his eye the memory of which will never fade.

THE SERPENT ON SECOND VIEW

The weather had been thick and nasty all the morning, the heavens heavily overcast threatening to pour forth a deluge at any moment, and the wind blowing from "all quarters" at once. But now there was a dead calm, and the surface of the sea undisturbed by a ripple. On approaching the side of the vessel, the captain saw in the water beneath a monster such as he had never seen before.

It was about twenty-five feet in length, and proportionately thick; its head was very large and flat, while at each side, on the extreme edge, were set two bright, scintillating eyes, which, he says, looked dangerous and wicked. Its back was covered with large scales, like the crocodile, about three inches in length, which hooked together and formed and impenetrable armor. Its belly was of a tawny yellow color, and altogether hideous.

It was accompanied by a smaller specimen of its own species and may have been its offspring. This was but a few feet in length, but in shape and color, closely resembled the larger one.

THE EFFECT UPON THE SAILORS

All the efforts of the captain to have the sailors make some attempt to capture it were abortive. They looked upon it as something supernatural, and were not disposed to meddle with it. The thing was about four feet from the vessel, was lying but a few feet below the surface of the water, and was easily discernible to all on board. The captain gave orders to have a boat lowered to attack the monster, but in the meantime the attention of the smaller one was called to the presence of the vessel. It raised its head a few inches above the surface, and then went toward its larger friend, and seemed to tell it of the circumstance; but whatever transpired between them the larger one raised its head as though to investigate its surroundings, and then, with an easy motion it dropped into the ocean. In disappearing, it went head downward, and its body described a circle like hook, its tail rising out of the water, which, the captain says, tapered off to a sharp point.

THE STORM THAT FOLLOWED

The calm that had beset the vessel in the morning now gave way to a strong northwest breeze, that as night closed around, burst into a storm, accompanied by vivid lightning and rolling thunder. The ship was tossed about by the waves which ever and anon broke over her with relentless fury, and during the whole of this fearful night the sailors would not go on deck without lanterns, such was their fear of meeting the monster.

Now and then they would go to the captain and ask his opinion on the probability of that occurrence; but he being no wiser than themselves, would laugh at their fears, and bid them go to their work. About morning did the storm die away, but until the following day, when they came in sight of land, the brave men entertained an unexpressed dread of the reappearance of the monster.

THE CAPTAIN'S THEORY

Captain Allen thinks that the monster came from the regions of Florida, where he has often heard of similar creatures from other shipmasters, and by following the warm current of the Gulf stream it reached the position where he found it. In his opinion, it is a deep water animal; and he accounts for its appearance so near the surface by the fact of the dark day, and the monster not knowing how high up he was.

STORIES FROM THE:
1870's

A BALLOON FISH.

Public Ledger – March 26, 1870 – Tennessee

Huge Piscatorial Pirate – One Hundred Feet of Serpent – A Marine Wonder.

From the New York Herald.

The monsters of the air, forest and sea have been illustrated by such great authorities as Buffon, Cuvier and Agassiz. They have classified species, determined the purpose, characteristics and propensities of the lesser life, and have even gone so far as to express the belief that all monsters of the past and present are known to the naturalist. The fallacy of this confidence is not only evident in the discovery of the fossil remains of the great hydrosaurus by Professor Waterhouse Hawkins, but also in the appearance of a vast sea-serpent in American waters, off Cape Hatteras, on the 12th instant.

The schooner Saladin sailed from Jacmel, Hayti, with a cargo of copper, bound for New York. On the 10th and 11th instant she had heavy weather; but as the morning of the 12th dawned there were only light airs and a swelling sea. About six o'clock the Captain was on deck alone, his hands being below safely quartered in their bunks, enjoying those visions that hover over heavy eyelids. The Saladin was now steering north-northwest, going along at an easy pace, about four knots an hour. Murky and foggy drapery obscured the brightness of the sky.

As the Captain scanned the horizon he described what he considered to be a wreck on the starboard beam, about five miles distant, bearing east-northeast. He immediately put down his helm and turned the Saladin's head to eastward, hoping to overhaul the object and render what assistance might be necessary. The Captain inserted his head in the cabin and called: "All hands on deck!" In a moment the crew was upon deck, rubbing their eyelids, and curious between hope and fear.

The Saladin had few provisions on board, but was only seventy-five miles from Hampton Roads, bearing south-southeast, and the Captain, unlike the Bombay's Captain, thought of performing an office of humanity and save those who might be clinging to an ugly wreck. Progress was made toward the point of interest for a few minutes when it was plainly evident that the Saladin was overhauling a huge piscatorial pirate, which they soon saw was the most remarkable specimen of a marine serpent probably ever seen since pre-Adamite man. The Captain exclaimed, "Is this a dream, is this a dream?"

The seamen, who had just been released from the bondage of a profound sleep, thought it was, for there dead ahead sat an enormous fish, larger than a ship, looming up in comparison with the Saladin as St. Peter's before a village parsonage. The serpent was making headway at the rate of about two knots an hour, and the Saladin was rapidly overhauling her. At half-past seven a.m. the schooner hove to, with the monster twenty feet on her starboard quarter. Then all hands strained their eyes from their sockets to see how the monster looked and would behave.

It was now in plain sight, with every portion clearly visible. Its architecture was accurately measured, and the serpent was found to be one hundred feet long, with a body forty feet in length, and a tail of sixty feet. But the most curious feature of the monster was an immense body of hard gristle matter twelve feet in height, forty feet in width, with the same length, which was entirely void within, forming a large bladder-shaped balloon, which, filled with air, buoyed the serpent on the water, and seemed to be an agent whereby it could keep the surface and commit its depredations either upon commerce or upon the harmless inhabitants of its own element.

This oval buoy had regular ridges, running from the apex ahead — for this bladder preceded the body of a fish — to where it joined the main body. These ridges extended fore and aft, at intervals of four inches, and gave to the surface the appearance of the network of a balloon. The bladder portion was elastic, and yielded to the movements of the sea, and was two inches thick, but of a hard, dense, impenetrable character that would resist knife or bullet. On each side of this floating dome were two heavy paddles, each five feet long, by which the monster made progress. This part described may all be considered as one of the most surprising wonders of the piscatorial world The fish proper, which was but an appendage tailed on to this blown-up bladder, consisted of a heavy fishy substance, with brown sides, and about ten feet from the dome were two eyes, one on either side of a large horn.

From this point the fish tapered off to a forked tail of material as heavy and hard as iron. Captain Slocum declares the tail would weigh 100 pounds to the cubic foot, and forks of the tail stood horizontally in the water, but submerged four feet, the rest of the monster sitting lightly on the ocean wave. Captain Slocum feared to fire at her, to disturb her in any way, as one movement of the docile pirate would have crushed the Saladin to the deep. He believes that the animal has some internal engine by which she fills her balloon with air and discharges it at pleasure, then sinking out of sight. Her touch is poison and her contact dangerous. She is like a sunfish, but is really new – a balloon fish. Had the Saladin encountered her it would have been, "Up in a balloon, boys, up in a balloon."

This discovery is valuable to science and was made by men of entire credibility, and the statements given are by those who understand the sea and are enthusiastic at the marvelous discovery.

A STRANGE MONSTER.

Knoxville Daily Chronicle – February 15, 1873 – Tennessee

Mountain People Alarmed and Fortifying.

From the Jonesboro' Flag and Advertiser.

A gentleman recently from the Shelton Laurel District of North Carolina, some forty miles from this place, informs us that the people in that "densely thicketed" country are greatly excited in regard to the appearance, upon several different occasions, and in several different places, of a huge mountain monster, the species of which is unknown. Mr. George Anderson, one of the gentlemen residing in the Laurel country, being one of the persons who saw the monster, also furnishes us with the following description of it:

"I was out in the jungle hunting up some lost hogs, when all of a sudden there came into my path a beast, the appearance of which I must confess, caused me to quake for the first time in many years. Aside from its strange and unusual appearance, the unearthly yell it uttered on perceiving me, which reverberated and re-reverberated through the forest, was enough to shake the senses of the most daring adventurer. The animal was some hundred yards distant from me, and appeared to be a huge black bear with mane and head like a lion, but had horns like an elk upon it. Its tail was long and bushy, with dark and light rings around it to its very extremity.

Its eyes gleamed like a panther's, and its size was that of an ordinary ox, but somewhat longer. Just previous to making its appearance, I had shot off my gun at a squirrel, and felt little prepared to meet such a ferocious beast without any weapon of defense. I immediately set about reloading my rifle, but had scarcely begun, when it started towards me. I retreated in as good order as possible, and must say I did some good running – not looking back until I had reached an open spot, when I found the animal had disappeared in the laurel thicket. This is no story, Mr. editor, gotten up to scare naughty children. I am not the only one who has seen the monster – several have seen it since I did; and as sheep and calves are lately missing, it is presumed to be a carnivorous brute. Many have fortified their homes to prevent a night attack from the strange monster – the like of which was never seen in these mountains before. Some think it has escaped from some rambling menagerie, while others superstitiously think it is sent to warn people of some great approaching danger."

We recommend that the citizens of the Laurel catch the animal and put a bell on it!

A MONSTER IN THE MOUNTAINS.

The Watertown Republican – October 7, 1874 – Wisconsin

Our readers will remember that about two years since a wild man was seen on the Welch Mountains, near Morgantown, in this county, and created quite and excitement at the time. A correspondent from Bethel township sends us the following description of one of the most hideous monsters in human shape ever seen in that section. It is written by a reliable gentlemen, and the story seems to have the foundation of truth:

On a recent Sunday while three young men were out on the Blue Mountains, near Swatara Gap, they met an old gentleman named Jos. Feshter, who resides in a small hut near the mountains. He informed the party that about an hour before a monster nearly seven feet high, and weighing over two hundred and fifty pounds, came within twenty yards of his cabin, and gave an unearthly yell, when Feshter looked out and saw the creature on all fours in the middle of the road, making all kinds of gestures. His hair on his head was very long, and his face covered with hair. His hands and feet were to all appearances double the size of ordinary hands and feet, and altogether he presented a horrible appearance. Feshter asked him what he wanted, and received merely a grunt for an answer.

He says that he heard a noise on Saturday evening, about midnight, in the rear of his hut, but paid but little attention to it. In the morning when he got up he found that two pigs, about ten weeks old, had been taken away, and also three lambs. He could not imagine what became of them, as he had no neighbors within three miles.

The monster, after sitting in the road a few minutes, gave another yell and a maniac laugh and leaped some ten feet on his hands and feet near to him, when Feshter became uneasy and ran down the road. He returned and found that two more of his lambs were gone, and the stove in his cabin overturned, and the fire burning the floor. He put the fire out and locked the cabin, and then started for his nearest neighbor for assistance, when he met the three men, one of whom was your correspondent. We all went to a house two miles distant and procured two guns and other weapons. We searched the mountains until five o'clock in the afternoon.

When we were about to return to the cabin, and when within a mile of it, and passing through a deep ravine, we heard some noise upon the bank, and in looking up discovered the monster grinning like a wild beast, and before we had time to take a second thought he gave one yell and a jump, and when we reached the top of the bank, nothing could be seen of him.

A party of some twelve are going out on Tuesday, and will remain until the brute is captured.

– Reading Eagle, 18th ult.

A BIG LIZARD.

Chicago Daily Tribune – June 18, 1876 – Illinois

Or a Bad Case of the Jim-Jams.

Correspondence Denver News.

LAS ANIMAS, June 8. – With an issue of the News of a week or since before me, in which the usual ridicule is made of the marine monster known as the sea-serpent, in connection with a Brobdingnagian specimen of the species said to have been seen comparatively recently in the Indian Ocean, I have but to marvel at the incredulity of my race. You are not willing to acknowledge the possibility of the vast caverns of the deep containing denizens, which, after all, are not constructed on much larger plan than the familiar whale, while the very plains that surround your city are the home of monsters of bygone ages. Within a short hundred leagues of Denver may now be found a reptile compared to which the famous African serpent that once kept Rome's legions at bay could not hold a candle. With my own eyes, hardly forty-eight hours ago, did I behold this terrible creature, the like of which I could not have conceived to exist in the heavens above, nor in the earth beneath, nor in the waters under the earth.

Last evening, just at dark, I was traveling horseback-wise along a stretch of country, about 200 miles east of here, which, for a long distance merits the appellation the old geographies gave this entire region, of the Great American Desert. As far as the eye could reach, not a living thing, or object created by the hand of man, could be seen. The solitude was as entire as if cattle on a thousand hills were not grazing within less than 50 miles, and the iron horse did not draw his heavy freight only just beyond the line of vision. On every side the horizon only bounded the view, and not even where the sky kissed the plain did aught but the scanty prairie grass, already burned to brown under the rays of the fast summering sun, life itself, dotted here and there by innumerable cacti, from mother earth. And the silence. Save the quickly recovering thud of my horse's hoofs as he loped over the prairie, not a sound was to be heard, and the stillness was so profound that I almost expected to hear the hissing of the sun, which was on the point of setting, as it quenched its fire, according to ancient science, in the Pacific Ocean.

But the silence and the solitude were not for long. As I was about to seek a place to build a fire and bivouac for the night, suddenly a long trailing form started from the earth in the very path of the setting sun, and a queer rumbling cry was borne to my ears upon the western wind. I at first thought it was the initial train of some opposition to the Banana Line Railway and tried to distort the noise I had heard into the whistle of a locomotive, but my horse taught me better. Hardly had the sound died upon the air when an intense trembling seized his every limb, and, with expanded nostrils and dilated eye, he began looking on all sides as if to find a way of escape. And now the same strange cry was repeated, and my terrified sight perceived that what I had taken to be a railway train was an enormous reptile, half serpent, half quadruped, that was now running, now creeping along the earth, with incredible rapidity. Although my limbs almost refused to perform their office for terror, I had turned mechanically to leap on my horse; notwithstanding that I knew that the pace of the monster was coming was far faster than that of a horse at full gallop, but the beast had broken away from where I had tied him, and was quickly devouring the earth with rapid feet. Not, however, away from the coming danger. Although destruction stared me in the face, I almost lost consciousness of my peril in viewing the strange scene that followed. As soon as the terrible thing perceived that the horse was able to run at a rate that compelled an inconvenient degree of speed to catch up with him, he suddenly stopped in his career and for a moment remained silent and motionless, and the only sound to be heard was that made by the retreating horse, which was growing fainter and fainter. Immediately, ere it had become quite lost to the ear, the cause of the brute's flight began to utter a sonorous roaring that one moment sounded like some brutish mother calling her young, and another a weird imitation of the cooing of a dove. Hardly had the sound been uttered when the horse, which was not almost lost to sight in the rapidly-growing darkness, stopped. Presently he turned around and began with hastening steps to return. The noise still continued, and even to my human hearing seemed to have a pleading, inviting note in it. The Brobdingnagian beast, too, had assumed the shape at once of a cat ready to play with her kittens, and of a serpent when trying to charm its prey into its folds.

And now let me describe the monster, more terrible than which never creature lived since those long past periods, when all of nature's animated formations were equally great and grotesque, huge and horrible. Like other saurians, it had the body of a lizard, uplifted on, as near as I could judge, eight feet, but its propelling power, as already noted, seemed to exist chiefly in its tail, which streamed behind the body at least 100 feet. The trunk of the monster must have been 30 feet long by about half that figure in width, and at least from 8 to 10 feet through. The feet seemed little more than paddles with which to push its huge body along and apparently had little supporting power, the creatures belly touching the ground, except when its rapid motion forced it forward in the air. And the head; It seemed as large as an ordinary omnibus, while it was flattened at the top as if having undergone in youth the experience of the papooses of the Flathead Indians, and towered high up over the body on a neck greater in diameter than a barrel, and fully 10 feet in length. The eyes, which, like those of the dog in Hans Christian Andersen's story, were as large as saucers, and appeared larger than millwheels, were about a yard and a half apart, and gleamed like lanterns on either side of a carriage. Thus far, the mouth was only partly open to emit the sound above as noted, so that in the comparative darkness I could not see it distinctly, but the opportunity to witness it to more advantage soon came. The color of this extraordinary elephant was a dark purple, such as is sometimes used in churches at Lenten time, mottled with black.

By this time the horse had come within the embrace of the seducer, and the charming all at once ceased. Another movement, and the terrible mouth, which I now could see was as large as a barn-door, opened, and a forked tongue darted out and pulled my poor beast within. Then came the sound of the teeth crunching and the breaking of bones, mingled with the stifled death-cry of as faithful a brute as ever man bestrode. Then all was still, and the frightful creature lay motionless, as if digesting its meal. Presently it stirred, and, giving myself up for lost, I made up my mind to be its next victim, when, turning, it rapidly rolled away in the direction from which it came, without as much as looking at me. More dead than alive with terror, I made the best of my way to this place, where I arrived, horseless as I was and nearly all my provisions gone, this morning.

VAMPIRISM IN SERVIA.

The Cincinnati Daily Star – August 14, 1876 – Ohio

A Horrible Story of a Young Girl Killed by a Vampire.

In Servia, as in the most Slavonic countries, exists a popular belief in vampires, dead folk who quit their graves at night to torment the living. The signs by which the vampire is known are the preservation of the body for a long time after it should have decayed, the fluidity of the blood and the suppleness of the limbs. Prosper Merimee, in the course of his travels, was the witness of a case of alleged vampirism, which he describes as follows.

In 1816 I was traveling on foot in Vargaraz and chanced to stop at the little village of Varboska. My host was one Vuck Poglonovich, well-to-do for the region, a good fellow and sufficiently drunken. His wife was yet young and fair, and his daughter, a girl of sixteen, charming. I would have remained with him several days, in order to study the ruins in the neighborhood, but he would not rent me a room, insisting that I should be his guest, and as this involved holding my own with him at the wine after dinner, true relation was not particularly pleasant.

One evening the women had left us about an hour and, to avoid being compelled to drink, I was singing to my host, when we were startled by the most fearful cries from the sleeping apartment, which, as is the custom of the country, was occupied by the whole household in common. Arming ourselves, we hurried thither, and beheld a frightful sight – the mother, pale and haggard, holding her still more pallid daughter, who was stretched on her straw bed as if dead. The woman was shrieking, without pause, "A vampire! A vampire! My poor child is dead!"

With great difficulty we restored Khava to consciousness; she had, she said, seen the window opened and a man, pale as ashes, and wrapped in a winding sheet, had flung himself upon her, bitten her and strived to strangle. She was only able to shriek aloud when the spectre fled, and she swooned away, but she fancied that she had recognized in its features those of a villager named Wiecznany, dead about a fortnight. There was a small red spot on her throat, but I did not know whether it might not be a natural mark or the result of the bite of an insect during the girl's nightmare. When, however, I hazarded this conjecture the father rejected it sullenly; the girl wept piteously, and wringing her hands and rocking to-and-fro, kept repeating: "Alas! To die so young and before one's wedding-day!" while the mother loaded me with reproaches, declaring that she had herself seen the vampire and known it to be Wiecznany. I considered it, therefore, the part of prudence to be silent. All the amulets in the village were soon hung around the sufferer's neck and her father took an oath that next day he would disinter the corpse of Wiecznany and burn it. Thus, the night passed in an excitement that nothing could allay.

At daybreak next morning the whole village was out, the men armed with muskets or hangers, the women bearing heated irons, and the children sticks and stones. With cries of rage against the dead man they all thronged to the graveyard; it was with great difficulty that I could obtain and retain a position whence I could witness the ceremony of exhumation. It was slow, for as all strove to take part in it each interfered with the other, and not a few serious wounds would have been inflicted by pick or shovel had not the Elders ordered two men only to complete the work. At the moment that the shroud was unrolled a horrible cry fairly raised my hair on end. It proceeded from a woman by my side. "It is a vampire!" she shrieked; "the worms have not eaten it!" and her words were taken up by a hundred mouths. Twenty musket shots shattered the head of the corpse to fragments, while the father and relatives of Khava hacked the body savagely with their long knives, and the women dipped linen clothes in the red liquid that oozed from the wounds to apply to the sufferer's throat. The body was dragged from the grave and firmly tied to the trunk of a small tree that had been cut down and prepared, then drawn to the house of Poglonovich, where a pile of faggots and straw had been erected. Fire was set to it, and the body tossed into the flames, while the people yelling madly danced around the pyre. The abominable stench from the burning flesh soon compelled me to take refuge in the house.

The house was crowded with visitors, the men all puffing at their pipes, the women all speaking at once and overwhelming with questions the sick girl, who sat pale and stupefied, the blood-soaked bandages round her neck forming a ghastly contrast with her white, half-naked shoulders. Little by little the crowd diminished till we were left alone. Khava grew more and more uneasy as night came on, and insisted that some one should watch by her bedside constantly. As her parents were worn out with fatigue and excitement I offered my services as nurse, and they were accepted gratefully.

I shall never forget the nights I spent by the bedside of this unfortunate girl. The creaking of a board, the very murmur of the wind made her start and shudder. She could not fall into a doze without seeing visions of horror, and from time to time would waken with a fearful start and a cry of anguish. She had had one horrible dream, and the village gossips had succeeded in completing the ruin of her mind by narrating to her all the frightful stories about vampires that they could remember or invent. Often as she felt her eyes closing she would say to me, "For God's sake do not sleep! Take my rosary in one hand and your sabre in the other and watch over me!" Nor would she sleep save her two hands locked about my arm, locked so tightly that the convulsive grip of her fingers would leave livid marks in my flesh. Nothing could distract her mind; she was abjectly afraid of death, and believed that she must certainly perish. In a few days she became shockingly thin; her lips were colorless and livid; her great black eyes seemed even larger and more brilliant; she was a pitiable thing to see.

I tried to impress her imagination by feigning to believe as she did, but, unhappily, as I had at first derided her credulity, I could not easily gain her confidence. I told her, however, that I was possessed of a paten charm against evil spirits and that, if she desired it, I would pronounce it. At first her natural unselfishness and gentleness would not permit her to allow me to draw the wrath of heaven on myself, but, finally, the fear of death overcame her scruples and she implored me to try my spell. I pronounced loudly and solemnly some lines of Racine as an invocation; then, after rubbing her neck, pretended to draw therefrom a small red agate I had concealed between my fingers, and assured her gravely that I had removed the source of her illness and that she was saved. But, with a sad smile, she said: "You have deceived me; you had that stone in a little casket; I had seen it before. You are not a magician." Thus my ruse did her more harm than good. From that moment she grew worse rapidly.

On the night before her death she said to me, "If I die it is my own fault. My lover (and she named one of the young men of the village) wished me to elope with him, but I would not and asked him to bring me a silver chain. He went to Marcaska to buy me one, and it was then that the vampire came. After all, if I had not been at the house, it might have killed my mother, so perhaps it is for the best." Next day she made her father promise himself to cut her throat and open her veins after her death, that she might not also become a vampire; she would have no other hand but his to commit upon her corpse these needless atrocities. Then embracing her mother she desired her to take a rosary to the tomb of a local hermit, or saint, there to sanctify it; then to bring it back to her. I could not fail to admire this peasant's thoughtfulness in finding such a pretext to keep her mother from witnessing her dying agonies.

She took an amulet from her neck and gave it to me. "Keep it," she said; "and may it do you more good than it has done me." She then received the sacrament devoutly. Shortly thereafter her breathing became more difficult and her eyes glazed. Suddenly she seized her father's arm and made an effort as if to cast herself upon his breast; then ceased to live. Her sickness had lasted eleven days.

A few hours later I had left the village behind me, consigning heartily to the devil, vampires, and all who believe in them.

A STORY OF THE DEEP.

Knoxville Journal – February 7, 1877 – Iowa

British sea captains are becoming famous by reason of their discoveries of sea monsters. Some weeks ago we published an amazing story of a monster marine frog seen by the officers and crew of an English steamer in the Straits of Malacca, and now Capt. Drewar, of the bark Pauline, of London, who has just arrived at Cork from a long voyage, favors the public with the following account of an ocean marvel:

Bark Pauline, July 8, 1875, latitude 5 deg. 13 min. north, longitude 35 deg. West, Cape San Roque, northeast coast of Brazil, distance twenty miles, at 11 a.m., the weather fine and clear, wind and sea moderate, observes some black spot upon the water, and whitish pillar some thirty feet high above them. At first sight I took all to be breakers, as the sea was splashing up, fountain-like, about them, and the pillar a pinnacle rock, bleached with the sun; but the pillar fell with a splash, and a similar one arose. They rose and fell alternately in quick succession, and good glasses showed me it was a monster sea serpent, coiled twice round a large sperm whale. The head and tail parts, each about thirty feet long, were acting as levers, twisting itself and its victim around with great velocity.

They sank out of sight every two minutes, coming to the surface still revolving; and the struggles of the whale and two other whales that were near, frantic with excitement, made the sea in their vicinity like a boiling cauldron; and a loud confused noise was distinctly heard. This strange occurrence lasted some fifteen minutes, and finished with the tail portion of the whale being elevated straight in the air, then waving backwards and forwards, and lashing the water furiously in the last death struggle, when the whole body disappeared from view, going down, head foremost to the bottom, where, no doubt, it was gorged at the serpent's leisure; and that monster of monsters may have been many months in a state of coma, digesting the huge mouthful.

Then two of the largest sperm whales I ever saw moved slowly toward the vessel, their bodies more than usually elevated out of the water, and not spouting or making the least noise, but seeming quite paralyzed with fear; indeed, a cold shiver went through my own frame on beholding the last agonizing struggle of the poor whale that had seemed as helpless in the coils of the vicious monster as a bird in the talons of a hawk.

Allowing for two coils round the whale, I think the serpent was about 100 or 170 feet long, and 7 or 8 feet in girth. It was in color much like the conger eel; and the head, from the mouth being always open, appeared to be the largest part of its body. It is curious that the whale, that lives on the smallest food of any fish in the ocean, should itself be but a meal for another monster; for I think it as feasible that the serpent swallowed the whale as that a boa-constrictor can consume a whole bullock.

I am aware that few believe in the existence of the great sea serpent. People think that as so many vessels are constantly on the ocean it would be seen oftener. But the northeast coast of Brazil, noted for its monster reptiles, is peculiarly adapted for the growth of sea monsters. The temperature of the air and water is seldom above 81, the shore for a thousand miles is bordered by a coral wall or reef, and numerous banks and reefs extend for a considerable distance from the land, while there are strong and various currents and no ports; so that ships for business or pleasure seldom go near it. It was unexpected circumstances led me to the home of the sea serpent, and I think it may be allowed that the serpent retains some portion of that cunning mentioned in scripture. At least it has wit enough not to leave a good feeding ground and secure home to go wandering about the ocean like a fish, and be tortured and captured for man's pleasure or profit.

I think Cape San Roque is a land-mark for whales leaving the South for the North Atlantic. The warm water is also good for its breeding; and if the Crystal Palace Company or some enterprising Barnum, offered a suitable reward for its capture, I am sure a steam whaler with suitable hooks baited with some animal and steel wire lines, would effect its capture while following a profitable whaling business.

I wrote thus far thinking I would ever see the serpent again; but at 7 a.m. July 13, in the same latitude and some eighty miles east of San Roque, I was astonished to see the same or similar monster. It was throwing its head and about forty feet of its body in a horizontal position out of the waters as it passed onwards by the stern of our vessel. I began musing why we were so much favored with such a strange visitor, and concluded that the band of white paint, two feet wide above the copper, might have looked like a fellow-serpent to it, and no doubt attracted its attention.

It was put on to keep the vessel's side clear and free from barnacles, which it does remarkably well; and if the agitators about the deep load line gain their wish, it would be both useful and practical to mark the vessel thus, in place of disfiguring it with plague spots that would be constantly rubbing off. If the ship owners, with two competent surveyors, so decide, must misery, uncertainty and perpetual lawsuits would be avoided. While thus thinking, I was startled by the cry of "there it is again!" and a short distance to leeward, elevated some sixty feet in the air, was the great leviathan, grimly looking towards the vessel.

As I was not sure it was only our freeboard it was viewing, we had all our axes ready, and were fully determined, should the brute embrace the Pauline, to chop away for its backbone with all our might, and the wretch might have found for once in its life that it had caught a Tartar. This statement is strictly true, and the occurrence was witnessed by my officers, half the crew and myself; and we are ready at any time to testify on oath that it is so, and that we are not in the least mistaken.

ANOTHER SEA SERPENT.

Watertown Republican – August 29, 1877 – Wisconsin

A Monster in Rice Lake, Canada. (Hardwood Cor. (Aug 10.) Cobourg, Ont. Sentinel.)

The most intense excitement has been created here by the appearance of a monster in the waters of our lake, which, according to the description given of it by those who have seen it, rivals any of the specimens of the great sea serpent.

Two American gentlemen, who are enjoying the lovely scenery of our lake and the good sport which it affords, were out yesterday on a fishing excursion, and when off White's Island they noticed an unusual commotion in the water, looking toward the south. Their surmises and doubts were soon set at rest on discovering the undulating portions of the body of a monster which was making his way up the lake toward Harwood.

They at once gave chase and were rapidly gaining on the creature, when their courage was tested by the monster turning around and making directly for them. The view they had of it, and it is described by them as having a head almost like a horse, but twice as long, eyes fierce and glaring, the color of the skin dark gray, the gullet pink and having large but apparently soft fins or long hair along its back as far as seen. They could not see more than about twelve feet of the animal's body, but think it must be over sixty feet long. They succeeded in reaching Idyl Wild, the monster having disappeared before they got to the shore. This was about 11 o'clock in the morning.

At 1 o'clock two ladies and two gentlemen standing on the piazza of the "Lake View House," saw the monster pass the north side of Tick Island going in the direction of Spoeke Island. With a good opera glass they were enabled to notice more accurately the movements of the monster serpent, for such now it appeared to be, and in a short time it had passed behind Spoeke Island and made directly for the mouth of the Otanabee, but disappeared suddenly when in that part of the lake which is considering the river channel, and has not since been seen from here. Captain Brady got his yacht, the Slug, under way at once, and cruised around the island for some time, but could discover nothing of the alarming visitor. I will let you hear if anything further is seen or heard of his snakeship.

Latest. - A gentlemen just arrived from Gore's Landing says the monster was seen disporting himself between Sheep Island and the shore. A party is being organized to attempt its capture. Two sportsmen fired at it when it at once disappeared.

I am told that the ladies and gentlemen who saw the monster are about making affidavits of the fact before a Magistrate. In the meantime, every effort is to be put forward to effect its capture. I will not fail to let you know any further particulars that I may learn about this wonderful visitant of our lake. I understand the Indians are so alarmed that some of them intend removing from the borders of the lake for a short time at least, or until they are better satisfied of their security from the horrid monster now in their vicinity.

THAT MONSTER.

Chicago Daily Tribune – October 7, 1877 – Illinois

The St. Louis Globe-Democrat's River-Leviathan.

An Effort by the Mississippi to Get Ahead of Lake Michigan.

St. Louis Globe-Democrat, Oct. 5.

Mr. Robert Mathison, a well-known business man of St. Louis, whose residence is at 2334 Olive street, arrived in the city last night by rail, from Memphis, and at a late hour called at the Globe-Democrat office and gave to a reporter a startling account of the recent exploits of the river monster which has created such an excitement during the last two weeks among the denizens of the Lower Mississippi. Mr. Mathison's narrative – and there seems to be no doubt of its literal truthfulness – is substantially as follows: Friday afternoon, at a late hour, - the sun being about a half-hour high, and the sky and air unusually clear, - Capt. John Carraway, of the towboat Bee Wing, having in tow six heavily-loaded coal-barges of the well-known Brown Barge & Transportation Company, of Pittsburgh, was passing a point on the river just above the village or landing known as Bradley's, five miles below Devil's Elbow Cut-off, and about fifteen miles above Memphis, when his attention was directed to a loud, puffing noise a considerable distance up the river. At first he thought it was the roaring of a broken 'scape-pipe or the wheezing of a disordered engine; but, seeing no smoke, and having reason to believe that there was no steam craft within hearing distance, below or above, he very shortly came to the conclusion that the sounds emanated from another source. Five minutes passed and the noise continued to be heard at brief intervals, and evidently getting closer. From the deck of the tow-boat a view could be had for 1,000 yards up the river, a gradual bend commencing at the distance. The sun was almost dipping below the western horizon when, around this bend, there rose to view the writing form of

A TERRIFIC MONSTER,

darting impetuously in mid-channel down the river. When first seen the leviathan seemed more like an immense uprooted tree, floating in a semi-perpendicular position along the mid-channel. As it neared, however, its horrid proportions became manifest. The hideousness of this aquatic monstrosity is stated by Capt. Carraway to be beyond the power of description. Its immense pelican bill, from five to ten feet in length, the gigantic bull-dog head, and the mammoth, slimy neck, upreared high in air; the vast tail lashing the water into fury, and the enormous fins, ten feet in length, sending out waves like the roll of a flying boat; the frequent dipping of the monstrous beak into the water, and spouting huge streams forty feet high in oblique directions, and the deep, cavernous roars that came thundering along at the briefest intervals − all these formed an infernal panorama that made the blood of the towboat Captain and his affrighted crew run cold, and their very hairs to stand on end. The monster was in the exact wake of the boat and barges, but it traveled with such tremendous velocity that turning out of the course was impossible. It is believed that its locomotion was at least twenty miles an hour, and Capt. Carraway at once realized that if the ponderous body, with its irresistible momentum, should strike his fragile vessel the boat would capsize in an instant or be shattered to splinters. He was making eight miles an hour. On the monster rushed, roaring with deafening effect, spouting from his horrid bill two streams of water that shot forty feet into the air, and fell in torrents into the river on either side.

THE SERPENTINE BODY

swayed tortuously and with frightful rapidity through the muddy waters, while the prodigious foreparts of the colossal reptile rose and sunk, and swayed like a Stygian horror, threatening to swallow and devour all that came within its reach. When within 150 or 200 yards, the horrid reptile, as if it had just discovered an obstacle in its track, slackened its precipitate pace, and for an instant paused to contemplate the nature of the obstruction. With a tremendous snort, so loud, and deep, and sonorous, that it gave the boat a tremulous motion, the huge creature came to a dead stop, and with its monstrous bill, head, and neck reared perpendicularly, seemed like a watery demon rising from the bosom of the deep. Here Capt. Carraway, despite the terror that had necessarily taken possession of him, obtained a good view of the monster, at least the parts that were above the water, and his description of the horrible spectacle is sufficiently minute and accurate to deserve reproduction. Carraway alleges that there is no doubt the monster has a pelican-shaped bill, but that its length, which has heretofore been described as being five feet long, will measure at least ten feet. It appeared more like an immense horn than a beak, and in shape was much like the pointed sword of the spear-fish, though larger and longer, and decidedly more formidable as a weapon of offensive warfare. It was from through this bill that the monster spouted water, the water being thrown from a point near the head. Capt. Carraway, who is an old whaler, stated that

THE SPOUTING,

unlike that of the whale, which throws its stream upward in a straight column, was made in oblique directions, and that the volume of water spouted, and the height reached, was twice as great as that thrown by the whale. The head is described to have been four or five feet across, black and shining, and its shape bearing a close resemblance to that of the bull-dog. Capt. Carraway thinks the animal bore on its head two short horns, but of this he is not certain, as the time for observation was very short. There could be no doubt, however, as to the canine shape of the head, and of the phenomenal circumstance that to this dog's head was attached a bill or beak, fashioned like that of a pelican. The neck appeared to be ten or twelve feet in length, narrow and serpentine, and swaying and writhing with a motion like that of a snake poised in water. The sides and under portions of the neck were evidently covered with burnished scales of changeable hue, but from the top of the neck there grew what had the appearance of a mane, resembling that of a horse, being thick and shiny, and of a greenish tint. This mane reached from the base of the head to the body, and depended from the neck in long strands. These were the only parts of the body that were visible except the fins. On the back there appeared to be a dorsal fin, fifteen or twenty feet in length, measuring along the back, and perhaps three or four feet in height.

THE BODY,

being sunk in the water, however, could not be seen, and Capt. Carraway says he may be mistaken as to the dorsal fin, and only describes it as it appeared to him during the momentary opportunity he had for observation. The side fins were of monstrous proportions, extending fifteen feet on either side, and while the monster paused they rose and dipped back into the water rapidly, throwing immense waves in a forward direction, the monster by this means poising and steadying himself with the current.

This attitude was maintained not longer than three or four minutes, and the distance being nearly or quite 100 yards, Capt. Carraway's description is necessarily imperfect, but, in the main, it is undoubtedly accurate, as it agrees almost exactly with the description which has heretofore been given of the monster by persons who have seen him wading in shallow water or outstretched on sand-bars. Suddenly the immense head and neck disappeared under the water with a lashing sound that could have been heard a half-mile down the river. For a few moments nothing was seen of the monster, but it was quickly discovered that he was making, in a direct course, for the towboat and barges. His track was indicated by a rolling, pointed wave that came rushing forward like water impelled by a great submarine upheaval. There was great excitement on board, and the Captain and hands were all on deck, looking, with terror, upon the extraordinary spectacle. A young German, named Henry Decker, was on the coal barge lashed to the right of the towboat, and it was under this barge that the monster plowed his irresistible way. First came a violent shock and then the barge was thrown with tremendous force above the surface of the water and almost careened, the rear end being hoisted twenty feet into the air, half the cargo of coal being

HURLED INTO THE RIVER,

and along with it the man Henry Decker. The lashings by which the barge was secured to the towboat were snapped, and the shock was so sudden and strong that the towboat itself was almost lifted clear of the water. In a moment the monster reappeared in front of the fleet, and, turning its body so as to face the barge it has passed under, again reared its body, suddenly dived into the water, and made for the boats. It was a fortunate circumstance that the barge had become detached from the towboat; for this seems to be a special object of aversion to the leviathan, for he attacked it with a fury that was terrible to behold. First he dove into the sides with his huge beak, lifting it almost entirely out of the water, and sending it fifty feet away. Then he lashed it with his tail, the blows resounding with deafening effect, while in the meantime the air was made hideous with successive roars and harsh, loud bellows. A second time he made an assault with his beak, striking it fairly in the gunwales and sending it scudding 100 feet down the river. This last attack seemed to satisfy the monster, for, with a howl, he suddenly sunk beneath the surface and shot down the channel, going at a speed which Capt. Carraway affirms must have reached forty miles an hour. As he moved away no part of the body was visible, but the pointed wave that rolled before showed its course, while in its wake the waters rushed like those of a mill-dam

SUDDENLY LET LOOSE.

In two minutes he was out of sight.

In the meantime, Henry Decker, the hand who was precipitated from the barge, swam to another barge and clambered safely up the sides, with no greater damage than a thorough drenching and a slight contusion on the head, made by a falling piece of coal. The engine had been stopped when the first shock came. It was put in motion as soon as it was apparent that the danger had passed, and Capt. Carraway set about securing the detached barge. By the time he reached it it was 300 yards down the river, and in a sinking condition. The front end had already sunk, and the stern was raised ten feet above the water. As the towboat approached the wreck swung around, and a close view showed that the bottom had been ripped in a half-dozen places, the portions of the gunwales still out of the water were split and splintered as if an ax had been used to cut and tear them to pieces. At one point the gunwale was torn off the entire depth. As the towboat floated against the wreck, one of the hands called Capt. Carraway's attention to a strange object that protruded from the rear end of the boat. It had the appearance of a huge splinter, but its appearance was so singular that Capt. Carraway's curiosity was aroused, and he steamed immediately by the object, in order to see what it was. Upon a close view, it was discovered that it was nothing more nor less than a piece of the monster's bill, which had been splintered off and left in the gunwale of the boat. An effort was made to pull the splinter out, but this undertaking was found too difficult to accomplish, as it was driven entirely through the timber, and was as fast and hard as if it were part and parcel of the barge. Axes were brought, and the gunwale chopped down on either side, and the piece containing the splinter split off. An examination showed the splinter to be four feet long, and undoubtedly a piece of

THE MONSTER'S BILL.

At one end it was twelve inches broad, gradually sloping until it reached a sharp point. It was quite thin and looked as if it might be a mere outward covering for the end of the lower part of the bill. It was neither horn nor bone, but appeared more like ivory, though almost as tough and hard as steel. In color it was dark green and brown, mixed and varied though the larger end was almost black. The piece weighed eighteen pounds, this heavy weight showing the unusual compactness of the material composing the beak.

An hour was spent at the wreck, when Capt. Carraway, seeing that the coal was a total loss and the barge in such a condition that he could do nothing then to save it, steamed on, reaching Memphis about 9 o'clock at night, where he related his strange adventure and exhibited the splinter from the monster's bill. Of course, the majority of people are skeptical about stories relating to monsters, and many were incredulous, but those who knew Capt. Carraway felt certain that whatever he might relate could be depended on as truthful in every respect.

There certainly cannot be longer doubt that the Mississippi is inhabited with a monster that not only ranks in horrid proportions with the fabled creatures of fiction, but one that may do much to interfere with free and uninterrupted commerce on the great river. It is undeniable that among river men there is a feeling of insecurity, and it has been suggested that the matter is of such importance that an expedition ought to be organized under Government management to hunt down and annihilate the leviathan. The New Madrid Gazette (from which place the Globe-Democrat published a special dispatch concerning exploits of the monster) of Wednesday says that a number of valuable horses and cattle were

MYSTERIOUSLY DESTROYED

while the monster haunted that part of the river, that no less than three boats were overturned, and one skiff shattered and its occupant drowned. The Vicksburg Pilot publishes an interview with Capt. Cuthbert, of the Ohio River trade, in which the Captain states that at a point ten miles above Henderson the monster attacked a flatboat, overturning the boat and throwing the ferryman and two passengers and their horses into the river. One of the men was drowned and the monster devoured one of the horses. These stories seem almost incredible, but they are so fortified by the testimony of unimpeachable witnesses, that all unbelief is necessarily dissipated.

THE MONSTER HEARD FROM AGAIN.

MEMPHIS, Tenn., Sept. 20. – A report was current yesterday morning that the river monster, which attacked Capt. Carraway's barges, had been seen to pass the Memphis wharf, though as the rumor could not be traced to a positive and reliable source, it was generally discredited. A courier just in from Flournoy's Landing, fifteen miles below here, and three miles below President's Island, brings intelligence that it was seen to pass that point at 4 o'clock this afternoon, and that it was traveling at a furious rate down the river, with its head high in the air, and bellowing so loud that it was plainly heard a mile away. No more damage has been done by it, so far as could be learned.

THAT RIVER MONSTER.

The News and Herald – October 20, 1877 – South Carolina

ITS APPEARANCE UPON DRY LAND.

Terrific Encounter in a Field Near Cahokia, Witnessed Throughout by a Member of a Well-Known Family – "Beware the Jabberwock, My Son! Beware the Frumious Bandersnatch!"

The St. Louis Republican gives an account of a terrific encounter between a bull and an unknown species of monster that has of late appeared in the Mississippi River and on its banks. The story is told by Mr. Jabez Smith, "one of the most reliable men of the community."

One evening recently, Mr. Smith's son went to a pasture to drive a bull home. Just on arriving at the pasture, he heard an unearthly noise in the woods. The boy dodged behind the fence, and the bull squared himself for the unseen enemy. In a moment more

THE MYSTERY WAS SOLVED.

From the edge of the woodland there upreared a head upon a swaying neck at least twenty feet in length. The head was that of a wolf or dog, save that there was a prolongation into a huge bill or horny jaws. This bill the Monster opened at intervals, displaying a row of immense fangs upon each division, while as he opened it on each occasion there was emitted a hissing noise loud enough to be heard for a great distance. From the back of the head and adown the neck depended a mane of coarse reddish hair. The monster retained its position for a moment or two, swaying its head gently back and forth, when its eyes fell upon the bull; then it at once showed signs of great excitement. It snorted fiercely, the hissing sound became almost continuous, and it would repeatedly open its immense jaws and snap them together with a sound like the report of a rifle. Its hesitation did not long continue. Maddened by the sight of the bull the monster advanced at once and

SWIFTLY TO THE ATTACK.

Raising its head still higher, it shot forward over the fence and thence over in swift, billow undulations, the fence seeming no obstacle at all. As the animal entered the field its whole body could be distinctly seen. The great neck terminated in a body of somewhat less length, supported upon four short legs armed with immense claws, though the motions of the animal seemed to resemble rather those of a snake, than of a thing with legs. To the body was joined a tail quite as long as the neck and terminating in a huge barb, hard apparently as iron, and having the bright red color of a boiled lobster. The neck and entire body were sheathed in scales of a dark blue color and as large as dinner plates. Most remarkable of all was a pair of huge membranous wings which were folded along the body of either side. The appearance of the great reptile was indescribably fearful and repulsive. It moved toward the bull, hissing loudly, and sweeping about the apparently doomed animal in circles of decreasing extent.

The bull meanwhile retained his position with lowered head and an occasional response to the hissing by a short bellow. He was alarmed, but evidently

FULL OF FIGHT.

His whole body was quivering, and his stump of a tail stood out like a limb of a sturdy oak.

As the monster swept about in circles, the bull turned slowly, always keeping his front toward the enemy. Suddenly the reptile raised its head to an immense height, opened its huge jaws and darted forward.

The boy in the fence corner saw the shock of the encounter and nothing more. Instantly there arose such a cloud of dust as almost to conceal the powerful combatants from sight. The ground shook as with some internal convulsion. The air quaked with a commingled bellowing and roaring. Dimly discerned through the dust-cloud could be seen portions of bull and reptile and tufts of flying hair and chips of shattered scales. There could be heard the snap of the monster's jaws and the rattle of the bull's horns upon its mailed sides. Flashing here and there through the dingy nimbus could be seen the blood-red dart upon the reptile's tail as it sought to transfix its active antagonist. It was a panorama of desperate battle; volume of sound, of fierce encounter. The tide of battle shifted insensibly to the vicinity of a huge oak stump which was near the centre of the field. Then the boy saw the tail of the strange monster suddenly whip

OUTWARD AND UPWARD

and dart the great barb downward with the speed of a thunderbolt. There was a crack like the report of a cannon. The barb had again missed the bull, and this time encountered a harder substance. The boy peering through the fence gave a wild yell of satisfaction.

The barb had buried itself in the stump!

The monster was at a disadvantage. It was fastened at one end to the stump, and had remaining only its claws and teeth, terrible indeed, but less so since the movement of the creature was necessarily restricted by its remarkable position. The bull had wonderfully escaped all fatal injury, and its horns now clashed upon the sides of its adversary like a forge hammer upon an anvil. The fight swung around the stump as a pivot, and the pandemonium of sounds and clouds of dust continued. Closer and closer to the stump the combatants drew continually, for, with each revolution another turn of the monster's tail was taken about the object, and its freedom of action became more and more impaired. The struggle was terminating oddly.

The bull was getting the advantage!

The rattle of the horns upon the scaly sides became more continuous, and the bellowing of the bull louder, but the roar of the monster reptile became less fear-inspiring. A gust of wind swept across the field and lifted the cloud of dust. Then the boy saw the fight end strangely. The unknown animal, in its last great strait, made one last fierce effort, tore its barbed tail from the wood and unwound its sinuous folds about the stump with the celerity of lightning. Then suddenly rearing its head again it unfolded for the first time the

GREAT MEMBRANOUS WINGS

Folded along its sides and rose in the air like a gigantic bat. With a wild, hoarse cry it darted upward to the height of hundreds of feet and took a southwesterly direction towards the Mississippi. A few moments later, from the direction of the distant river, came the sound of a tremendous splash and swash of waters, as though some heavy body had fallen into the river from a great height. The baffled monster had reached again his native element.

Cautiously the boy in the fence corner emerged from his retreat and approached the scene of the late encounter. The bull, nearly skinned, with but one ear and one horn remaining, stood there, weak, but fearless still, stamping, lashing its sides with what little remained of its tail, and gazing in the direction where his antagonist had disappeared over the wood. There was hair enough on the ground to stuff a mattress with, and fragments of great scales were scattered about over an area of half an acre, while the oak stump was absolutely riven in twain in the effort of the monster to release its forked tail from the tough wood. The boy flourished the stick, and the bull started home quietly. It had been engaging in two grand a struggle to fool with boys any more, and besides it didn't seem to be feeling quite well. Twenty minutes later the father, "Truth Jabez," knew all about the remarkable occurrence.

AN ANTEDILUVIAN JOBBERWOCK.

The Opelousas Journal – December 1, 1877 – Louisiana

Discovery of a Monster Containing the Remains of a Human Being.

Mr. Henry Woodard owns a stock ranch in the Indian territory, in that Peoria nation, on which is situated the big Sulphur spring. The spring is surrounded by quagmire, which is very deep and "slushy," and so soft that it will not bear any considerable weight. Mr. W. lately undertook to curb up the spring in order to get water more easily, and while working in the mire came upon what appeared to be an enormous bone. He at once began an examination, which disclosed the startling fact that it was the head of some mammoth beast. His curiosity was aroused, and, with the assistance of three other men, he began the work of excavation.

For four days they worked, but did not succeed in bringing the monster to the surface. They threw off the marl, but could not lift the head of this golitic giant. They found the skeleton well preserved and the immense teeth still in the jaws. The jaws were both in place, and the spinal column attached to the cranium. The earth was thrown off from the body to the length of twenty feet, but still the gigantic skeleton remained beneath. Three of the front ribs were forced out, and proved by measurement to be each eight feet in length. The dirt was removed from the inside of the osseous structure, and there lay the skeleton of a human being, with one hundred and two flint arrow points and fifteen flint knives.

The cranium indicated that it was the skeleton of an Indian. It would have been impossible for the man to have been inside the animal without having been swallowed by him, and his theory is substantiated by the fact that the bones of his right side of the skeleton were broken and mashed apparently by force. The monster, therefore, must have been carnivorous, which is also proven by the teeth, which exhibit the marked characteristics of a flesh-eating beast.

A large molar and two incisors, taken from the upper jaw, were exhibited to us at our office yesterday, the largest one weighing eight pounds and measuring eight by four inches in size. There are two large molars and two blunt tusks on each side of the jaw; the teeth between the molars and the tusks are incisors, having from two to six points and corresponding prongs to each tooth. In front of the tusks the teeth are similar to those of most carnivorous animals in shape.

All the bones indicate that they have lain buried for an incredibly long period, as they crumble rapidly when brought in contact with the atmosphere. Every circumstance goes to show that these are the largest animal remains ever resurrected, and the teeth, tusks and structure of the head and jaws prove unmistakably that it was of the carnivorous class.

—Carthage (MO.) Patriot.

STRANGE INHABITANTS OF A WELL.

Knoxville Daily Chronicle – September 13, 1879 – Tennessee

Mr. Jeff K. Clark, a well-known farmer and stock-raiser of Florissant Valley, came to the city yesterday, bringing with him a horrible-looking monster of an unknown species, which he had taken from his well. The creature resembles a fish more than anything else, but has legs like a bear's and a tail like a scorpion. It has long black hair on its back, and its eyes are prominent and fierce looking. The shape of its body is like that of a sunfish, and from around its mouth seven or eight long arms or suckers, radiate, giving it the appearance of a devilfish. The animal was alive when taken from the well, but died in a short time when exposed to the air, and was placed in a brass tub with a glass cover. Mr. Clark had a bottle of water which he said was full of the same kind of monsters, and he intended taking it to Dr. Dean at the City Hospital, to have the contents examined through a microscope.

– St. Louis Globe-Democrat, September 3.

TWO TERRIFIED HUNTERS.

The Cincinnati Daily Star – October 30, 1879 – Ohio

Chased by an Enraged Maniac on Whom They Fired.

[New York Sun]

Two Vermont hunters, John Simmons and William Shegan, aver that they met with a strange adventure a day or two since on "Pine Crabble Peak," just east of Blackinton village, four miles north of North Adams. This pine-capped peak was, some years ago, the resort of wild animals, and of late it has been seldom visited. The story of the hunters is that, while hunting in the vicinity of this mountain, they heard a slight noise near a rugged cliff and saw a huge, hairy object, apparently half man and half beast, spring from behind the cliff and start for the woods, running with the speed of the wind. Mistaking it for a wild animal, one of the hunters fired at it. The shot appeared to take effect in the arm, for, with a scream of pain, the creature halted, tapped the wound, and, turning, charged its pursuers, who, with empty guns in hand, dared not measure strength with such a foe. Dropping their guns, both sought safety in flight, and stopped only when compelled to do so for lack of ability to run further. The men say that they are positive that the creature resembled a man in its general appearance. It was wild-eyed, and very fierce in its disposition, judging from the short time they saw it.

The hunter's story revives a long-forgotten but now distinctly recalled yarn to the effect that many years ago a lunatic, then a young man, escaped from his keepers from somewhere near the New York State line, and gained the mountain fastnesses, where he evaded pursuit, and, it is thought, subsisted on berries and the flesh of animals killed through some means best known to himself. Several years later a strange creature, answering the description of the being recently seen, with the exception of the grizzly beard, was discovered by a party of children who were berrying on the mountain, and it is thought that this may be the same.

The hunters say that they are positive that it was no optical illusion, but a genuine wild man, and a very fierce one at that. The creature's arms, they say, were long and hairy, and looked very much like a full-grown gorilla. They aver that it ran with remarkable swiftness, all the time uttering loud cries, as though in pain and enraged. They declare that it was only by their utmost exertion that they escaped their pursuer, and they say that there is not money enough in Massachusetts to hire them to again venture across its path.

There is talk of organizing an armed force in Williamstown to go in search of this creature.

EXCITEMENT OVER A MYSTERIOUS ANIMAL.

Helena Weekly Herald – December 11, 1879 – Montana

[From the Philadelphia Times.]

Quite a large searching party has been organized in Easter Berks for the purpose of scouring Muhlenberg and Ruscombamane Townships to hunt up and capture, if possible, one of the strangest looking beasts ever heard of within the borders of this country. What gives emphasis to the sincerity of the people engaged is the fact that responsible and reliable parties were first to report having seen the so-called monster. A son of Prison Inspector Schmehl was the first to bring the intelligence to Topton Station. O.H. Hinnershitz, proprietor of the leading hotel there, and a number of others went in pursuit of what Mr. Schmehl described. The monster had been reported on previous occasions, and when Mr. Schmehl saw it it was lying near a gate entrance to a field through which he was about driving a lot of cattle. The "what-is-it" is represented to be about four feet tall, long arms, with but two talon-like fingers on each paw; feet without toes, furrows on its head, body smooth and naked, quite yellow, looking as though it had been wallowing in the clay.

John Rissmiller heard of the animal. It had run up toward Schmehl with extended paws, and then darted into a corn-field and was lost to view. The two men went in search, and discovered the animal on the other side of the field, lying near the fence. Rissmiller says it is yellowish brown in color, has no hair, small eyes and face, arms about fourteen inches long, legs somewhat longer, the hands and feet resembling those of a human being, and has two horns on the top of the head. The young men made a raid on the monster, when they saw it dart toward the forest and was soon lost in the foliage. A Mr. Hickman also residing near there, is reported to have seen the beast, and he is inclined to believe that it is a large sized ape, that may have escape from some traveling menagerie. Every cornfield is to be searched, together with the neighboring swamps, for the purpose of ascertaining what the young men have really seen. After the recent rains the farmers plainly saw strange-looking tracks in the sand on the roadside. They have also heard very unusual howls at night, and the dogs of the neighborhood have been trying to hunt down the beast without success. At first a large number of people were disposed to view the thing as a joke, but this feeling is gradually changing. No effort will be spared to solve this matter and discover all there is in it.

STORIES FROM THE:
1880's

A MONSTER.

Claiborne Guardian – September 22, 1880 – Louisiana

The Most Horrible Being of the World Found in Oregon.

(East Portland (Oregon) Vindicator.)

Long years ago, when the first settlers came to Oregon, there were stories told to new-comers of the existence of a monster that had been seen in the wilds of the Coast range. He wandered over every part of the vast domain between the mouth of the Rouge river and the Columbia, going as far east as the Willamette river and the boundless ocean on the west. When the people began to settle the rich fields and vales of this part this monster went deeper and deeper into the wilderness, and was only seen at long intervals as some venturesome hunter would suddenly come across him in the mighty jungle of forest that covered his vast range. His appearance, frightful in the extreme would so inspire his beholder with terror that in his fear he would make all haste to leave the spot of horror with only an indistinct remembrance of the vision he had beheld of the greatest monster on earth. His story told by the campfire on his return to his comrades would only be hooted at, and he would retire amid their derision for being such a coward.

THIS FEARFUL FIEND

would sometimes venture near the settlements, and in the night would commit some depredation that would bring out the hunters and their dogs for a chase, but after several hours the hounds would come back dragging their tails in terror and slink crouching to their masters' feet. For long years this demon monarch held his sway of the forest, and his fame grew from the north to the south, from the east to the west, and many would start out to conquer him. Some came back regarding him as a myth, others with fear written on each lineament of their features, and others went out and never returned. Those who had seen him were unmaued forever, and their skill as hunters gone; nor could they ever be induced to go beyond the settlement again to seek the bear or elk for fear of an encounter with this inhuman monster. It was reserved for a party of tourists and hunters from California to meet him face to face, and to them we are indebted for the tale of their adventure. Two weeks ago a party of four, renowned as mighty hunters of the grizzly in the Sierras, came ashore from the Oregou and took boat for the Nehalem valley. Intent upon being the first to tread many portions of this wild country, they went on and on deep into the wilderness. One day last week, when far from the mighty Columbia they

SENT OUT THEIR DOGS

to chase the game, and each took a stand by a "run." One more full of curiosity and adventure than the rest of the party began to look around, and soon he saw in the soft mud near the spring the print of a monster foot; but one track was visible, but its size and resemblance to a human foot made him start back in horror and clench his trusty rifle as he held his bated breath. He remembered the stories he had heard and calling his companions and hounds around him they decided to give the monster chase, nor rest until he had been brought to bay. The track in the mud was shown to the dogs, and soon their deep baying betokened that they had found their quarry. On through the tangled woods rushed the men, and soon they were face to face with the horrible form that had haunted this place for years.

Of giant height, with hair falling in grizzled locks, his arms of the size of saplings, and covered with a coarse red hair all over his body, he stood facing the men with an expression of hate and ferocity. His teeth were set, and his two long tusks on each side showed that a life would be of little worth to anything into which they might be set, and with a sweep of his long arm one of the baying hounds was caught up and those fearful tusks sent crashing through his brain.

The men stood awed with horror. The remaining dogs seeing the fate of their comrade, drew back, and this horrible figure throwing the dog from him, moved away, and then they saw what they had not noticed before — that one foot was backward and the other forward, and that he could run one way as well as the other. Fleet of foot, he could dodge first one way and then the other, and springing by the mighty trees of the forest, he was soon lost to view. His track was measured and found to be twenty-seven inches in length. His height was estimated by measuring a small tree near which he stood, and found to be eleven feet and five inches. His terrible eyes and ferocious teeth, that grinning mouth and the swelling muscles of his body so inspired the hunters with a wholesome fear that they returned to the city, and on last Wednesday morning returned to their own State, content to hunt the grizzly and mountain sheep amid the hills and rocks of the Sierra Nevada's.

A MAN WITH A MERMAID.

The Lexington Dispatch – November 24, 1880 – South Carolina

The Strange Creature, Half Woman and Half Fish, Now in St. Louis.

Mr. Chas. A. Doyle is a San Franciscan, lately returned from Japan. He is registered at the Lindell Hotel from Yokohama, and in addition to the interest that attached to him, owing to the strange country he hails from, he enjoys the further distinction of being known as the man with a "mermaid." A *Globe-Democrat* reporter learned yesterday that Mr. Doyle not only enjoys the distinction mentioned, but really is the possessor of a genuine mermaid. The reporter hunted up Mr. Doyle and had a pleasant chat with him. He had been in Japan for several years and was greatly interested in the many modernizing influences at work in the Orient. Mr. Doyle, who is an art critic and collector, went into raptures over the richness of Japans' art products, and this is just what was expected from him, as he is here with a large quantity of rare Japanese articles, as curious as they are costly.

But these lost all interest to the reporter when a long deep glass cage, in the shape of an aquarium, was exhibited, which held the most curious and the rarest of all the objects in the collection. It was a wonderful looking thing, almost hideous to look upon, but possessing a powerful attraction for the beholder, owing to the queer amalgamation of species displayed in its formation. Those who have seen the old-time geography illustration, which has recently been used as a trademark for a certain patent hair restorative and which represents the mermaid rising from the sea and combing her long locks with one hand while in the other she holds a small looking-glass, can recall this picture and thereby form an idea of what the present monstrosity looks like, barring however, the beauty, which is a distinguishing trait of the ideal mermaid. Mr. Doyle's strange curiosity is half human, half fish. The head, chest, abdomen and arms are unmistakably human, but from the abdomen down the creature is a fish, scaly, finny and formed like the extremities of a dweller in the water. The arms are covered with scales to the wrist, and the backs of the small hands have the same scaly covering to the finger tips. The head is small as that of a baby but is perfect in every detail; the forehead does not recede, but is high and straight and is of the class that indicates an unusual degree of intelligence. The eyes are soft, swimmy and lightless, as those of a fish; but the mouth, the ears, the nose, and in fact all the other features, are pronounced human, regular, clear cut, and as perfect as a beautiful woman's face. A light covering of brown hair, several inches in length, and eyebrows of the same color, are the only hirsute of appendages. The spinal column is clearly seen running up to the base of the skull and falling down the back until it is lost in the fishy extremity. Ten ribs are easily counted upon the breast, and the mammalian female development for feeding the young is readily discernible. The mermaid measures almost three feet from the crown of the head to the extremity of the caudal fin, and is said to be larger than the only other specimen of the kind ever seen in this country. The other mermaid is now on exhibition in the New York Aquarium, and attracts a vast amount of attention from scientists as well as from the general public.

Mr. Doyle is very proud of his mermaid, and, although a great many attempts have been made to induce him to sell the curious creature, he has thus far refused to part with her. He says the monstrosity has been subjected to the closest scrutiny by scientists of the Pacific slope, all of whom have pronounced her the most wonderful natural phenomenon ever brought to their notice, and have concurred in declaring mermaids no longer myths. The curiosity was captured two years ago by three fishermen, near Urishaba, in the great island sea.

They had seen her many times and had made many attempts to capture her, and succeeded in taking her after the most persistent efforts. When taken she was placed in the museum at Tokio and remained there for a year and a-half. She had been heard by the fishermen to sing a peculiar song while on the rocks, but never spoke, except to feebly try to articulate after her capture. She was fed on a peculiar sea-weed, the secret of which is known only to the Japanese, and thrived under the great care taken of her. Mr. Doyle purchased her from the authorities of Tokio at the extravagant figure of 5,000 sat, or dollars. The purchase was made to satisfy a sudden desire to possess the strange creature, and Mr. Doyle does not know what special advantage he enjoys in being one of the very few men who own a mermaid.

THE GYASTICUTIS.

Wheeling Register – September 21, 1882 – West Virginia

Loose in the Woods of Northern Pennsylvania.

**Wild Excitement Among the Grangers Near Erie – Startling Rumors of a Hairy Monster Prowling Through the Forests.
SEEKING WHOM IT MAY DEVOUR.**

ERIE, PA., September 19. – The wildest excitement prevails here in consequence of startling rumors that came flying in from the western suburbs that an immense wild animal, of terrible proportions, was roaming the woods and tearing the roads and lands of McKean township. The wildest story heard was that the savage monster, said to walk erect on its hind feet, had seized three children on their way home from school, and had

Dismembered and Devoured Them

in sight of their parents. Before noon this wild horror had so multiplied that it was said the entire village had been mangled and torn by this fearful animal. The coming of Barnum's circus here to-morrow gave room for surmise that the dreadful thing was one of the wild men depicted on the glaring posters that illustrate the city just now, or that one of the strange Asiatic or African beasts had broken loose. An investigation developed the following facts, which, as usual, fall considerably below the sensational rumors that were circulated:

The True Story.

About 5 o'clock last evening residents of the village were terrified by seeing an immense, wild and fearful-looking animal rushing toward them from the south, across the meadows of H. Dewalt. It crossed the road and entered the wheat field on the farm of Mrs. E. Vorsie, tearing down the fence, strong barbed, without any effort. It turned from the direction of the spellbound people and went down to the creek, where it was lost sight of.

The Alarm Was Raised

and the people armed and turned out to track and kill the ferocious animal. A pack of hounds were put upon the scent, and amid their yelping and the cries of the beaters, the hunt was commenced. Across the meadows and farm lands traversed by the brute its tracks were plainly seen, the impress of its feet being clear and well defined. The reporter measured one of these tracks. It was found to be 16 inches long and 8 inches wide at the ball, each of the footprints being about five feet apart.

An Exciting Chase.

The chase grew more exciting as the evidences of recent exhibitions of its terrible strength grew thicker, and it was noticed that many of the valorous hunters fell off. At last the hounds refused to proceed, and no amount of discipline could induce them to take up the chase. Darkness came on before the hunters were aware of it, and excellent time was made in getting out of the woods. Extra attention was paid to locks, bolts and bars when the farmers got home, and

Doors and Windows Were Barricaded.

It was a sleepless night for the people at McKean, about 2 P.M. to day, the utmost terror reigned. Terrible noises were heard, and Mrs. S. Skinner, looking from her window, saw her cows rushing in great haste from the woods in which they had been grazing. Henry Koehler, a thoroughly reliable person, says he caught a

Glimpse of the Creature

at this time, and that it was unlike any monster he had seen even in a circus, and that it stood erect on its hind feet. Fright is the worst that the people of McKean have had to suffer. There have been no deaths or hurts of any kind, the positive assertions to the contrary notwithstanding. It is generally believed to be some circus animal at large. In the meantime the good people of McKean don't stroll far from home, or indulge in lonely walks abroad. Evening promenading of lovers has ceased for the time.

A MONSTER REPTILE.

The Grenada Sentinel – July 14, 1883 – Mississippi

Last Saturday G.B. Shaw, of Vermilion Parish and Will Cook, Frank Hausen and Fritz, the keeper of the Lake Catherine Club, were out hunting on Bayou Bobb, Lake Catherine, when their attention was attracted by a great disturbance in the water of the bayou. Rushing to the banks of the stream they saw, beyond the reeds which grew out into the water, a reptile whose immensity and revolting ugliness amazed them beyond measure.

As nearly as could be judged from that portion of the monster which was exposed above the water, it was thirty feet long; its breadth in the thickest part about three feet; its back was rough and corrugated with mottled and horny barbs, apparently from six to ten inches long, studded thickly down what was evidently the column of a vertebrate. The tail was not visible, but its length was made apparent by the movement of the waters as the monster used it in propelling itself rapidly down the bayou. The proboscis and eyes were visible and in the shape and position seemed much like those of an alligator.

As the monster moved great waves rose and broke among the reeds. Their guns were heavily loaded, fortunately, with buckshot. At the first fire there was a terrific result. The waters of the broad bayou were lashed from bank to bank and the great waves shook the reeds as strong as wind. The monster reared its huge, repulsive head full six feet above the water, and its red, glittering eyes glared fiercely toward its enemies. They were almost paralyzed with the horror of the dreadful apparition but directly summoned the nerve to fire their second barrel at the frightful muzzle of the monster, which, wide open, displayed a cavernous throat, from which flashed a long slender tongue.

As the smoke cleared from this second discharge it was seen that the monster had again subsided, and its huge back passed through the water with incredible swiftness toward an unusually thick and broad bunch of reeds, some score of yards down the stream and on the opposite side. As it disappeared the gentlemen were still further terrified with a muffled roar. They hastened to the spot opposite that at which the monster had disappeared and continued to fire into the reeds for a long while in the hope that the monster would reappear; but it was of no avail, and none of the party thinking the occasion demanded a nearer approach, they departed.

— N.O. Times-Democrat.

A DIABOLICAL CREATURE.

The Benton Weekly Record – October 6, 1883 – Montana

An Arizona Monster that is as Savage as a Bull Dog, and Fights Like a Viper.

Virginia City Enterprise.

William Blackheath, when he returned from a six month's sojourn in Arizona, brought to the Comestock, Nev., the skin of what he, for want of a better name, calls a Gila monster, but which is evidently that of a saurian of a different species. The skin now measures seven feet from tip to tip, and it has evidently shrunk some inches in drying. Though about the color of an ordinary Gila monster, the reptile is evidently a kind of inland crocodile, or, more properly, cayman, as it had not the webbed feet of the crocodile.

The strange saurian was found in a small valley in the Wheatstone mountains. When alive it stood two feet high, and its body just back of its forelegs was over three feet in circumference. The creature was as savage as a bull dog, and as full of fight as a viper. It was found by the dogs of Mr. Blackheath and partner. When the men arrived at the haunt of the reptile – to which they were attracted by the fierce and peculiar barking of their dogs, three in number – they found that one dog had already been killed and the others were badly cut up and covered with blood. The creature displayed such activity, and was so diabolically vicious, that the two prospectors feared to go near it, being armed with nothing better than a prospecting pick and a shovel with a small handle.

Finally the thing got one of the dogs by the fore leg, and finding that it held on like a terrier, with no signs of loosing its hold, Mr. Blackheath ran forward and stuck his pick into its head. Even then the reptile held on, and it was not until it had been struck several blows with the pole of the pick, that its jaws relaxed and it gave up the ghost. When the dog was released it was found that his fore leg had been broken at a point about two inches above the knee.

Mr. Blackheath says that he has met with several of the creatures known as Gila monsters that were two and a half feet in length, but never, before or since, saw, or even suspected the existence of one so large as that whose skin he possesses. It was a surprise to all white men in that section, but some of the Indians asserted that far to the south in the Sierra Madre mountains they had seen some that were as large or larger.

Unfortunately, in flaying the saurian, Mr. Blackheath's only idea was to have the hide tanned and made into boots and gaiters, therefore he did not preserve the feet, otherwise the skin might be stuffed and mounted by a taxidermist. He says the teeth of the creature were over an inch in length, were sharp as needles, and in shape resembles the teeth of a shark.

A WESTERN MONSTER.

Savannah Morning News – August 17, 1884 – Georgia

A Mysterious Creature in British Columbia.

The village of Yale, B.C., is situated at the head of navigation on Fraser river, 90 miles above New Westminster, which was the capital of British Columbia until it was changed to Victoria. About 20 miles from Yale, on the line of the railroad, is a locality roughly known as "Tunnel No. 4," where the extraordinary occurrences about to be related took place during the early part of the present month.

Notwithstanding the improbability of any amount of prospecting resulting in turning up even the bones of the "missing link," much less in finding an actual living specimen of this much-debated being, the actual facts which are related concerning the remarkable appearance near "Tunnel No. 4" would tend to bear out this theory of the subject. At different times during the past two years there has been seen in the hilly country about the settlement a being whose personal appearance is variously described.

One day about a year ago a party of young people from Yale went up on the road as far as Tunnel No. 4, and there, disembarking from the ears, proceeded to spread themselves over the country in the form of a picnic party. The tempting meal had been spread upon the ground, and the young men and girls were seated in a circle preparing to enjoy the viands, when there was heard a loud, crashing noise above their heads, and in an instant, without further warning than was given by a most fiendish yell – something between the shriek of a hyena and the Indian war-whoop – there dropped into the midst of the spread a horrible creature as large as a man, covered with hair from head to foot, with long arms, which he brandished about in formidable style as he vainly tried to extricate himself from the canned fruits, cold meats, jam-pots, and oleomargarine into which he had unexpectedly tumbled. This was a "surprise party" for which no intentional preparation had been made, and in a moment there was a stampede. Tumbling headlong down the hill on whose crest the elaborate meal had been laid, the frightened picnickers so hastened their departure as to be utterly unable to give any coherent description of what had frightened them to the railroad men whose assistance they implored. A party fully armed was at once made up, and the scene of the sudden onslaught was carefully approached. The unwelcome visitor had fled, but before leaving he had plainly helped himself to everything that took his fancy, and that seemed to have been guided by nothing but the opportunity. If he were a human creature and had eaten what was certainly gone, selected from every imaginable article of food, his remains would undoubtedly be found in a few hours. No idiot, Indian, or other kind of man could possibly have eaten such a mixture and live.

But if such was the case, the most careful search failed to result in finding the body, and after a protracted search, which lasted, after a desultory fashion, for several weeks, the idea of his having died of indigestion or gout was reluctantly abandoned. One fact which was demonstrated by the circumstances of his visitation caused the believers in the Indian theory to be very deeply shaken in their convictions. This was that he had fallen from an overhanging limb of a tree, carrying a large piece with him, and the size of the limb was a good indication that the creature must be as heavy as an ordinary-sized man, and hardly an Indian, as they do not usually climb trees. A few months later another view of this strange being was had by some workmen on the railroad, but, though they gave chase, they were not able to come up with him. He was not seen again until about three weeks ago, when he was not only seen, but caught. The spot where he was discovered was a series of bluffs, deemed inaccessible. A train was running from Lytton to Yale, when the engineer saw what he supposed to be a man lying close to the track. He whistled down brakes, but just as the train stopped the object sprang to its feet, and in an instant was climbing the side of the precipitous declivity with the greatest ease. The conductor, brakemen, express messenger and a number of passengers at once gave chase, and after some perilous climbing succeeded in corralling the creature on an overhanging shelf of rock, from which he could neither ascend or descend. The ingenious, though rather cruel, method was now adopted for securing him of dropping a piece of stone from above, which, falling on his head, stunned him, and he fell insensible.

The bell-rope was now procured, and, after some expert climbing, he was reached, tied, and lowered gradually down to the foot of the cliff. He was placed in the baggage-car and successfully transported to Yale, when it was found that he had recovered from his insensibility, and was tractable and docile. One of the men in the railroad machine-shop assumed the care of him, named him Jacko, and very soon made his friendly acquaintance. And even then, and up to the present time, it has not been satisfactorily ascertained to what race the new discovery belongs. He is of the gorilla type, but not definitely enough to be declared a gorilla, which is, moreover, a creature unknown to the latitude of British Columbia – while there has been no menagerie there to introduce even a monkey. He is about 4 feet 7 inches in height, and weighs 127 pounds. His entire body, except his hands and feet, is covered with black, glossy hair about one inch in length. He greatly resembles a human being, but his forearm is much longer than that of a man, and so strong that he will break a stick – by wrenching or twisting it – so large that no man could possibly accomplish this feat. He makes a noise, half bark and half growl, but is generally quiet. His favorite food is berries, and he drinks fresh milk with evident relish. His captor intends taking him to London for exhibition, when his exact position in natural history will probably be discovered.

BADLY FRIGHTENED.

Evening Capital – September 13, 1884 – Maryland

As two farmers of the second district were returning to their homes late on Tuesday night, when near Spa Branch, they encountered what they supposed to be his Satanic Majesty, in all his hideousness of sulphurous flames, horns, hoofs, tail and all. One was more courageous than the other and determined to meet the hideous monster, and, with a revolver in one hand and a club in the other, advanced towards the Satanic looking object, while his companion took to his heels and made reindeer speed up the country road. He called to the object in front of him, but it made no reply; he then fired his revolver at the "infernal thing," when lo and behold a cow jumped from the bush. The animal had taken rest for the night at the foot of an old stump of a tree which had been burned, and the other with the bark off, the cow lying at its base switching its tail, made a hideous looking object in the glimmer of the dim moonlight. – The fellow was terribly frightened, but he succeeded in getting his breath, and called for his companion but he had fled. The sight was so appalling and blood curdling, says our informant; that his companion was so badly frightened, he was confined to his bed for several days, after witnessing the fearful spectre.

SUB-MARINE MONSTER.

The Florida Agriculturist – November 5, 1884 – Florida

STRANGE FISH OR REPTILE CAUGHT IN THE MISSISSIPPI RIVER.

A strange marine monster was brought to this city yesterday, says the Nashville American, and will be put on exhibition this week, in a building near the square. Bill Orley and Nick Moley, two old fishermen, caught it in the river just above the water-works a few days ago, and since that time it has been fastened securely to the river bank by stakes driven around its body, in addition to which it is hog-chained by the tail to the bank.

When seen in this position yesterday it appeared to be about the size of a Newfoundland dog. It had webbed feet, that were attached to the body by legs without joints. Its body and back, except the stomach, is covered with large, diamond-shaped bony scales. The long, coarse yellow hair growing out of these scales and the skin, which bulges out in welts between the scales, hangs together like that on an Angora goat, and is as coarse and tough as coconut skin fibers. But its mouth is well worth a detailed description. It is certainly the most hideous opening that is developed in the countenance of any animal extant or told about by scientists.

It is about the size of that of a large alligator, but shaped like that of a shovel-nosed shark, being very blunt at the end. And the teeth! There are no less than three rows of them in both the upper and lower part of the mouth. The teeth are all jagged, the upper rows fitting into the lower rows, and the jaws working laterally, so as to make the teeth grind to powder everything that falls into them.

The reptile, devil-fish, or whatever it is, crawls sideways like a crab, and its eyes are placed one above the other in the top of the skull, and bulge out like pegs on a hat rack. There are no lids to the eyes, so that the animal cannot wink, but it pops its eyes in and out of the sockets so fast when the monster is angry that the noise made by this working of the eyes is similar to the sound made by a cow's feet when the animal is wading in soft, deep mud. The tail is shaped like that of a beaver's and is covered with warts of various sizes, the smallest being about the size of a dime, and the largest about the size of a half dollar. Each one of these warts seem to possess the power of moving separately from the other, and when the whole mass gets to working it is something frightful to behold. It has rather more the appearance of a swarm of bees hanging from the limb of a tree, than anything else, and is altogether the most sickening sight imaginable.

The whole animal is covered with a thick green slime, which seems to ooze out of its body, and especially its tail, where it seems to originate from the center of small mouths or openings, one of which is the center of each of the warts mentioned. When prodded with a stick the animal snaps its eyes, grinds its teeth, and each particular hair stands on end, and every inch of its body seems to writhe, squirm, and jerk on its own account and in the manner and direction that seem to give it most comfort. The tongue is forked and black, and darts in and out like that of a sea-serpent.

The two fishermen who captured it have followed this means of making a livelihood for many years. It seems that the existence of this animal has been known to them and a number of old rivermen in this city for a number of years. They say it has made its abode under a high bank on the left-hand side as you go up the river in a place suitable for such a terrible, uncanny looking thing to live without much hesitation. They have been much annoyed by this reptile and have been put to a great deal of experience in repairing their lines, as fish-hooks seemed only to whet its appetite. As if by instinct it knew when and where the lines were set and would go to devour the bait and destroy the lines, which it did almost every night.

But lately a new method was resorted to for dealing with this monster, which resulted in its capture, to the great delight, as well as astonishment, of both the fishermen. Instead of resorting to the old method of fishing, they procured a long, heavy clothes-wire, and stretched it midway across the river. It was attached at the end of a ten gallon keg, that acted as a buoy. To anchor it down an old iron cog-wheel was used. About sixty feet from the shore the bait was set in a large steel trap and let down. It was not long before it was gobbled, as a fisherman, who was looking after his other lines, discovered.

The keg was seen bobbing up and down, and suddenly disappeared altogether. They commenced to haul in their line, and came very near upsetting their skiff. The reptile by this time was furious, and lashed the waters into a white foam. It was found impossible to land it with the boat, and it took two hours to pull the beast out on dry land. An old fish-net was promptly thrown over it, and secured by driving stakes around the outside. The monster bit, snapped, and struggled all night to free itself, until finally, when it was exhausted, five men brought it across the river in a flatboat, and left it at an old sawmill, just below the water-works, where his satanic majesty now reposes. There the reptile has since been viewed by the curious hundreds of people who have been going there to see the brute.

A TOUGH YARN.

Northern Tribune – November 27, 1884 – Michigan

Chicago Inter Ocean.

Last season marine circles were all torn up over the discovery of an alleged sea monster a few miles off the port, and subsequently when it was seen again off Death's Door by some fishermen. The original discovery was made by Captain Dick Brewer while he was towing a big mud scow past the Marine Hospital. Looking ahead out of the pilot house of his boat he saw a large, black object about a quarter of a block distance which he at first took to be a log. There was something in the appearance of the object, however, which impelled him to a closer inspection, and picking up his marine glasses he leveled them in the direction of the supposed log. To his astonishment it began to move rapidly towards the tug, and when within a hundred feet it stopped, raised its head, and dove beneath the surface of the water. A lookout was kept on all sides of the boat, but the strange monster did not reappear.

Captain Brewer described the animal or fish or whatever it was as being about eight feet in length, covered with long black hair, and possessed of an immense head, which was a cross between the head of a horse and cow. A great, gaping mouth, fringed with two sets of long, threatening teeth and two large eyes set close to the center of the animal's forehead, gave it a ferocious appearance. Subsequently an animal of pretty near the same description swam alongside the boat of two fishermen off Death's Door and frightened the pair so badly that they were taken sick and nearly died. Others claimed to have seen this inland sea monster, but their statements were not credited, and whenever the story was repeated the narrator was scoffed into silence. The story was very forcibly received yesterday by the experience of the crews of the tugs Miller and Tom Brown, and, coming as it does from two direct sources, it can no longer be doubted that a marine monster, rivaling even the most hideous of

Jules Verne's deep-sea animals in point of ugliness lives in the waters of Lake Michigan.

Yesterday afternoon when about a mile east of the crib the steward of the tug Miller was engaged in filling his water barrel. He was startled all of a sudden by a huge black object rising to the surface of the water right under the tug's port bow. At first a black hairy body, about eight or nine feet in length, was visible, and then an immense head with distended jaws, which snapped viciously at the tug's wale, was thrust out of the water. The cook recoiled and called to Captain Weiman and the engineer to look at the monster. They all ran to the bow of the boat, and corroborate the story of the cook, whose description of the monster tallies closely with that of Captain Brewer's.

Captain Weiman ran for the boat's pike pole, but before he could use it the strange object had disappeared. A few minutes later it was seen leisurely rolling about in the water, a few hundred feet from the boat, on the starboard side. As the miller had the Mediator in tow he could not give chase to the fish, or animal or whatever it is, but he watched it until it dived beneath the surface of the water and disappeared.

An hour or so afterward the tug Success was passing Lincoln Park about two miles in the lake with two vessels in tow. The deckhand Ed Burke, was leaning over the rail contemplating the water when he was startled by a huge animal rising out of the water with a roaring sound. It roared as loud as a circus lion and darted toward the tug with a ferocity and force which threatened to sink it. Captain Everatt's attention was called to the monster by the noise it made, and he says he saw it also, it disappeared into the depths of the lake. Marine men regard this story with undisguised incredulity, notwithstanding that the crews of both tugs stoutly maintain that it is true in every particular.

The thing to do now is to capture the monster and bring it ashore, so as to give scientists a chance at it. Everybody who has seen the thing says it bellows like a bull and can be heard half a mile away.

THE SLAUGHTER OF A MONSTER.

The Butler Weekly Times – January 28, 1885 – Missouri

A monster animal was killed near Oskaloosa, in this State recently. It measured from end of tail to tip of nose 81 feet. Its heart weighed 80 pounds and had four cavities. After being hunted for a long while it was finally killed with a twelve pound cannon loaded with railroad spikes. It required a team of twelve strong oxen to pull the monster to the river bank after its death.

It was skinned and a taxidermist is stuffing it, when it will be sent to the Academy of Natural Science at Philadelphia. The flesh is being removed from the bones, and the skeleton will be properly wired and kept, at present on exhibition at Oskaloosa. Dr. Peck, of Davenport, calls it the Cardiff Giant, and says it belongs to a species of gigantic lizards supposed to have been extinct many thousands of years.

The monster had been swallowing farmers' hogs, weighing from 300 to 400 pounds each at one gulp. Thousands of people have been gunning for the monster, but it was proof against everything until the cannon brought it down.

THE POULP IN PALATKA.

The Palatka Daily News – April 1, 1885 – Florida

A Great Cephalopod on Our Wharf – The Monster on Exhibition – His Proportions and Features – His Habits and His Home.

As we were going to press last night, a great noise arose on the wharf, near Lane's warehouse, and the whole force of The News rushed out to find a large area of the dock covered by a vast slimy mass which was strange to all the assembly. Long whip-like arms lashed the air, and curved and twisted in snaky tangles around a dark body in the center. Then the arms fell rattling on the hard planks, and tried in vain to seize the hard surface, while the central mass rose and fell in uncertain expansion: two large eyes stared horribly at us, and a long curved beak snapped and snarled in anger. From a hundred blowholes the air rushed with hissing noises as the thing breathed and the whole struggled to draw itself along the wharf. It seemed to feel no alarm at the increasing number of spectators, and paid no heed to their wondering exclamations. Several negroes left, thinking that "De Debbil's come," and probably ran far beyond their homes before fatigue compelled them to stop.

Meantime no effort was made to stop the monster, and he continued his way across the wharf until he reached the deep sand in the rear of Marrion's hotel, on Water Street. Here he settled himself and rested. But his great eyes still kept angry watch and emitted a dull green phosphorescent light. Occasionally the hooked beak snapped viciously and protruded itself from the tangled mass of legs seemingly larger than a man's hand. The crowd drove him with sticks and brickbats further from the water, and as he lay with his arms expanded a stout rope was drawn around one, and he was tied securely to a strong post. He was evidently badly wounded, probably by the wheel of a river steamer, and had betaken himself to the first land for recuperation. His slimy trail showed that he had climbed one of the supports of the wharf and thence was drawing himself along when the watchman saw him.

These animals are generally found only in the depths of the ocean, but one was killed at New Smyrna some years ago, and several small ones have been seen on the Florida coast. The one which has come to us so strangely this morning will weigh about 300 pounds, and his utmost spread would be 25 feet. But all of this is conjectural, for none of us have ventured near enough to his terrible beak and horrible arms to make an exact description. They have been seen more than one hundred feet from one extended tip to the other, and then the monster weighs three or four thousand pounds.

Our visitor probably lost his way as porpoises have twice done, and became entangled in the wheels of a steamer so that it was too much injured to return. The great Cephalopod will no doubt attract crowds of visitors to-day, and furnish a new reason for remembering the First of April, 1885. Our naturalists – Fry, Kersting and others – will give us scientific particulars, which we will publish tomorrow.

A HUGE SERPENT.

Barbour County Index – September 24, 1886 – Kansas

A Reptile Which Chases Cattle and Drives Grown People Nearly Frantic.

(Cincinnati Commercial Gazette.)

Butler, Ohio, has been in a feverish state of agitation since last Sunday by the report of a monster snake that has been seen in the immediate vicinity. Last Sunday Nick Corbin, one of the oldest and most esteemed citizens, and whose veracity is unquestioned, went about a mile out of town in search of a lost pig, and as he was passing through a thicket of blackberry bushes his attention was attracted by some cattle that were rushing frantically toward the river, and on searching for the cause of the strange action of the cattle his attention was called to a strange, whirring noise in the bushes behind him, and on looking round was almost paralyzed at the sight of an immense monster of the snake species.

It was of a dark-brown color, with a flat head, and at least twenty-five feet long. It was standing with its head about teen feet from the ground, waving from one side to the other in an excited manner. Corbin suddenly thought of some business in town that needed his attention. He succeeded in getting away without attracting the monster's attention, and with all the speed he could command he rushed to Butler and spread the report; and the people having the utmost confidence in his veracity, armed themselves with guns, clubs, and other weapons that were handy, and about 4 p.m. about seventy-five men started for the place where the snake had been seen.

The place was surrounded and with the utmost precaution, led on by Uncle Nick, the men gradually closed in, but no snake; but there were unmistakable signs of its having been there a short time before, and after searching for a short time a trail, which looked as if a log had been drawn on the ground, was found leading toward the

Ohio river. Several men followed the trail till dark set in and then returned to town. It is thought by a great many to be the same snake so often seen by residents of Mosco, O., as the trail led in that direction. The excitement has not yet subsided, and the blackberries are going to waste in the community.

SCARED BY A BIG GORILLA.

Daily Evening Bulletin – November 3, 1886 – Kentucky

A MUSEUM MONSTER AT LARGE IN LONG ISLAND WOODS.

The Residents About Setauket Afraid to Go Out at Night Because the Gorilla Infests the Neighborhood – He Kills Sheep and Has Fun with Everybody.

New York, Nov. 3. – The villagers of Setauket, L.I., believe there is a gorilla lurking in the woods which border their town, and they are fearful of their lives in consequence. The farmers go armed to their work in the fields and do not venture out alone after dark. Their wives would as soon defy an army of mice as leave the shelter of their homes, and the children are afraid to go to pasture for the cows, and in some cases have to be escorted to and from school. The nutting season is at its height, but the children dare not venture near the woods. The colored natives, many of whom go nightly to Stony Brook, two miles distant, to buy rum, now make the trip in groups armed with axes and pitchforks.

Selah Strong is a farmer of Setauket, who has a fine flock of Southdown sheep. Two weeks ago, the pick of the flock was found one morning dead in the field with its throat horribly mangled. There were marks of claws in the flesh; and on a spot of soft ground near by was an almost human footprint. The sheep was skinned and then it was found that its back was broken. Farmer Strong was puzzled. A man he argued, might have broken the animal's back and left the footprint in the soft ground, but he could not have torn the flesh about the throat and left the claw marks. He finally concluded that a man had started the job and that later a beast had finished it.

Two nights afterward Jacob Satterlee, who lives about a mile from Farmer Strong, heard a fearful squawking in his chicken house. He loaded a double-barreled shotgun and went forth. The chickens had quieted down, but on the floor beneath the roost were three fat hens whose heads had been literally torn from their bodies. There was nothing to indicate who or what had been guilty of the slaughter.

The "bloody butcher," as the unknown trespasser came to be called, remained veiled in mystery for several days. A few evenings since, however, Farmer Jim Addis met with an experience which has satisfied his neighbors as to the true character of the intruder. This is what occurred, as told by himself to the reporter:

"I'd been up in the hills all day plowin', and about dusk I put the team to the wagon and started for home. My off mare was a little lame in one foot and I was drivin' easy. We came down through the lane to the highway, and I stopped and closed up the bars after me. Then I climbed back into my wagon and we headed down into the holler. I was nigh onto the big white oak at the edge o' the swamp when the nigh hoss, Billy, pricked up his ears and took a scent o' the air. He did not seem to like it, and the mare was up to something pesky, too. I naturally looked to see what was wrong, and the first thing I knew we passed within twenty feet of a big ape of some kind. It was just in the edge of the bush and stood on its hind feet graspin' the limb of a saplin' with one hand. It made a move towards us, and my nigh hoss gosh durn near jumped through his collar. The mare was frightened, too, and they lit out of that holler like they was colts. I wasn't exactly scared, but I looked around and saw the brute watchin' in the middle of the road, and I thought I would let the team git out as quick as they was a mind to. I had two good, square looks at the animal. He stood high onto five feet high. His legs was thin up to the knees and then they was quite full. His arms was the same, and he had a little head. He was hairy all over, and I didn't see no tail."

This was the story which, connected with the inhuman butchery of the sheep and chickens, frightened the quiet village folk. Then the natives began to wonder where the animal had come from, and a party of Sound fishermen was discovered who alleged that a few night previous a South American trader had sought shelter in the harbor of Port Jefferson, three miles down the coast, and that they had a couple of good sized gorillas on board. It was further alleged by the fishermen that the animals had escaped while exercising on the deck, and that only one of them had been recaptured. Nobody could be found by the reporter yesterday either in Setauket or Port Jefferson who knew who the fishermen were that had told the yarn.

There are many of the villagers of Setauket who have been exercising their imaginations to increase the sensation. A darky named Jerry Woodchuck, a famous hunter, is at present in the lead. He has paralyzed the colored colony by a tale that on Thursday, while hunting for coon in Nassakeag Swamp, he came across footprints in the mud which measured twenty-two inches in length. He followed them, so he says, and came across a tremendous gorilla, at least nine feet in height, who stood up to his knees in water, and pounded his chest with both fists. Jerry Woodchuck discharged his gun at the beast and fled, or at least that is what he tells his neighbors. Henry Sanford, a farmer, told a grocery crowd at Stoney Brook the other night that the gorilla had stood in the middle of the road and refused to allow him to pass. The animal, he said, slapped its chest violently, producing a sound like a blow on a hollow log. Farmer "Hi" Calkin's son and a schoolboy named Sherman Hawkins each told their playfellows that they had met the gorilla in the woods. Two strange men passed through Setauket on Wednesday, who said they were looking for a gorilla which had escaped from a Brighton Beach museum.

THE WILD MAN OF OHIO.

The Midland Journal – March 11, 1887– Maryland

A Curious Creature Seen Among the Hills of Holmes County.

A party of hunters, who have just returned from a hunt in the hills of Holmes County, Ohio, say they encountered a curious creature on their trip. According to their description, a wild man, or some other strange being, is at large in Holmes County. The party who reported seeing this strange creature claim that he or it looked like a man, but acted like a wild beast. The creature was encountered near a brushy thicket and willow copse near what is known as Big Spring, where General Buell rested on his march through Ohio, at a point a short distance south of the Wayne County line in Holmes County.

The hunters were beating the brush for pheasants when the attention of one of the party was attracted to an object that suddenly darted across an opening in the brush. Later on the object was again seen along the edge of the brush. By this time the hunters had reached open ground, and were surprised to see what they describe as a man, entirely nude but covered with what appeared to them to be matted hair. When seen he was some distance away, but on discovering the hunters he started toward them on a run, and gave forth queer guttural sounds. On seeing the strange being moving toward them the party of hunters, which included four persons, all armed with shot guns, broke and ran.

The strange creature pursued them for a short distance until the party had reached a public highway, when he turned back and was seen to enter Killbuck Creek, which he swam, and then disappeared in the brush again. On approaching the water he dropped on all fours and plunged in like a dog, swimming in a manner similar to a canine. The hunters did not have the nerve to return, but got away from the place as soon as possible. They are emphatic in their assertion that they encountered a wild man and describe him as above, but they are of the impression that he is no relative of the famous wild man of Rockaway.

GREAT LAKE MONSTER.

Omaha Daily Bee – May 20, 1887 – Nebraska

A Huge Amphibious Animal Seen on the Beach of Lake Erie.

Toledo. O., May 13. – There was great excitement among the French inhabitants along the lake shore in Ottawa county over the reported discovery of a marine monster by two French fishermen named Dusseau. The brothers were returning from the fishing grounds late last night, when they noticed a monster on the sandy beach of Lake Erie.

They fastened their boat and upon examining the monster found it to be an immense fish between twenty and thirty feet in length. It was shaped like a sturgeon, but had arms which were thrown wildly into the air.

The fishermen say the light must have been caused by phosphorescence emitted in its death struggles. They hurried away for ropes and aid, but when they returned the submarine monster had evidently thrown itself into the lake in its dying struggles and been carried away by the waves. No trace of the animal could be found save a half dozen scales as large as silver dollars.

Tracks on the beach where it was discovered made it perfectly plain that the lake serpent was of great size, and it was undoubtedly in its death struggles when first seen.

HERE'S A SNAKE.

St. Paul Daily Globe – May 31, 1887 – Minnesota

Unless the Eyes of Reliable Witnesses Have Been Deceived.
Dwellers at Lake Minnetonka Say They Saw a Monster.

With a Terrible Head and Fins That Moved Like Wings.
A Great Leviathan Sporting the Big Water This Year.
On Several Occasions He Has Lashed the Lake to Foam.
The General Topic of Conversation at the Lake.

Snake stories are always disbelieved, save by those who actually come in contact with representative reptiles, and the writer of a communication to the GLOBE doubtless felt the same way, for he not only signed his own name, but gave information which yielded good fruit in an investigation. In the mail that reached the GLOBE Saturday was the following missive:

Wayzata, Minn., May 27, 1887.

Daily Globe, St. Paul, Minn. Inclosed we send you a picture of the lake serpent as seen by a party of fishermen in Lake Minnetonka on the evening of the 23d inst. The immensity of this strange amphibious animal frightened the party from the lake. We have the names of about fifteen persons that have seen this serpent.

MARTIN V. HENRY. one of the party.

The picture referred to was a pen and ink sketch of a monster not unlike a gigantic snake with two fore paws, or flippers, and a forked tail similar to that usually delineated in representations of the prince of darkness, and in the middle of the body were two gigantic fins, which at first glance looked like wings. The dimensions of the monster were given as thirty feet in length and about as large round the belly as a full-grown man.

Armed with the document and picture a representative of the GLOBE set out for Wayzata and was fortunate enough to find, upon leaving the car at the depot, an eye-witness of the maneuvers of the monster in the person of A.P. Dickey, at present engaged in building a bridge across Shafer's narrows, a point opposite to Wayzata on the west. According to his statement, several days ago while at work on the bridge with Messrs. George McLean and Jacob Snow, the narrator saw what at first looked like a log moving down Lake Minnetonka from Cedar point.

"You will all say this is another snake story," he said, looking around at a group of open-mouthed rustics who had been attracted by the advent of a stranger and a note book, "but what I am telling you I saw with my own eyes. My companions on the bridge did not see the thing, whatever it was, until I directed their attention to it, and finally it came within 200 yards of us. Raising its head several feet, for by this time it gave unmistakable signs of life, the monster began to thresh the water violently, and at the same time flopped over, showing its white belly. This was repeated several times, and the time occupied was fully five minutes. From my observation I should say that

IT WAS THIRTY-FIVE FEET LONG

"Closer inspection made it look like the head and fore-shoulders of an alligator, for it came within six or seven rods of the bridge before it finally dived out of sight, and we did not see it rise again."

All the details were listened to with the deepest attention by the crowd now gathered about the story-teller, who was an honest-looking, well dressed fellow, and too much in earnest with his subject to give the faintest suspicion of intoxication. Then it occurred to one of the group that a lady named Thurston had also said something about seeing a monster last Saturday in the lake. A walk of a few minutes over a pleasant stretch of sward soon brought the GLOBE'S representative to a brown painted cottage on a bluff overlooking the lake and surrounding country.

In response to a knock at the cottage door Farmer Thurston appeared and ushered his visitor into the parlor, where the mistress of the house was sitting.

"Last Saturday afternoon, the 21st of May," she began, "just after the shower, I had occasion to go to the edge of the bluff to look after my children. I did not see them for a few minutes, and stopped to listen for sounds from them. While thus waiting my attention was attracted to what at first seemed to be the struggles of a man drowning in the lake, a few feet beneath where I stood. The water was lashed to a foam by something, and while I looked more intently, I saw it come up out of the water, with head erect, several feet. What I thought were two flippers were moving continually, and I at once saw that it was a snake, or big water monster of some kind. It turned over several times, showing it to be very long, and kept me fascinated by the unusual spectacle for several minutes. There were no boats or fishermen near by, the storm of a few minutes before having driven them all ashore, and I could not call any one to see the monster. As soon as my husband returned from his work I related to him what had occurred, but he advised me to keep it quiet, as people would think it was only an optical delusion. I saw the reptile, or, whatever you might term it, as plainly as I ever saw anything in my life, and it was fully thirty feet long and as large round as a man's body. Mrs. Gallagher, up on the hill, has also seen the monster, but she was closer to it than myself and saw its outlines better."

ANOTHER EYE WITNESS.

A trudge up a steep declivity to the Arlington hotel, which covers a high bluff on the Huntington estate, was rewarded by a sight of Mrs. Mary A. Gallagher, who is in charge of the premises, and she promptly acceded to a request to tell what she knew about the lake terror.

"One afternoon I was down on the wharf below the boat house with my children," said Mrs. Gallagher, "and they were amusing themselves wading and splashing about in the water. Several other children were with them engaged in the same manner, when something caused me to look up suddenly. What at first looked to me like a colored man floating in shore caused me to shout to the children, 'There is a man swimming toward you; come ashore.' My first impression was that some one had jumped off the steamer, intending to have a swim, and as I did not want to see him land I naturally called to my children. At first they misunderstood me, but eventually they saw the object which was now several feet above the surface of the water, and they screamed with terror. Their shouts evidently scared the serpent, for such it appeared to be, having a large flat head with what seemed to be bushy black hair, and it lashed the water violently and disappeared. I was very much frightened, and a party of fishermen, attracted by our noise on shore, looked up from their lines, and as they did so the monster passed their boat. One of the ladies of the party screamed in terror, but the snake swam by without attempting to injure anybody. At least that was what they told me when they came ashore. I could have at one time hit the serpent with a long stick, for it was not further from me than the length of this room, about twenty-five feet, and I distinguished its eyes to be light. Its belly glistened as it turned over apparently, and the color seemed about that of a catfish, and I should say it was between twenty-five and thirty feet long. This was my first, and I hope it will be my last, look at the serpent or whatever it was."

Conversations with numerous denizens of the locality elicited the information that the people whose statements have been given were thoroughly reliable, but they had refrained from repeating their experiences, because they feared the ridicule that might follow.

But the adventure of the fishing party the evening of the 23d inst. had recalled the incident more vividly than ever, and now it was the principal topic of discussion whenever a party assembled for the evening. No fishing party at Wayzata considers its make-up complete unless there is a heavily-loaded gun in the bow of the boat ready for use, and many of the fishermen have additional security in the form of revolvers worn in belts around their waists.

THE SEA SERPENT.

The Daily Morning Astorian – November 13, 1887 – Oregon

A Desperate Battle with a Monster on the Louisiana Coast.

WASHINGTON, Nov. 7. – information has reached this city that a sea serpent or an unknown marine monster was shot in the Gulf of Mexico, but on account of its immense size only the head could be secured. The head will soon be in possession of the National Museum, there to be "sat on" by the scientific sharps. To Captain James P. Hare, who is in charge of the Trinity Show Lightship, off the Louisiana coast, belongs the honor of securing this prize. He has relatives in this city, and to them he has written a very interesting letter describing his encounter with the monster of the sea. He says that while his ship was lazily rolling on the ground swell, one of the seamen came to him and told him that he had seen a strange object in the sea, a couple of cable-lengths from the ship.

The Captain, with the aid of a pair of powerful glasses, saw, to use his own words, "As hideous a creature as ever the human eye rested upon. The first casual glance convinced me that, although from boyhood following the precarious vicissitudes of a seaman's life, and having visited all the prominent waters of the globe, and naturally seeing many strange inhabitants of the sea and land, I found it impossible to name or classify this monster in view."

Determined to investigate further, the Captain called for a volunteer crew and a boat was immediately manned. In addition to harpoons and axes, Captain Hare took his rifle and fifty rounds of ball cartridges. When they got within fifteen yards of their prey the boat stopped and Hare fired. "Simultaneously with the sharp crack of the rifle and the thud of the striking bullet," he writes, "it suddenly reared its head high and began lashing the water with intense fury. Never have I seen such fury displayed by any creature exhibited. Its motions were so rapid and furious that it was impossible for the eye to retain its form. All that was distinguishable was a huge, dark, writhing mass, surrounded by seething foam, into which the water was lashed by the stricken and enraged monster." In a few minutes the Captain fired another shot, which only seemed to further enrage the beast. By this time the blood was spurting from a number of wounds in the head, and the surrounding waters were dyed a deep crimson. Suddenly it turned, and with distended jaws, which showed its huge, tusk-like teeth, commenced to approach the boat. The crew stood ready for the attack. Hare realized that it was a fight to the death, and the chances were even if not in their adversary's favor.

He threw out for empty water-breakers, hoping thereby to distract its attention long enough to enable him to strike a vital part. The ruse worked to a certain extent. The sea-serpent chewed up the breakers one after another, and the Captain kept up a constant fusillade, but without being able to reach a vital spot. "As it reached the side of the boat," he writes, "it slowly raised its hideous head, erected its neck, and with wide-extended jaws it seized the side of the gunwale of our boat and crushed it as easily as though it was made of glass. The crew rained in blow after blow in rapid succession with their axes and hatchets. The harpooner thrust his keen weapon to the hilt in its eyes, while I shot into its quivering body ball after ball. It was not long that this strange and curious battle continued. After a few spasmodic tremblings the animal suddenly, with one convulsive jerk that carried away the side of the boat, fell with a splash along side, a huge dead, repulsive mass. As it slowly settled beneath the surface of the water we hastily attached a tow-line and tried by every effort in our exhausted condition to secure it for other and more scientific investigation.

Although we went to work with a will I soon found that the strong southerly current, together with the cumbersome body of the monster, our almost dismantled boat and our exhaustion was rapidly setting us to leeward and on the shoals, and being now some distance from the ship and night fast setting in, I was most reluctantly compelled to order the reptile cut adrift. But before we did so we severed its head from its huge body, which we soon saw disappear in the dark water."

Captain Hare says he cannot form any idea of the creature's length. At no time did he see more than forty or fifty feet exposed, and how much more was submerged is only problematical. Its color was a rusty-black on top, fading to a yellowish-white on the under part.

A MONSTER OF THE WOODS.

The Omaha Daily Bee — November 29, 1887— Nebraska

Two Otoe County Men Make a Hideous Discovery.

PARALYZED HIM WITH HORROR.

Sensations of a Woodchopper Who Stumbled on the Animal in the Brush — An Ineffectual Hunt — Nebraska News.

Neither Beast nor Human.

NEBRASKA CITY, Neb., Nov. 28. – [Special to the Bee.] – Two woodchoppers, John Huff and Lewis Mann, who have been at work on the bottoms near Peru, for several months, were in the city last night and related to the BEE correspondent a strange story of their discovery on Friday night of a hideous wild boy. According to Huff's story, which was corroborated by Mann, for some weeks past their shanty had been frequently entered during their absence and the greater portion of their eatables either devoured or carried off. At first they blamed several other woodchoppers who were camped near by, but their denial and the frequent repetition of the depredations put them at a loss for a solution. They securely barricaded their hut and the annoyance ceased. Then their neighbors began to complain of the same mysterious disappearance of their "grub." A farmer near by accused the woodchoppers of robbing his hen roost and even said he at one time at night had seen one of the men running away from one of his corn cribs on his hands and knees.

Last Friday evening, as the men returned from work, they discovered that some one had made attempts to break open the door of their hut and tracks in the fresh earth about the place indicated that their visitor had been there very recently. While Mann remained, Huff went in search of the depredator, and having beaten about in the brush and undergrowth for more than an hour in all directions, was about to give up his search and return home when he almost, as he says, stumbled over the form of the most frightful and hideous looking creature that ever met the gaze of human eyes. He says the sight for a moment paralyzed and rooted him to the spot, and not until the animal disappeared in the thick underbrush could he even find voice and call for his companion. He describes it as undoubtedly of human form in face and body but so frightfully deformed as to leave only a faint resemblance. The head bore a slight resemblance to a negro, the eyes almost protruding from their sockets, and fangs stood out from a horribly shaped mouth. The monstrosity in locomotion used its feet and what were undoubtedly its arms, using the portion from the elbows to where the hands should have been, as fore feet.

The two men notified their neighbors and together they followed the direction taken by the creature, but gave up the hunt when night came on without finding a trace of it. Owing to the thick and entangled brush they say its capture is an impossibility unless accomplished while it is out in search of food. The cold weather and heavy fall of snow of last night will undoubtedly drive it out if it does not freeze or starve to death.

Those living in the neighborhood of the discovery associate it with a colored family named Jacksing who resided in the bottoms for several years and left sometime last spring for Kansas. They were known to have had a boy of such horrible deformity as to be frightful in its ugliness, and the boy was often known to had disappeared and remained away for weeks at a time to the utter indifference of his parents who often expressed the wish that he would never return, and it is believed he was left behind when the family went to Kansas, and that this monstrosity and the creature seen by the woodchoppers are identical. Another hunt will be made.

THE BANSHEE'S WARNING.

The Times – June 8, 1888 – Michigan

Michael Phelan, the vigilant night watchman at the Planters' house, tells some queer stories of his experiences in Ireland before he decided to emigrate:

"Once I saw a banshee. It was many years ago, in King's county, Ireland, about forty miles from Dublin. During the summer months there the twilight is very long, and late one afternoon, when the sun had gone down, I happened to walk over to the farm of a man named Michael Burns. Well, as we stood and talked, my friend suddenly said: 'Mike, do you want to see a banshee?' Of course I did, and when I looked where he pointed, sure enough, there in the lane, creeping along near the hedge, was a wee bit of a thing not more than three feet high. It looked like a little girl, only its hair, which was long and yellow, fell down its back clear to the ground, and as it crept along it whimpered and moaned just like a child in pain. My friend looked very grave, saying: 'That's a family banshee, and I'm afraid some of my relations are going to be sick.'

"Pretty soon I left, but not before a neighbor had come riding up and told my friend to make haste, as his mother had been taken very ill. The next day I learned that the poor woman had died before her son reached her. Oh, the banshees are queer things, and they never let any one come near them. Another man I knew came across one sitting in a corn field, near the fence. When he suddenly appeared it ran out of sight among the corn, but it dropped its comb from its yellow hair, and the man picked it up and put it in his pocket. That night the banshee came near the house and whined so piteously that the man dropped the comb out of the window. The banshee then left, and when a search was made next morning it was found that the comb had disappeared, too."

– St. Louis Post-Dispatch.

MAMMOTHS IN ALASKA.

Wichita Eagle – July 26, 1889 – Kansas

VALUABLE DISCOVERY MADE BY THE ALAKSA FUR COMPANY.

Monster Creatures Twenty Feet High and Thirty Feet in Length – Tusks Weighing 250 Pounds – Garden "Sass" and Glaciers Side by Side.

"Alaska is a country of paradoxes!"

That is what Mr. Cola F. Fowler, of the Alaska Fur and Commercial company, said in answer to the question of a reporter respecting his late field of operations.

"During all that time, up to two months ago, when I resigned and started for home," said Mr. Fowler, "I have had my headquarters at Kodiac, which is the most northern station occupied by agents of our company. We have our headquarters in San Francisco, and trading stations all over Secretary Seward's purchase. As yet Alaska is almost a terra incognita. The country immediately surrounding some of the principal rivers like the Yukon, Snake and Stickeer has been explored, and a few miles inland from the coast line, but the great interior is almost unknown. What we have learned of it is a surprise, and was the foundation of my answer to your question.

"Alaska is certainly a country of paradoxes. You who live here in the states look upon it as a land of perpetual ice and snow, and yet you would be astonished if I told you that I grew in my garden at Kodiac abundant crops of radishes, lettuce, carrots, onions, cauliflowers, cabbage, peas, turnips, potatoes, beets, parsnips and celery. Within five miles of this garden was one of the largest glaciers in Alaska, and between the fertile coast slip and the interior is reared along the entire sea boundary a continuous mountain of perpetual ice and snow.

"During your twelve years' residence in Alaska what was the most wonderful thing you ever saw or heard there?"

Mr. Fowler smiled at this question, and, after a moment's hesitation said: "Two years ago last summer I left Kodiac for a trip to the headwaters of the Snake river, where our traveling agents had established a trading station at an Indian village. The chief of this family of Innuits was named To-lee-ti-ma, and to him I was recommended. He received me hospitably, and I at once began negotiations for the purchase of a big lot of fossil ivory which his tribe had cached near the village. The lot weighed several thousand pounds, and was composed of the principal and inferior tusks of the mammoth, the remains of thousands of which gigantic animals are to be found in the bed of interior Alaskan water courses. I subjected the ivory to a rigid inspection, and upon two of the largest tusks I discovered fresh blood traces and the remains of partly decomposed flesh.

"I questioned To-lee-ti-ma, and he assured me that less than three months before a party of his young men had encountered a drove of monsters about fifty miles above where he was then encamped, and he succeeded in killing two, an old bull and a cow. At my request he sent for the leader of the hunting party, a young and intelligent Indian, and I questioned him closely about his adventure among a race of animals that the scientific people claim are extinct. He told a straightforward story, and I have no reason to doubt its truth.

KILLING A MONSTER.

"He and his band were searching along a dry water course for ivory, and had found a considerable quantity. One of the bucks, who was in advance, rushed in upon the main body one morning with the startling intelligence that at a spring of water about a mile above where they then were he had discovered the 'sign' of several of the 'big teeth.' They had come down to the spring to drink from a lofty plateau farther inland, and had evidently fed in the vicinity of the water for some time. The chief immediately called about him his warriors, and the party, under the leadership of the scout, approached the stream.

"They had nearly reached it when their ears were suddenly saluted by a chorus of loud, shrill, trumpet like calls, and an enormous creature came crashing toward them through the thicket, the ground fairly trembling beneath its ponderous footfalls. With wild cries of terror and dismay the Indians fled, all but the chief and the scout who had first discovered the trail of the monsters. They were armed with large caliber muskets and stood their ground, opening fire on the mammoth. A bullet must have penetrated the creature's brain, for it staggered forward and fell dead, and subsequently, on their way back to their campground, they overhauled and killed a cow 'big teeth,' which was evidently the mate of the first one killed.

"I asked the hunter to describe the monster, and, taking a sharp stick, he drew me a picture of the male animal in the soft clay. According to his description it was at least twenty feet in height and thirty feet in length. In general shape it was not unlike an elephant, but its ears were smaller, its eyes bigger and its trunk longer and more slender. Its tusks were yellowish white in color and six in number. Four of these tusks were placed like those of a boar, one on either side in each jaw; they were about four feet long and came to a sharp point. The other two tusks he brought away.

"I measured them and they were over fifteen feet in length and weighed upwards of 250 pounds each. They gradually tapered to a sharp point and curved inward. The monster's body was covered with long, coarse hair of a reddish dun color. I took a copy of the rude sketch made by Indian.

"By the way, our late governor, the Hon. Alfred P. Swineford, has pretty carefully investigated the matter, and he is certain from a thorough sifting of native testimony that large herds of these monsters are to be found on the high plateaus in interior Alaska about the headwaters of the Snake river."

— *Philadelphia Press.*

A MONSTER ANIMAL.

The Enterprise – August 21, 1889 – Ohio

He Was Seven Feet High, Covered with Hair and Walked Erect.

During the time the Indians were in the South, a hunting party established a camp east of Tugalo river, in what is now Oconee County, S.C., says the Clarksville (Ga.) Advertiser. One day they all went hunting, leaving a deer they had killed the evening pervious at the camp. At night when the Indians returned to the camp the deer was gone, and the next day the same thing was repeated, when they concluded to leave an old Indian to guard the camp and see what went with their deer.

That day the old Indian saw a monster animal come and carry off the deer, and was afraid to make any attempt to kill the monster, which was about seven feet high and walked erect like a man, hairy all over, and its mouth was in the chin and great claws on the fingers and toes. The next day all seven of the Indians stayed at the camp, and, as usual, the monster came, gathered up the deer and started off, when one of them fired at it, the ball taking effect in the back. The animal dropped the deer and turned and started toward them, when the other six poured volley into its breast and it fell dead.

About three hours after that the Indians heard a noise like some one hallooing about a mile distant: "Yaho, yaho, yaho!" The Indians left the camp and called on the posse comitatus for protection, when a party of whites on horses, with all the dogs they could get, went in search of the other animal and found it. It was like the one the Indians killed, and they put the dogs after it. When the men appeared in sight the animal would run, but it could whip every dog they could get after it. The party pursued it to the river and at two jumps it went across the river over into Habersham County, and was shot by a party soon after it crossed the river.

A MONSTER TURTLE.

St. Landry Democrat – November 9. 1889 – Louisiana

The Cape Sable Advertiser reports that the crew of a fishing schooner a short time since, while a few miles from Cape Sable saw what at first sight they took to be the genuine sea serpent come up to the surface for an airing. They could see the immense black mass was propelling itself slowly away from them, and they resolved on giving chase and having a closer view. The captain and another man sprang into a boat and were soon alongside, when they discovered that it was a turtle of rather vast dimensions, being fully fourteen feet long, eight feet broad, and between five and six feet in thickness. Then a wicked looking head protruded from under the shell to the length of four feet or more. After vain efforts to catch the creature with a gaff, a harpoon was tried, but the iron rebounded from the solid shell, and the attempt had to be abandoned. During the struggle, the monster made the spray fly on all sides and it was not safe to get near him.

A MARVELOUS STORY.

The Anaconda Standard – November 27, 1889 – Montana

Has the Great White Dragon Reappeared, Portending a General Smash-up?

A story which savors strongly of the marvelous comes to us from the interior of Asiatic Turkey. Three Mussulman travelers were lately journeying to a point near Poulank. On arriving at a spot called Ahlat, on the Lake of Van, one of them approached the water and began his morning ablutions. As he was dipping his feet for the last time he suddenly uttered a scream and informed his companions that he was being dragged into the lake by some unseen marine monster that was holding to his leg. His friends rushed to his assistance, and taking him by the hands and arms succeeded in bringing him ashore, but what was their surprise to see the monster also emerge from the water firmly attached to the man's leg by its teeth.

It was a horrid-looking creature, with the legs and body of an alligator and the head and restless, lidless eyes of a serpent. Between its fore and hind legs, on either side, were large, ribbed, leathery-looking wings. The tail was scaled, but not barbed like that in the picture of the typical dragon. With the exception of the under part of the throat and the tips of the wings, feet, and tail, the creature was a beautiful creamy white and its skin soft as velvet.

Knives, sticks, stones and everything else which were brought to bear upon the monster proved unavailing, and at last the ingenious travelers bethought themselves of a heroic measure. They built a good fire and pulsed the neck and belly of the beast, bird, or fish across it, taking good care not to burn the leg of their comrade in the operation. After a while the scorching heat aroused the animal from its torpor. It began to move its body and to stretch out its leathery wings after the manner of a bat, and suddenly flew into the air, still holding the man by the leg.

After arising to the height of about 200 feet it took a "header" downward toward the lake, into which it plunged with a mighty splash, burying itself and victim out of sight.

The natives are greatly excited, believing that the great white dragon has reappeared and that the end of the world is near at hand.

STORIES FROM THE:
1890's

A SERPENT IN A CLOUD.
Democratic Northwest – July 3, 1890 – Ohio

A few days ago Atkama Yatzry, a Bengalese gentleman residing on the flat seven miles north of Shuttezat, saw, as he affirms, an enormous serpent floating along the sky in a fleecy white "tezarer" or "wind cloud." The cloud and its shiny passenger passed directly over Mr. Yatzry's farm, and bore off in the direction of the "Blue Jungle." Over a score of men, women and boys working along the flat attest that they saw the same hideous monster while in his ethereal flight. One witness describes the serpent as being at least four "tsongs" (200 feet) in length and as big around as a man's body, with a head as large as that of a large alligator. He was yellow and black striped, according to all witnesses, and kept continually rolling over and darting out his head in genuine snake fashion. The natives are much excited over the matter.

– *Calcutta Indian Gentleman.*

MARINE MONSTERS.

Democratic Northwest – July 31, 1890 – Ohio

THE STORY TOLD BY A VERACIOUS SEA CAPTAIN.

A Hand-to-hand Encounter off Hatteras with Long-armed Monsters of the Deep – Several of Them Captured.

Captain Gheen, of the Schooner Abby Gheen, now lying at Bulson street wharf, Camden, saw strange things off Cape Hatteras on his voyage to this port. He does not claim to have seen the sea-serpent, but he did see a number of monsters of the deep that put all well-credited sea stories in the shade. The captain is a man whose veracity is not to be doubted. The captain brought his vessel from Rio de Janiero, and it was when twenty miles off Cape Hatteras that he ran into a school of sea monsters such as he had never before seen.

The monsters were sighted by one of the crew. They were nearly a hundred yards ahead of the vessel and were apparently rushing toward her. When first seen by the sailors they thought the ship was running into a floating island, some of which are often seen at sea. They soon changed their minds, however, when they got closer and saw a school of big fish that no one on board could recognize as having seen before. The school opened to let the ship pass, and then at once closed in and followed her. They floated all around her and greatly impeded her progress.

Although the vessel was going at a speed of seven knots an hour, the monsters followed along in its wake, and several more daring ones seemed to clutch hold of the vessel's side and let themselves be carried along. After they had followed the boat for several hours the crew began to grow uneasy as to their safety, and called upon the captain, who heretofore had not been aware of the chase.

He sent for his glass, and, going aft, made a survey of the school, which he describes as resembling a low, rocky island. He said they were larger than the average-sized sharks, being about ten feet in length and varying from the size of a bucket to a tub in circumference. They seemed to be running a race, and were having a great battle among themselves.

They had four long arms, on the end of which were claws that resembled the hands of an ape. These arm-like things extended from each side of the body. Discovering that they were a new species of fish, he immediately communicated the fact to the first mate with orders to try and capture some of the strange monsters.

The mate gave orders to the crew, who were more or less frightened, but were waiting for the chance to "skeer" the brutes, and when they were told of the captain's orders they nearly jumped out of their shoes. The boat was searched for weapons, and soon the deck was covered with harpoons, boat hooks, fish hooks, and every other kind of implement used in catching fish.

The boat hooks were first used in their attempt to catch the fish, but unsuccessfully. The fish seemed to know what was needed of them, and they used their "hands" to protect themselves from being caught. Groups of two and three of the monsters would grab the rod of the boat hook and pull it away. Eight of these hooks were taken from the sailors. The arms of the fish were about six feet long, said Capt. Gheen.

The sailors became alarmed, thinking that some ill omen had caused the serpents to follow the ship, and they thought they were going to be lost. They told the captain that they thought the ship would never reach port. Some rushed to the forecastle and others to the captain's cabin in their endeavors to escape from the supposed "Jonah."

By this time the fish had become more daring and would swim alongside the boat and grab the sail tenions and traces. At last the captain became so exasperated at the men that he ordered them to cast the lines which they use in catching drum and sturgeon. This the crew reluctantly did. The lines were baited with huge pieces of codfish and cast over the side. They were handled by the fish the same as they handled the boat hook. They would grab the line with their "hands," and try to tear them apart, and if one was not successful two or three would come to his aid.

"All the time we were trying to capture one of them," said the captain, they would keep up a yell that sounded like the bark of a coyote. At last the men were successful. They had, indeed, caught one of the fish, and they began to haul him in. When the remaining fish saw their captured brother they made great efforts to rescue him. They grabbed at him while the men were hauling him up along the side of the boat, and once or twice one of them succeeded in getting his claws over the side of the fore rail. At last we had him on deck, and such a hilarious yell as the crew gave out at that happy moment, and the scene on the deck is indescribable.

The captured monster floundered all over the deck, but his maneuvers were quickly stopped by the use of an axe; we soon cut his head off. In another hour we had caught two more of the huge monsters, but these must have been young ones, as they were a great deal smaller in size than the rest, and probably did not know how to evade the hook."

"This was a strange monster," said Captain Gheen. "The body was round and about the size of a small barrel, and the bark was covered with thick scales, resembling the scales of a drumfish, while the belly resembled the hid of a porpoise. The head was about as large as an ordinary sized bucket and was horrifying to gaze upon. The eyes were as large as a dollar, and greenish in color. They made my blood run cold when I saw them.

"We all held a consultation and decided to have the fish cooked. One of them was carefully cleaned and cut into huge chunks, and I ordered the cook to prepare it for supper. I thought that they would not be fit to eat and ordered the others thrown overboard, which was done. But they weren't in the water ten seconds before the others, which were still following us, began a battle over which should have the feast. They grabbed them with their 'hands,' and in the battle a number of others were killed, and in their wild attempt to get a meal they chased after one of their dead number, and they were lost from our view in a short time, and we continued our voyage unmolested.

"But to go back to the eating of the fish. Why, when the post stew was served up no one could tell it from a mess of boiled codfish, and when boiled by itself it tasted like shad."

Capt. Lehman Lake, who for a number of years commanded the pleasure yacht of W.L. Elkins, of the Atlantic Refining Company, stats that three years ago, while cruising in South America, he had a similar experience.

– Philadelphia Times.

KILLED A WINGED MONSTER.

News and Citizen – July 31, 1890 – Vermont

A winged monster, resembling a huge alligator, with an extremely elongated tail and an immense pair of wings, was found on the desert between the Whetstone and Huachuca Mountains, last Sunday, by two ranchers who were returning home from the Huachucas. The creature was evidently greatly exhausted by a long flight, and when discovered was able to fly but a short distance at a time. After the first shock of wild amazement had passed the two men, who were on horseback and armed with Winchester rifles, regained sufficient courage to pursue the monster, and after an exciting chase of several miles succeeded in getting near enough to open fire with their rifles and wounding it.

The creature then turned on the men but owing to its exhausted condition they were able to keep out of its way, and after a few well directed shots the monster partly rolled over and remained motionless. The men cautiously approached, their horses snorting with terror, and found that the creature was dead. They then proceeded to make an examination and found that it measured about ninety-two feet in length and the greatest diameter was about fifty inches. The monster had only two feet, these being situated a short distance in front of where the wings were joined to the body. The head, as near as they could judge, was about eight feet long, the jaws being thickly set with strong, sharp teeth. Its eyes were as large as a dinner plate and protruded about half way from the head.

They had some difficulty in measuring the wings, as they were partly folded under the body, but finally got one straightened out sufficiently to get a measurement of 78 feet, making the total length from tip to tip about 160 feet. The wings were composed of a thick and nearly transparent membrane, and were devoid of feathers or hair, as was the entire body. The skin of the body was comparatively smooth, and easily penetrated by a bullet. The men cut off a small portion of the tip of one wing and took it home with them.

Late last night one of them arrived in this city for supplies, and to make the necessary preparations to skin the creature, when the hide will be sent East for examination by the eminent scientists of the day. The finder returned early this morning, accompanied by several prominent men, who will endeavor to bring the strange creature to this city before its mutilated.

– *Tombstone, (A.T.) Epitaph.*

A WATER MONSTER.

The Morning News – November 2, 1890 – Georgia

From the Pittsburg Dispatch.

A frightful story has just come to light which confirms an old Indian tradition. About six miles southeast of Mullen, Id., and within a stone's throw of the Montana line, is a small lake which for beauty, grandeur and tradition is unsurpassed by any point of interest in the wild west. It is to be found at the head of Willow creek, a north branch of the Coeur d'Alene river. St. Stephen's Peak, the most elevated point in the Coeur d'Alene mountains, towers over it, and the famous St. Joe range of mountains prevents its waters from flowing south into the St. Joe river.

The Indians long ago often frequented this point, and obtained quantities of almost pure lead, from which they made bullets to be used in the chase and raid of warfare against other tribes and the whites. Some years ago two prospectors left the gold placer camp of Eagle. It was a hot, sultry afternoon, and they proposed a bath in the lake. One of the men, being a very poor swimmer, kept close to the bank, and was soon standing near the shore watching his partner swim in the lake. When he had swam about 800 yards from shore he suddenly turned about and started back toward the shore he had left, and his friend, who was standing on the shore watching, saw to his horror some water monster pursuing his partner, who was making every exertion to reach shore, but without avail. A few undulations and a low rumbling sound, and the monster raised a part of its body out of the water, closed its mighty jaws upon the unfortunate man, and both disappeared beneath the lake.

The water was dyed with blood and the waves wriggled against the shore for a moment and all was still as before. Several weeks ago a camping party was located at the spot. Both fishing and swimming were indulged in. Toward evening cries were heard, and upon investigation it was found that a monster had pulled one of the party under the water. The unfortunate was a miner from Helena. Since then large searching parties have industriously dragged the lake, but no trace of the man-eating beast has been discovered.

A MEXICAN CENTAUR.

The Daily Independent – June 30, 1891 – Nevada

The Strange Creature Killed in the Woods of Arkansas.

According to an Arkansas journal Dr. Collins of Little River County, that State, killed a most remarkable quadruped near his place in the spring of 1877. From the time of the war up until the year named, several persons claimed to have frequently seen an animal in the form of a large red deer, with the head and neck of a man. On the day that the animal was killed, Dr. Collins' wife and a negro girl were going along an unused path when they saw the queer creature peering at them through the underbrush. They made haste and informed the doctor what had occurred. He took his gun and started in search of the beast, which he soon overtook and shot. Closer inspection showed that the head, instead of being that of a man, more nearly resembled that of a baboon. Its eyes were large and very prominently set to the sides of its head. A long fringe of brown beard covered the chin and neck. Dr. Collins says that when he came up with the creature and leveled his gun at it, it seemed to be aware of its great danger, the large eyes melting into tears as it saw the utter hopelessness of the case. When shot it uttered a heart-rending scream and leaped high in the air, expiring with awful groans which closely resembled those of a man in distress. It is generally believed that the creature was a species of Mexican centaur, a semi-legendary creature of the post-conquest era.

FOUGHT A SEA MONSTER.

The Meriden Daily Republican – August 4, 1891 – Connecticut

A Greenport Captain Tells a Strange Story of a Recent Encounter.

Capt. Edward Reeve has the contract to light the beacon on the breakwater every night, says a Greenport correspondent of the New York World. He is an industrious and reliable man, not looked upon as one likely to see visions or deal in blood-curdling sea yarns.

Every day as the sun is sinking he rows in a little skiff to the breakwater and, after lighting the beacon, pulls back up the bay. In the morning he rows down the bay, puts out the light, and cleans and fills in preparation for the night.

The other morning, the captain says, while pulling leisurely toward the breakwater, he was attracted by a commotion in the water near him. He rested on his oars and looked to see what it was. He saw what looked like the hard shell back of a monster turtle. A moment later he saw the head and eyes of the strange object. As the head protruded above the surface the water was churned into foam by the flapping of what appeared to be long flippers. The head of the marine animal, the captain says, was covered with protruding horns.

The monster came toward the boat and apparently mediated an attack, when the captain hit it with an oar. It paid no attention to this assault, but ran its head against the boat with a force that caused the skiff to keel over. The captain weighs over two hundred pounds, and managed to keep the boat right side up. Then the fight became fierce. The tide was carrying the contestants toward the breakwater. One after the other the oars were broken by the captain by striking on the hard back of the monster. Finally, without anything to defend himself, the captain managed to throw a noose over a projecting rock on the breakwater, and so pulled himself a shore.

The monster continued its attacks on the boat and remained in the vicinity for some time after the boat had been drawn up out of the way. When last seen the ferocious marine monster was churning the water into foam as it sped off toward Gardiner's island. The captain puts the monster down as a sea turtle, but of enormous size.

PTERODACTYLS.

Los Angeles Herald – August 5, 1891 – California

Sport Gunning for Dragons Near Fresno.

Monstrosities Which Are Half Alligators, Half Birds.
The Wild, Weird Story of a Fresno Newspaper Man.
Two Screaming Dragons Snap Their Jaws and Show Their Teeth –
Six Feet Long and Look Like Frogs.

The Fresno sportsman now goes gunning for pterodactyls. These are dragons who lived in the carboniferous age, but who forgot to get petrified when the Fresno man and woman went through that process for the special benefit of nineteenth century dime museum owners. A letter from Fresno to the San Francisco Chronicle of Monday tells the Munchausen story, and from it the following excerpts are taken:

Fresno, July 31. – The report that two strange dragons with wings have recently appeared in the swamps east of Selma was at first regarded by many as a sensational story without foundation in fact, but after different persons at different places had claimed to have seen the strange creatures it began to be thought worth investigating.

The history of the unusual visitors, so far as reported, is as follows:

The men who live along the swales and sand hollows east and southeast of Selma on the evening of July 13th heard strange sounds in the air just after dark, like the rushing of wings when some large bird passes swiftly through the air overhead. At the same time a cry was heard, resembling that of a swan, though enough different to make it plain it was not a swan. But on that evening nothing was seen. The sound of the rushing of wings and peculiar cries were heard at intervals for two hours, when about 10 o'clock all became still. The last cries heard were far away in the direction of King's river.

On Monday night, July 21st, Harvey Lemmon and Major Henry Haight were out looking after their hogs that feed in the tules. As the men were returning to Selma they were surprised to hear a strange, strangling noise in the deep swale under the bridge. In a moment there was a heavy flapping of wings and the two monsters rose slowly from the water and flew so near the men that the wind from their wings was plainly felt.

Mr. Haight described the dragons as resembling birds, except that they had no feathers, and their heads were broad and their bills long and wide. He judged that the expanse of their wings was not less than fifteen feet. Their bodies were without covering. Their eyes were very large – Mr. Haight was sure not less than four inches in diameter.

J.D. Daniels, of Sanger, heard of the matter, and on Wednesday went over to Selma and joined those who were going out to capture the dragons. Your correspondent saw Mr. Daniels today and had from him the account of the searching party. It is better given in Mr. Daniels's words:

"When I reached Selman I found the company, which, with me, consisted of five persons, preparing to go down to Hog lake to set watch. This is a small pond of water, and was considered as liable as any to be visited by the monsters.

"We drove out to the lake, and there being no brush convenient for a hiding place, we dug holes in the bank, and soon after dark we took our places in the holes with our guns, ready to see what could be done in the case the visitors put in an appearance.

"We remained there till 3 o'clock in the morning, and nothing of an unusual nature having taken place we returned to Selma, somewhat disappointed.

"About 10 o'clock that day, Thursday, Emanuel Jacobs came in and reported that the monsters had evidently been in Horn valley, about four miles above, the night before. They had killed a number of ducks, and the banks of the pond were strewn with feathers.

"We had no intention of giving over the plan of capturing the dragons, and Thursday night two of us returned to watch – Mr. Templeton and myself. We secreted ourselves in the holes which we had made the night before and waited patiently with our guns, determined to secure one of the strange visitors at least, should they make their appearance.

"About 11 o'clock the cries were heard in the direction of King's river, seeming two or three miles away. The ominous yells drew nearer, and in a few moments we heard the rush and roar of wings, so hideous that our hair almost stood on end. The two dragons came swooping down and circled round and round the pond in rapid whirls, screaming hideously all the while. We had a good view of them while flying. Two or three times they passed within a few yards of us, and their eyes were plainly visible. We could also see that instead of bills like birds they had snouts resembling that of the alligator, and their teeth could be seen as they snapped their jaws while passing us.

"Evidently the dragons were trying to decide whether or not they should come down in the pond. They were probably examining if there was any food to be had, such as ducks, mudhens and fish.

"At length they came down with a fearful plunge into the pond, and the mud and water flew as though a tree had fallen into it.

"They dived and floundered around in the water, and as nearly as we could judge at the distance of thirty yards they were about six feet long, and while wading in the water they looked not unlike gigantic frogs. Their wings were folded, and appeared like large knobs on their backs. Their eyes were the most visible parts, and seemed all the time wide open and staring.

"They were very active, and darted about among the tules and rushes catching mudhens. One of these fowls was devoured at two or three champs of the jaws.

"As soon as we saw a good opportunity we leveled our guns at the one nearest us and fired. One rose into the air with a yell and flew away, every stroke of the wings showing immense strength.

"The other floundered about in the water till it reached the edge of the pond, when it crawled out, dragging a long wounded wing after it, and started across the plain. We loaded our guns and gave chase. We soon lost sight of it, for it went much faster than we could.

However, we were able to follow by its dismal cries in the distance. We followed it half a mile, when it passed out of our hearing.

"The next day a company went in pursuit and trailed it by the blood on the grass. It was followed three miles to the Juniper slough, which it entered and all trace of it was lost. Whether it is yet concealed in the tules or whether it has died is not known.

"Where it passed down the bank it left several well-formed tracks in the mud. One of the best was cut out with a spade, and, after drying, was taken to Selma, where it is in the possession of Mr. Snodgrass. The track was like that of an alligator, though more circular in form. It had five toes, with a strong claw on each. The track is eleven inches wide and nineteen long."

The most probable solution of the matter is that these dragons are solitary specimens of some geological animal supposed to be extinct. It most nearly fits the description of the pterodactyl, a weird nocturnal vampire, half bat, half lizard, that infested the vast swamps of the earth in the carboniferous age. The pterodactyl is described by geologists as attaining a size often four times as large as the eagle, while the bill became a snout, and its mouth was set with ghastly teeth that devoured birds, reptiles and all small animals that came in its way.

It may be that this species of animal has not become entirely extinct, as has been supposed, but that these are veritable pterodactyls. It is now recalled that a strange monster resembling these was reported a few years ago in the vast swamp between Tulare lake and Kern lake.

WHISTLING ANIMALS.

The Yazoo Sentinel – September 10, 1891 – Mississippi

Strange Creatures That Infest the Olympic Mountains.

The Whatcom (Wash.) Reveille has the following: After lunch we passed through a beautiful piece of bottom land, teeming with flowers, red and yellow monthly musk, fringing the banks of the stream where it spread out over the meadow in a dozen different channels. Charlie wanted to stop and take up 100 acres, but Campbell told him, "Too much plenty snow in winter," and after vainly trying to drink the creek dry, we passed on. Another turn brought us to the base of a steep, bare, stony mountain. Skirting this and climbing over some big rocks we suddenly came into a lovely grass country. Like the prairie in summer, every conceivable flower seemed to bloom and blossom in the grass; the place was ablaze with red, blue, yellow and white.

We must have passed through 500 or 600 acres of it, and every here and there a rippling stream ran wildly through it. The place was a perfect paradise, and, thank goodness, we had got out of the dark valley and stood in the bright, warm sunshine. We were now close to the head of the Quileene, and we eagerly pressed on. Presently we met a dog, and close after him his master, who turned out to be Mr. Ransom, going from the head of the Dungeness of Port Townsend. He gave us cheerful accounts of the elk and also kindly took a letter into town for us. At 5:30 o'clock we camped under Sentinel rock, about a mile from the divide. This rock stands boldly out alone, like a massive fortress, guarding the entrance to the valley of the Dungeness.

Suddenly the mountain sides seemed to be alive with men whistling to one another, when – and one would turn sharp around only to hear another and a shriller whew – on the other side; and soon we saw lots of animals; about the size of a fox, with long, bushy tails, running about from rock to rock, sometimes lying down, but more often sitting bolt up, erect, as a ferret does. We shot a couple of small ones that night, and afterwards shot several more larger ones. Campbell called them whistling dogs, and declared they were good to eat but the smell was enough for us. Their odor is peculiar, but not fragrant. They have two long teeth in front like a beaver, and feet almost shaped like a squirrel's feet. I believe their right name is mountain beaver.

Wherever we went afterwards in the mountains, as long as there was grass, we saw these whistling dogs, as we got to call them. I liked to see them; they seemed to make the place cheerful and lively and were very amusing to watch. In winter they have long burrows under the snow, and their coats get a dark grey; in summer they are yellow. Their skins should make a good fur, and I think would pay for being trapped in the winter months. Our altitude this night was 5,450 feet, and we christened the place "Stone Camp," from the terribly stony ground we had to sleep on. The night was warm until about 4 o'clock a.m. when it got fearfully cold, and we were almost frozen.

MONSTER OF THE AIR.

The Forrest City Times – September 11, 1891 – Arkansas

AN INDIANA TOWN TORN UP BY A TERRIBLE SIGHT.

Crawfordsville People Think the End of the World is at Hand – A Preacher's Strange Tale.

CRAWFORDSVILLE, Ind., Sept. 9. – There is great excitement in Crawfordsville over a horrible monster which has been seen hovering over the city about midnight for the last two nights. It was first seen Saturday night. It was about three or four hundred feet in the air and it was about eighteen feet long and eight feet wide. It moved rapidly through the air by means of several pairs of side fins which it worked most sturdily.

It was pure white and had no definite shape or form but resembled somewhat a great white shroud fitted out with propelling fins. There was no tail or head visible, but there was one great flaming eye and a sort of wheezing, plaintive sound was emitted from a mouth that was invisible.

It flapped like a flag in the wind as it came on and frequently gave a great squirm as though suffering unutterable agony. It circled about, hovering over one house and then another, sometimes descending with a hundred feet of the ground.

The story when told yesterday on the streets was hardly credited, but last night several unimpeachable witnesses saw the monster reappear. The Rev. Dr. G. W. Switzer, pastor of the Methodist church, together with his wife, watched its movements for over an hour, as did several other highly respected citizens.

Some think that the strange visitor portends some terrible calamity. Others say that it is a sign of the near approach of the last great day when the world will be destroyed.

So great is the excitement that not an eye will be closed to-night until this monster of the air has appeared and once more taken leave of the town.

WINGED MONSTERS.

The Princeton Union – September 24, 1891 – Minnesota

A Remarkable Bird Seen Recently in California.

At the last meeting of the Amalgamated Association of Fish Liars the member from the north side who goes out twice a year with rod and gun but never unpacks the former, asked and received permission to read the following from San Francisco:

"A well-authenticated story comes from Selma, Fresno County, of the appearance at that place of two huge-winged monsters that resemble the fabled dragon. They live on ducks and chickens and have been seen by a score of persons. One party watched for them on several nights and at last got a close view. The birds are said to have wings fully twelve feet long. Their bodies are six feet high when they walk about. They are not covered with feathers, and instead of a bill they have a hogs snout, with sharp teeth. Watchers saw two birds descend to a pond and chase mud hens in among the grass, crunching and devouring those they caught. Their eyes are very prominent. As soon as they men could get a shot they fired. One bird was wounded but escaped by running through the marshes. The track which it left was like an alligator's, with five toes and strong claws on each foot. The track is eleven inches wide and nineteen long. It is thought the birds might be survivors of extinct species like the pterodactyl which lived on the shores of Tulare Lake, which has never been thoroughly explored."

WEIRD DESERT MONSTER.

Los Angeles Herald – May 19, 1892 – California

Prospectors in Search of a Gigantic Reptile.

Which Wears a Head Like a Cracker Box.
It is Over Thirty Feet Long – Makes a Track in the Sand Eighteen Inches Across – Its Trail About Newbery and Hazlitt.

George Nay, the well-known mining man, for fifteen years a resident of the Needles, on the Colorado river, is at the Grand hotel, San Francisco, and tells a remarkable story of the discovery of a strange monster in the vicinity of Daggett.

Mr. Nay stopped at Daggett twenty-four hours on his way up. A party of prospectors headed by E.W. Spear had just arrived. Spear reported the finding of a curious trail eighteen inches wide in the sand of the desert, twenty miles toward Death Valley from Daggett.

He followed the strange trail for some distance, when suddenly turning almost at right angles around a sand dune he beheld a monstrous reptile, or animal, at least thirty feet long, with a head, so he expressed it, "larger than a candle-box" and "eyes as big as teacups" and luminous in their brightness. Spear was alone and being scared ran for camp as fast as his legs could take him.

When he had told his story, he was greeted with loud laughter, for nobody believed it. Next day, however, Henry Brown, who was coming across the desert in the lead of another party, saw it. Both reported it at Daggett.

The Daggett people had taken no stock in Spear's story, although he was always known as a truthful man. They thought, however, he was trying to play a practical joke on them. He stoutly persisted, however, that he had really seen the strange monster.

When Brown arrived the next day and corroborated it in every detail and added particulars as to how it appeared, they remembered having seen curious trails in the sand over the Atlantic and Pacific track thereabout for two years past. Also, that these trails were particularly numerous between Newbery and Haslett, nearby stations on the Atlantic and Pacific.

The greatest interest prevailed, and at once a party was organized to go and search for the monster, be it snake or some surviving specimen of a supposed long-extinct desert animal resembling one, and only found now in the large museums.

Horses and pack animals were at once secured. Two cowboys were among the party, and they took out with them a number of riatas, intending to ride close enough, if safe to do so, to lariat the monster and take him alive. It was the intention to exhibit him at the world's fair.

Mr. Nay says the people of Daggett are fully convinced that there is some monster of the kind set forth loose on the Mojave desert, and they fully expect that the party they have outfitted will secure it.

Its trail looks almost exactly as if a sack of grain or ore had been dragged through the sand. What the unique denizen of the desert lives on is not known.

A 30-FOOT MONSTER.

Alexandria Gazette – June 14, 1892 – Washington D.C.

Tuesday morning last the Examiner published a statement made by George Nay, of Needles, in relation to a large reptile that had been seen in the vicinity of Daggett. According to Mr. Nay, E.W. Spear had discovered a peculiar trail, and, following it, came upon a gigantic creature, unlike anything he had ever had the pleasure of meeting. He described it as thirty feet long and thoroughly unprepossessing.

Spear withdrew without formality and told his story, only to be laughed at. Later, Harry Brown saw the monster, and Mr. Brown scratched the desert sands quite hastily in retreat. At the time Mr. Nay left Daggett a party was being organized to hunt this strange denizen of the valley. Now appears Oscar W. Clark, scientist, with a weird tale and word painting of the animal.

"The announcement of the experiences of Messrs. Spear and Brown rather anticipated me," aid Mr. Clark yesterday. "I had a fine opportunity of seeing this strange denizen of that mysterious land known as Death Valley Desert, and I desire to say that this animal is the most wonderful living proof of the exact authenticity of the researches made by savants into the field of paleontological study.

"This animal is really the only living link between prehistoric times and the present. It is virtually a marvel of the ages, the eighth wonder of the world, a marvelous illustration of the profound economy of nature. It was six weeks ago that I had the pleasure of seeing this remarkable animal. I was some 30 miles distant from Daggett, and stopped at 6 o'clock in the evening to rest, having made some valuable additions to my collection of fossil remains.

"Happening to glance to the southwest through the haze peculiar to the desert I saw a strange body moving along about one mile away. I went toward it and was soon both elated and horrified by seeing an animal fully 30 feet long that differed from any of the known forms of the present epoch. It was an immense monster, walking part of the time on its hind feet and at times dragging itself through the sand and leaving tracks of a three-toed foot and a peculiar scratchy configuration in the sand whenever it changed its form of locomotion and dragged itself.

"The forelimbs of the animal were extremely short, and it occasionally grasped the nearest shrub and devoured it. The thumb of the three-pronged fore foot was evidently a strong conical spine that would be a dangerous weapon of attack. Whenever the animal stood upright it was fully 14 feet high.

"The head was as large as a good-sized cask, and was shaped somewhat like a horse, while the body was as large as that of an elephant, with a tail extending from the hind quarters something like that of an alligator.

"When I saw it the strange animal was on the edge of a great sink-hole, of alkaline water – a sink-hole, by the way, that my guides told me was a bottomless pit, and evidently a remnant of the days when Death Valley was in inland sea. I approached within 300 yards of the monster, crawling cautiously over the sand, and watched it for fully half an hour. Suddenly the beast began to bellow, and the sound was of a most terrifying and blood-curdling character. Its immense eyes, fully as large as saucers, projected from the head and gleamed with a wild furious fire, while from the enormous mouth of the monster streams of steam-like vapor were exhaled, and as they drifted toward me the effluvia was something awful.

"The animal was liver color, with bronze-like spots. The monster dragged itself to the edge of the sink-hole and lashed its tail, and finally fell off into a quiescent condition. I left the scene and attempted to secure the assistance of my guides in an effort to capture the monster, but they were absolutely terrified and refused to do anything.

"From what I saw of the animal I am perfectly satisfied that it is one of the species of the Iguanodon bennissantensis, of the European Jurassic, an animal presenting many points of structure in common with the iguana of today. In fact, that is the report that I have sent in, and knowing full well the geological environments of the Pacific slope and the very remarkable and peculiar conditions regarding the Death Valley section, I am satisfied that my deductions are correct and that there is to-day living in the desert of Death Valley one of the most remarkable animals now on the face of the globe – none other than one of the monsters of the prehistoric epoch, a wonder of the centuries."

– San Francisco Examiner.

A MAN EATING PLANT.

The Democrat – August 18, 1892 – North Carolina

NATURALIST DUNSTAN SAVES A POOR DOG WHICH WAS CAUGHT.

Horticultural Times.

There has been discovered in Nicaragua a flesh-eating or rather man-eating plant, which is called by the natives "the devils snare." In form it is a kind of vegetable octopus or devil fish, and it is able to draw blood of any living thing which comes within its clutches. It appears that a Mr. Dunstan, a naturalist, has lately returned from Central America, where he spent two years in the study of plants and animals of those regions. In one of the swamps which is surrounded the great Nicaragua Lake he discovered the singular growth.

He was engaged in hunting for botanical and entomological specimens when he heard his dog cry out as if in agony from a distance. Running to the spot whence the animal's cries came Mr. Dunstan found him enveloped in a perfect network of what seemed to be a fine, rope-like tissue of roots and fibres. The plant or vine seemed composed entirely of bare interlacing stems, resembling, more than anything else, the branches of the weeping willow denuded of its foliage, but of a dark, nearly black hue and covered with a thick viscid gum that exuded from the pores.

Drawing his knife Mr. Dunstan attempted to cut the poor beast free, but it was with the very greatest difficulty that he managed to sever the fleshy muscular fibres of the plant. Mr. Dunstan saw to his horror and amazement that the dog's body was blood-stained, while the skin appeared to have been actually sucked or puckered in spots and the animal staggered as if from exhaustion. In cutting the vine the twigs curled like sinuous fingers about Mr. Dunstan's hand and it required no slight force to free the member from its clinging grasp, which left the flesh red and blistered.

The gum exuding from the vine was of a grayish dark tinge, remarkably adhesive and of a disagreeable odor, powerful and nauseating to inhale. The natives showed the greatest horror of the plant and recounted to the naturalist many stories of its death-dealing powers. Mr. Dunstan said he was able to discover very little about the nature of the plant owing to the difficulty of handling it, for its grasp can only be shaken off with the loss of skin and of even flesh. As near as he could ascertain, however, its power of suction is contained in a number of infinitesimal mouths or little suckers, which ordinarily closed, open for the reception of food.

If the substance is animal the blood is drawn off and the carcass or refuse, then dropped. A lump of raw meat being thrown in, in the short space of five minutes the blood will be thoroughly drunk off and the mass thrown aside. Its voracity is almost beyond belief.

CAUGHT A WHAT IS IT.

St. Paul Daily Globe – March 20, 1893 – Minnesota

Thrilling Tale of a Dakota Man at the Merchants' Hotel.

Encounter with a Mysterious Animal Unknown to Science.

Final Capture and Disposition of the Unseen What-You-Call-It.

Arrival of Two Officials Sheds Light on the Strange Story.

"I have a story which may be of interest to the readers of your paper," said Doctor W.W. McIntyre, of New York, Wednesday afternoon to a GLOBE man as he settled himself back on one of the comfortable seats in the lobby of the Merchants.

"I have just returned from a visit to Bismarck S.D., where I have been making an investigation of one of the most interesting affairs it has been my luck to meet with in the history of my professional career. I have in my possession a cast, made in plaster, of an unearthly creature which was found in a house in the vicinity of Bismarck. I was written to in regard to the existence of the strange 'thing,' and it was alive at the time of my arrival in Bismarck. It died a day or two after I got there. If you care to hear the story, I will tell it to you.

"About three weeks ago a man who lives in Bismarck, or, rather, in the immediate vicinity of that city – I will not give his name, by request from him – rented a house located on a farm twelve miles from the city. He was making plans for living on the farm during the coming summer in company with his wife and family. He went to the farm, accompanied by a friend, for the purpose of seeing that everything was in order, and expected to return in the course of a day or two to Bismarck. His friend was employed in one of the banks of Bismarck, and he took the trip with the expectation of enjoying a hunt for a day or two. They arrived at the house all right in the course of the forenoon, and while the banker, whom I will call John Wilkins as that is not his name, went out to kill some partridges, the other man, whom I will call Allen, went through the house. The building had been furnished in an elegant manner by an Englishman, who started a ranch there, but he had moved away after living there for about a year without giving any excuse for so doing. He left orders with his agent to dispose of the property at any price he could get but did not give any reason for doing so. However, some of the servants had told stories of the house being haunted, and they ascribed the precipitate leaving of the Englishman to this cause. All kinds of stories were in circulation about the mysterious sounds about the house, but Wilkins and Allen, the latter being a physician, did not believe in the supernatural. They laughed at the stories, and called the tellers of the yarns old women, after the custom of the Indians.

"Allen made a trip through the house and found in one of the rooms a quantity of bed clothing, carefully packed away in the drawers of a bureau. He proceeded to make up two beds in adjoining rooms, and then waited for the return of his friend. They cooked supper – all Dakota men can keep their own houses properly – and after a good smoke they retired. Allen took one of the rooms and Wilkins slept in an adjoining room. They were tired and went to sleep almost immediately after touching their pillows.

"Allen was awakened during the night by a strange sensation. He could not see anything, as the room was dark, but he felt that there was something in the room. A strange and uncanny feeling took possession of him, and the cold perspiration stood out on his forehead in large drops. It was not a man; he could feel that, but it was some unearthly presence which he could not help but know was there. He sat up in bed, tried to light a candle which he knew must be there, but his hands shook so that he could not find the matches. He was frightened, very much so, although he was known as a brave man, and had been in more than one personal combat during the early days of the settlement of the Dakotas. Suddenly he felt that something was coming near to him. He could feel that something was in his immediate vicinity, when suddenly some body dropped onto his breast. The feeling of the thing was cold and clammy. It was not very large, but it was possessed of an immense and superhuman strength. The skinny fingers seized his throat with a death grip, and he was at first powerless. The feeling that he was dealing with something of an unnatural form unnerved him, but as he felt his breath being stopped by the pressure of the fingers of the being on his windpipe he was aroused to a sense of his danger, he threw off the lethargy which seized his muscles, and gave a shout for help. He seized the skinny hands which clasped his neck and tried with all his strength to loosen their grip. Finally, after a terrible struggle he gained the mastery of the strange being, and, clasping the wrists of the creature in his hands, he waited for the arrival of his friend, whom he could hear stirring in an adjoining room. Soon the door opened, and Wilkins stepped into the room.

"'My God, have you got a fit?' he asked, as he held his candle in the air above his head and peered at Allen. The candle gave a good light in the room, and Allen looked at the creature which had tried to choke him. Horrors! There was nothing there. Nothing which he could see, although he could feel the struggles of the thing and hear its breath. His fingers clasped something and the forms of the wrists which he held could be seen in the air, but, to his eyes, nothing was there.

"'Get something so that I can tie it,' he gasped, as he was almost out of breath from struggling.

"'Tie what?' asked Wilkins with a laugh. 'You had better go back to bed as you are dreaming.'

"'But I am not. Can't you see where my fingers were clasping something. It can't be seen, but there is something there. My God, man, I am not crazy. Look at the bites on my arms and wrists where this creature has bitten me. Feel of it yourself.'

"Wilkins stepped up to his friend for a moment and put his hand out towards where the creature was. He suddenly withdrew his hand with a cry of pain, and the red blood spurted out of his hand. He had been bitten.

"They took one of the sheets from the bed and tied it around the arms and legs of the creature. Then the body was laid on the bed. It was a strange sight. There could be seen the folds of the sheet as they were wound around the body. The twists and turns which had been given were all there, but they seemed to surround nothing but air. On the pillow and bed clothing could be seen the outlines of something which pressed into them in the form of a child, but no body could be seen. The panting of the captured thing could be heard, exhausted with its struggle, and if the hand was placed in the vicinity of its mouth the snap of teeth could be heard. It had lungs, the form of a human being, and on touching it the same sensation as of contact with a dead person could be felt. It made no sound and did not utter a cry during the entire struggle.

"The remainder of the night was spent in sitting by the side of the bed and watching the movements of the wrappings. They could not imagine what it was or what it could be, as Allen, the doctor, had never heard of anything of the kind. When morning came, they wrapped it up in several blankets and took it to the office of the doctor. They wondered if it could eat, or if it desired to eat anything. Food was offered, but it would not partake of it. Allen then wired for me, as he knew I was interested in freaks of nature and all kinds of queer things. I started at once for Bismarck and arrived as soon as the train could take me there.

"I found everything as had been represented in the short dispatch which I had received. We examined it from every standpoint, but I could make nothing out of it. It was decided that it would be proper for us to preserve it in the interests of science, but the question was how could we do it? Finally, a happy idea was hit upon. It had a form which, although it could not be seen, could be felt. Why not make a plaster cast of it. We decided to do this, but as we were afraid of killing the creature by taking a cast while it was alive, we decided to try the effects of chloroform on it.

"We succeeded. The chloroform which we administered put it into a deep sleep, and we took the cast. But on removing the plaster we found that it had stopped breathing. We were unable to resuscitate it in any way, and after keeping the body for some time it was buried in the woods in a carefully marked spot.

"I shall present the cast to the Smithsonian institute after it has been examined by my friends in New York. Quite a yarn, isn't it? I supposed people will think I have been drinking some of the North Dakota whisky, but it is true, every word of it.

"The cast? That has been shipped by express to New York."

As the doctor concluded his narration two muscular men, with the air of officers stepped up to the doctor, and one of them tapped him on the shoulder.

"Better go to bed and get some rest," he said, and the doctor quietly went up the stairs accompanied by one of them.

"A good fellow, but —"

He tapped his forehead in a significant manner and then followed the doctor and his companion. They left on the evening train for New York. The doctor had escaped three weeks before and was found in Fargo.

A DEEP SEA MONSTER.

Bridgeton Pioneer – June 8, 1893 – New Jersey

Thrilling Experience Vouched for by a Diver.

(Special Correspondence.)

ST. JOHN, N.B., May 9. – Sailors are said to be superstitious, and perhaps they are, yet who is the landlubber who has not read Jules Verne or Victor Hugo's "Toilers of the Sea?" The monster described was identical with the octopus, or giant squid. Once in a while newspapers contain articles about sea monsters and their doings. So, too, Newfoundland men and men living on the coast of Maine relate that living in the deep and silent caves of the sea is a huge lobster resembling the smaller fish in structure but being very voracious. It is said that he seldom comes near the shore, but that enormous lobster shells are sometimes found thrown up on land after a gale. All northern fishermen have heard of the monster, and I have seen them shiver in the cuddles of their fishing smacks as some one described the size and appearance of the fish. Never having seen it myself, I do not know how far the general impression is correct, but I have no doubt that it exists, and I will relate the story as it was told me by a Newfoundland diver:

"When the Anglo Saxon, a ship laden with costly merchandise, as many will remember, ran into Chance cove on the Newfoundland coast, striking a reef, and sank, the government at once took steps to have all that the unfortunate vessel contained removed. There were over 100 persons on board but not a single one escaped.

"As soon as possible divers were brought to the spot, but it was difficult to go down. The first day we got below we could do little but lay out the plan of operations. The ship was on her side, the stumps of the mast turned toward land. I had never gone down before in water so far north, and the place was so wild that I was timid. Lines were attached to our bodies and the ends fastened in the skiff above, so that if any diver pulled his line he was at once drawn to surface.

We walked around the bottom and around the ship with our feet weighted to keep us from rising. The water was a pale green, and I could notice objects, quite plainly for many yards distant. There was a huge break in the bottom of the ship, while her stem was staved in, and so was her stern.

"One afternoon while my two men remained above repairing their diving apparatus, I went down alone. We were now removing the bales from the after compartment by the break in the stern. The method of raising the goods was to lower down heavy hooks, which could be fastened into the bales after they were pushed outside. Some of these bales or cases, would float and some would rest lightly on the bottom. I had selected a large case which I was about to move when, happening to turn my eyes, I saw outside a huge creature moving toward the vessel. I had never seen anything like it before. Its body seemed to be several feet high and about eight feet long, and it had on each side an enormous arm.

"There seemed to be an unlimited number of legs attached to the hideous beast. Its color was a dull brown, mottled over with dark spots. Two round shining black eyes were in its forehead, and two supple horns, each resembling and enormous whip, likewise came out of his head. All this I noticed in once glance. A numb terror seized me, and involuntarily I moved for the outlet from the ship. But, as if knowing what I intended, this brute, looking straight at me with its frightful, motionless eyes, walked or rather crawled directly toward me. I hurried in the hope of being able to seize the hanging hook, now my only means of signaling the skiff, but I had barely put my foot upon a gray rock outside when the two writhing horns of the detestable monster were twining about me and again untwining. Then he would touch me with these and sweep them up and down as if feeling what kind of prey I was.

"In my hand I held a crowbar, which I used to loosen the cargo. In my belt I carried a heavy sheath knife. These were my only weapons. Suddenly and without any warning the monster threw out one of its arms and seized me below the shoulder. I felt as if my bones were being crushed. The more I resisted the more terrible was the pain. I still had the crowbar in my right hand, but it was of no use to me. So, I let it drop. The monster's arm terminated in a claw, which opened and shut convulsively. This horrible mouth shaped thing had two rows of shining white teeth, as seen often on the inside of the two fingers of a lobster's claw. Several of these were piercing my arm almost to the bone. Some distance above the mouthlike hand I observed a joint, and then – I drew my knife. But alas! The heavy shell so overlapped the fleshy tissue that I could not injure my captor.

"For the first time I saw those terrifying eyes move and turn upon me. The whip-like arms again began to move and curl about my body. His head was now only about a foot distant from my body and drawing my knife once more I plunged it into the eye near me, turning the blade round and round. I saw that I had destroyed the eye for an inky fluid issued out of the socket, darkening the water about his head. This checked the aggressive movements of the animal, but it did not seem to hurt it. I waited until its head turned, so I supposed, that he might be able to see his prey with his other eye.

"This was what I wanted, and with a swift thrust I sent my knife into his other eye down to the hilt. The creature reeled, and the grip on my arm slightly relaxed, but though totally blind my captor did not release me.

"The agony of my arm soon grew unbearable. Then the light went out of my eyes, and I remembered nothing more.

"When I recovered my senses, I was in the skiff and learned how the divers, alarmed at my long silence below, had come down. They saw my plight, and after a time succeeded in severing my arm from the body of the fish, which they both declared was the awful deep sea lobster."

—LIEUTENANT F. DE T. – CLOTH.

STORY OF A CURIOUS BATTLE.

The Herald – August 25, 1893 – California

Fighting with a Monster Eagle in Mid Air.

**When Even Fear Gave Place to Thoughts of Self-Preservation.
Bert Barnes Tells in Detail the Story of His Battle from the Tip of a
Telephone Pole – A Lively Fight.**

Bert Barnes, the telephone lineman who has come into prominence as the hero of an encounter with an immense eagle in a lonely part of the San Fernando valley a few days ago, spent the greater part of yesterday surrounded by a group of admiring friends, who listened to his graphic recital of the encounter with eyes greatly bulged out, and injected into the intervals of the recital many exclamations of surprise and astonishment.

The exclusive publication in the HERALD of the details of the strange battle between man and bird in mid-air only made the friends of the brave lineman eager to hear more, so gradually he was forced to tell the whole story in minutest detail.

"I had been sent alone," he said, "into a lonely part of the valley to repair some lines that had become detached. It was a sultry day; not a breath of air was stirring, and I had reduced my apparel just as much as was possible, so that the upper portion of my body was protected by only a thin shirt. As I aimed to protect it only from the burning rays of the sun this was all that was necessary.

"I had not the least fear or even a thought of danger, and, indeed, why should I have, for apparently there was not a living thing within rifle shot of the place where my work was to begin. Even the jack-rabbits and the lizards had deserted the place.

"The work upon the pole occupied all my attention for some moments. I did not look up until about to descend. I had heard not the slightest sound save the noise made by my hammer at the work before me.

"Suddenly I noticed a great shadow moving across the stretch of sand below me, moving in a great circle, sometimes fast and again slow. I knew the shadow was that of a bird; 'it is certainly a very large one,' I said to myself, and from curiosity, merely, I turned my head to locate the feathered monster – for such I was convinced it was.

"I had not the least bit of fear. If I had felt fear then I might have quickly slid to the ground and probably have escaped the attack, which came only a moment later.

"One more circle the flying monster made and then, spreading its great wings, darted directly for me.

"Even then I believe I was not afraid.

"I had a feeling that in some way I must protect myself from the attack of the bird, but there was no fear in the thought. The fierce, venomous eyes of the bird were never turned from me. Even when it circled, as I first glanced upward at it, I was attracted by those eyes, and I noticed that in whatever position to me the huge body might be, the head turned so that the two fierce eyes were full upon me.

"For a weapon I had only my hammer, but even in the brief instant allowed me, I resolved to make that as serviceable as possible, and I had no time for misgivings as to the outcome of the encounter.

"Twice the monster came to the attack. A sudden turn and a setting of the wings brought the immense body very close to me. The talons were curved, and the legs drawn up ready to strike. The heavy beak was half opened.

"I could turn only part way around, as my 'climbers' of ankle spikes, upon which I depended for support, were firmly driven into the wood. It was fortunate that at the second attack the bird was directly before me, for it allowed me the full swing of my right arm, and swing I did, with a vengeance.

"It's no use for me to say where the blow struck. Things were too confused for me to judge just exactly, and I only know that a moment later the great bird lay fluttering on the ground at the bottom of the pole and my hammer lay before it.

"The bird was not dead – only stunned. I climbed quickly down and securely tied it with some pieces of twine, and I have it now alive. I will sell the eagle if anybody wants it.

"They say that when a man is drowning," continued Mr. Barnes after a moment's pause, "thoughts of various kinds come to him; you've all heard that. Let me tell you another curious thing. When a man is on top of a telephone pole and a great brown bird with glittering eyes and opened beak comes swooping toward him, all the stories he has ever read or heard of people being carried away by mother eagles to the nests of their young come popping into his head quicker than you could say Jack Robinson, and, between you and I, perhaps I was a trifle scared about the time I aimed that second blow."

A FRESH WATER SEA SERPENT.

The Weekly Thibodaux Sentinel – September 23, 1893 – Louisiana

The latest from the sea serpent, comes from the upper Ottawa river. Mrs. Lahey, a farmer's wife, according to the Ottawa Free Press, went down to the river to do her washing. Going to dip a bucket of water out of the river, she found a great log in the way. She took a pole and undertook to push the log out of the way, and to her horror found that the side of the log sunk inward under the force of her efforts, but the log itself would not give an inch. While she stood considering what to do suddenly the log rolled over and about 10 feet from her the head of a hideous monster rose 5 feet above the surface of the water, hissing in a snakish way, and then with another roll and a splash of its tail, which was fully 20 feet from where the head appeared, the animal plunged toward the middle of the stream and disappeared. The lady was so terrified by the sight that she fainted and was confined to the bed for several days.

A MONSTROUS BRUTE.

The Columbian – November 30, 1893 – Pennsylvania

Nothing Like It Known to the Most Eminent Zoologists.

It Has a Broad Body, Flat Head, Big Fiery Eyes, Woolly Hide, Bushy Tail, Powerful Limbs and Bleeding Mouth.

The "dog eater," panther, or whatever it is that has created consternation time and again throughout this section among the country folks, has again made its appearance, after an interval of something like a year, says a Danville (Ky.) dispatch to the Cincinnati Enquirer. The existence of this strange animal has been scouted at by the skeptics, but persons of undoubted veracity who claim to have seen the monster during its midnight prowling say they are willing to make oath to the statements concerning it.

About five years ago it made its appearance in this county, and several parties were organized in the vicinity of Perryville to hunt the strange beast down and exterminate it, but none were successful in their mission. From the fact that it seldom, if ever, attacked anything save dogs, the people gave it the name of the "dog eater," and by this it has been known for about seven years. Persons versed in natural history say they can recall nothing like it, and seem to think, from the descriptions given by those who have caught glimpses of the animal, that it is a cross between a panther and a mastiff, though the descriptions vary so at times that such a conclusion cannot be relied upon.

Its last appearance was in Mercer county, a short distance from this city. James O'Connor and the colored driver of R.E. Coleman's bus were returning from Burgin with several passengers aboard, and had just passed the old Walden farm and were coming down hill at a moderately rapid gait, when suddenly the team stopped, reared, snorted and plunged about, almost upsetting the bus and badly frightening the passengers, acting just as horses have been seen to do when scared by some strange beast.

In a moment the occupants of the vehicle were startled and almost paralyzed at seeing an animal of enormous size and ferocious looks spring out of the woodland into the road, glare at the conveyance a moment and then leisurely leave the scene without molesting anything. The animal was distinctly seen by Mr. O'Connor and the driver, who were sitting upon the front seat. They described it as being of a dark color, with a broad, flat-like body and head, large, fiery eyes, woolly hide, powerful limbs, bushy tail and a monstrous head and mouth. There can be no doubt of Mr. O'Connor having seen this animal, as he would not concoct such a strange story, and his testimony about the appearance of the beast is corroborated by others who have seen it.

The question asked by many is: What is this monster that comes and goes, and still molests nothing except the worthless curs of the country, except now and then destroying a fancy setter? It is no stranger in Mercer county. Several years back there was a current report that some strange animal had taken up its abode in Boone's cave, and the people there about, especially the colored portion, were very much alarmed and afraid to venture out after night. A few determined ones, however, explored the cave, but failed to find the monster, though they discovered strange-looking tracks in the moist earth on the floor of the cave.

Two other gentlemen, Mr. Phil Marks and Edward H. Fox, the artist, claim to have seen this remarkable beast one night as they were returning from a coon-hunting expedition. They were riding leisurely along the pike, engaged in conversation, their fine pack of hounds following behind, weary and worn out after the chase, when suddenly Marks' horse reared up and had it not been for Mr. Marks' expert horsemanship he would have been thrown backward against the ground. Mr. Fox, who preserved his presence of mind, soon saw the cause of the trouble. The dog eater had steeped out into the road ahead of the party and began drinking out of a small stream, and right here this animal's strange influence over dogs was illustrated. The hounds following along seemed to become paralyzed with fright. They huddled together, trembling with fear and whining piteously. Mr. Fox drew his revolver and shot at the dog eater, which jumped over the fence and disappeared. The artist is confident that he hit the monster but thinks that the thick coating of hair on it was too much for the small bullet used. After the animal had got out of the way the hounds struck for home at a 2:40 gait. Mr. Marks can be found at his place of business in this city at any time and will cheerfully detail the story of his experience with the now noted animal. Mr. Fox, at the request of the reporter, made a rough sketch of the dog-eater as it appeared to him.

SAW A SEA SERPENT.

The Jersey City News – March 23, 1894 – New Jersey

Atlantic City Life Savers Discover the Monster Near the Shore.

Special to the Jersey City News.

ATLANTIC CITY, March 23, 1894. – That *lusus naturae,* a sea serpent, a sight of which is so seldom accorded human eyes, and then usually under circumstances that envelop its existence in a cloud of mystery, is reported on the authority of five of the crew of the Lower Absecon Government Life Saving Station to have been observed disporting in the ocean yesterday morning about fifty feet from the shore.

According to the story as related by Captain Gaskill, who has charge of the crew, the monster was first seen about 10:30 this morning by two young men who were walking along the beach a short distance below the station.

Scared at the frightful looking object, which was wriggling its way landward, they ran back to the station and first informed Surfman Nicholas Jeffries. The latter was joined by Surfman Robinson, Young and Loder, and procuring guns, they were guided to the place where the monster was seen.

Sure enough, the marine monster in all its hideousness was plainly visible and had come within fifty feet of the beach. It reared its ugly head high above the water and exposed about twenty feet of its scaly body, which was of a slimy, greenish hue. A further description made its eyes about as large as a silver dollar and of a reddish color.

Taking careful sight, the several surfmen discharged their guns in the hope that they could capture it. While they deny that their shot was heard to rattle against the monster's hide, they aver that the leaden pellets apparently had no effect whatever. After lashing itself about in the surf for a few minutes the serpent set its face seaward and swiftly passed out of view.

It was at least a foot in diameter in the thickest part of its exposed body, and they estimated that it was at least fifty feet in length. Owing to the fact that the story is vouched for by Captain Gaskill and his crew as being true, people here are in a quandary whether to give it credence or not.

The only other instance of a sea serpent being seen along this coast on record was the one which appeared in the Brigantine Shoals in 1879, but it was not supported by such authority as the account of the one observed today.

MONSTER OF ISSOIR.

The Madison Daily Leader – August 31, 1894 – South Dakota

MYSTERY OF THE FOURTEENTH ARRONDISSEMENT OF PARIS.

Singular Disappearance of Many Inhabitants of the Quarter – Enticing Its Victims with Music – Death of the Gigantic Spider.

For many years it is undeniably stated that in the fourteenth arrondissement of Paris – called the tomb of Issoir – a number of persons living in that quarter had mysteriously and periodically disappeared. The most careful researches, the most minute inquiries, the most skillful agents of the police had failed to discover the least trace of them.

Every year successively some inhabitants of this quarter would suddenly disappear, leaving their friends overwhelmed with grief and anxiety. It is also stated that these strange, inexplicable facts always occurred in the early spring – from the 20th to the last of March – and without regard to age or sex.

First a notary disappeared. It was thought he had used his client's funds and fled to parts unknown. Then an old woman, returning late one night from market, was the next victim, then a laborer going home from work. The last victim had been a young girl – a flower maker out late delivering her goods. From that time, she had completely disappeared as if the earth had opened and swallowed her up. Strange to say, no children had been among the victims.

This peculiar fact was accounted for in this way. These mysterious disappearances always occurred last at night, when the children were at home asleep.

As the time was drawing near for one of these periodical mysteries the chief of police became very anxious and instituted a strict surveillance, confiding the matter to a number of the most skillful of his assistants, hoping the combined efforts of so many zealous agents would surely be crowned with success. You will now see the result.

One night – this fact can be verified by applying to the office of the prefecture – a policeman about 3 o'clock in the morning heard a distant musical song, which seemed to come from the bowels of the earth. He listened and fancied the sounds came from and opening in the center of the street, at the foot of an enormous rock called the tomb of Issoir, or the Giant's cave.

It may be interesting to state that this rock derived its name from a legend that great giant had been buried there many years before the Christian era, and this rock had been placed there to mark the tomb.

Surprised at this strange discovery – for the opening had never been noticed before – the policeman waited, listening to the peculiar song, when he suddenly saw a young man approaching. He knew from his costume that he was a countryman lately arrived in the city. This young man also seemed to hear the subterranean sounds, first walking slowly with a peculiar wavering step, as if in cadence with this musical chant, then faster and faster as he drew near the fatal rock, until he ran with such velocity that in spite of the warning cries of the policeman he was swallowed up in the mysterious opening. Without taking a moment to consider the policeman recklessly followed, first firing his revolver and giving one or two vigorous blasts on his whistle.

At this signal several of his comrades quickly arrived. The musical chanting had ceased, but they could hear in the dark, cavernous depths the muffled sounds of desperate struggle.

By the aid of ropes and ladders they succeeded in entering this mysterious chasm. The light of their lamps revealed a sickening sight.

The countryman was lying on his back writhing in the grasp of an unknown monster, whose horrible aspect froze the agents of police with terror.

It was as large as a full grown terrier, covered with wart-like protuberances and bristling with coarse brownish hair. Eight joined legs, terminated by formidable claws, were buried in the body of the unfortunate victim. The face had already disappeared. Nothing could be seen but the top of the head, and the monster was now engaged in tearing and sucking blood from his throat.

As soon as they recovered from their horror and surprise a dozen balls struck the body of this sanguinary beast.

He raised up on his legs, a greenish, bloody liquid flowing from his wounds, and, with a frightful cry, expired.

The first policeman, who had given the alarm, was lying unconscious in one corner of the cavern, where he had fallen, a distance of 30 feet.

It was with great difficulty they succeeded in removing the two bodies and the unknown monster from the cavern. The poor countryman was dead, but the policeman was soon restored to life.

The agents immediately sent for the commissioner of police, who summoned a naturalist in great haste.

The first established the identity of the victim; the second declared the creature lying before him was a gigantic spider. The species had been considered extinct for centuries – ever since the days before deluge. It was called "Arachne gigans" and was said to have the power of enticing its victims by a peculiar musical song. None had been seen or heard of for ages, but it is now believed some of these sanguinary beasts still exist in the deepest galleries of the catacombs.

The dead body of the spider was conveyed to the Museum of Natural History, where it was carefully prepared and stuffed and is now on exhibition – once a week.

BATTLE WITH AN OCTOPUS.

Chicago Eagle – September 8, 1894 – Illinois

Five Fishermen Have a Terrible Experience.

A huge octopus was hoisted on Fisherman's Wharf on Thursday afternoon from Capt. Charles Collins' boat, and the four members of the crew shuddered as they handled it and told of their terrible fight far out from the land. The monster covered a large section of the wharf, and its long tentacles were avoided by the curious crowd with dread. Several of the fish are caught each week and brought to the dock by the curious boats of the fishermen, but never had so large a one been carried in through the Heads as the one caught by Captain Collins and his crew. "The long tentacles when spread apart measured about twenty-five feet from tip to tip, and they were armed all the way along with dreadful saucer-like mouths that sucked the life from their victims.

"It was a fearful fight that we had with the monster," said Captain Collins, in his broken Greek, "and it is only by a miracle that I am here to tell of it. Wednesday morning, we commenced to take up our lines as usual. There came a violent tug at the line, and a huge arm of the monster flashed out of the water and landed across the gunwale of the boat. In an instant it fastened its tenacious suckers, while the water about the boat was lashed into a foam.

An octopus can be killed almost instantly if it can be stabbed just below the eye, even if the weapon be only the small blade of a pocket knife, and when the fellow rose so close to me and presented such a good opportunity for the death blow, I reached for the boat-hook and made a lunge for the vital spot. As I did so the boat careened violently, and instead of dispatching the brute only inflicted a wound that maddened the monster the more. The battle then became one of life or death between us.

A couple more of the arms of the octopus had by this time been wound around the boat and they reached from stem to stern. The boat was completely enveloped by them, and all hands were kept busy to escape being caught in the clutches of the relentless suckers. The small craft rolled and rocked in the arms of the monster, and every moment it threatened to throw all five of us into the water. Blows had no effect on the huge tentacles. The men belabored what parts of the fish they could reach with clubs, but the effect was like pounding a piece of rubber.

"One of the stout fishhooks had caught securely in the body of the brute and a couple of the men began to haul it on the stout line. Steadily the men hauled away until the body was dragged upward and as it reached the surface the sharp spike of the boat hook was driven with a hand of desperation deep into the brute's body just below the eye and the victory was won."

— San Francisco Examiner.

HIDEOUS MAN-EATER.

The Neihart Herald – June 22, 1895 – Montana

Along the Classic Banks of the Teton the Monster Frolics.

From time to time vague rumors have reached Great Falls of the depredations of a horrible monster which is reported to be roaming at large in Choteau county. Such fear has seized the people along Teton river that they have made every preparation against the monster, be it man or beast. Women and children are reported to have been frightened by the strange creature to such an extent that they have become seriously ill. Antelope and coyote hunters claim to have seen it skulking along the brush along the Teton, and ranchers claim that at night, hearing disturbances in the sheep pens, they have hastened forth, but just in time to see the brute escaping with a choice mutton wether clutched in his strange talons.

Many scoff at the stories circulated and profess to believe that the animal is a wolf of great size and unusual courage, but others, more credulous, claim that the animal has avoided bait which would tempt any wolf and say that it is invulnerable to bullets from any ordinary rifle.

One rancher claims that recently, while his wife was returning from the hen house, about noon, she heard a commotion among the poultry, and returning to the hen house to investigate, as she opened the door a monstrous beast leaped over hear head, its hot breath being plainly felt upon her face, and with a sound like a human moan, it disappeared around a building before she had recovered from her fright. A lady who was riding along a trail recently saw a queer beast loping along ahead of her and gave chase to it. She had nearly overtaken it, when it turned and with a cry, more of agony than of terror, rushed past her, frightening her horse so that he threw his rider.

The Ford Benton River Press say of the beast: "Morgan Williams, who came in from the Teton to-day, reports there was great excitement in his neighborhood yesterday. A sheep shearer came in on horseback at a breakneck speed, dashing through wire fences and other obstacles, and explained his hurry by declaring that he had been chased over the prairie by a hideous man-eating monster. From the description given of the animal it appeared to be a cross between a mountain lion and a buffalo, its size comparing with that of a 2-year old heifer."

Others declare that the animal is nearer the size of a Norman stallion, with the agility of a monkey and the grace of a panther. It is said to have the voice of a human being, but no one has been able to get an accurate description of it.

A HAIRY JABBERWOCK.
The Morning News – September 26, 1895 – Georgia

Winsted's What-Is-It Appears in Pat Danchy's Corn Patch.

From the New York World.

Winsted, Conn., Sept. 17. – Pat Danchy, of Colebrook, saw the famous wild what-is-it early this morning. He was in his barnyard hitching up his horses. The nigh horse began to shiver and snort, and Pat looked about to find the cause. He saw something running among the stalks of sugar corn in his garden. As he began to move in that direction a huge creature, with an enormous head and very small ears, appeared. Pat moved hastily into the barn and closed the door. Looking out through a crack, he saw that the monster had one great, hairy arm (it was covered with dark red hair from head to foot), crooked and filled high with ears of corn.

It made off at an easy gait and was soon hidden in the woods. Pat went into the garden and there found vast tracks, the like of which no man hereabouts ever made. All day farmers have been calling at Pat's, on their way from the County fair. All have been much perturbed by the sight of these mighty tracks. Late in the afternoon a half-hearted expedition beat the woods with a vague idea of starting up the monster. But nothing came of it.

It has nothing to do with the jabberwock, apparently, but is nevertheless highly interesting, that a number of young men of Winsted have formed a bald-headed club. All the members are young men, and all have shaved their crowns, and have vowed never to have anything to do with women. One member of the society, William Gordon, is down with the brain fever and is not expected to live.

A ROARING WHALE.

The Anaconda Standard – December 3, 1895 – Montana

Which, According to Reports, Stood on Its Head and Waved Its Tail in the Air.

From the Portland Press.

"No," said Captain J.A. Crossman of South Portland last evening, "we didn't encounter the sea serpent, but we had a strange experience with a whale, and I don't believe anybody ever had the like before. I've been at sea, man and boy, since I was 9 years old, but I never saw the like of the whale we encountered. I never saw a whale before that didn't blow, but the one we met didn't, but it did give a roar that was awful."

"It sounded like the lions in Central Park, New York," said Miss Houston, who was one of the party that had the strange encounter.

"It certainly was more like the roar of a lion than anything else I can think of," said Captain Crossman.

The schooner Grace Webster, Captain Crossman, was on her way from New York to Portland with 414 tons of coal. Besides the captain and crew, Mrs. Crossman, her daughter and Miss Houston were on board.

The schooner was about 10 miles off Wood island and making good headway under full sail, the mate, Merrill Crossman, at the wheel, when there was a sudden commotion ahead, and then a great head shot up into the air and was on a level with the deck.

One of the crew first sighted the strange creature and called Captain Crossman, and in a moment all on board but the man at the wheel were looking at the strange sight. They saw before them an enormous head, one mass of great bunches, through which the wicked looking eyes of the creature gleamed. They expected the whale, if such, would "blow," but it didn't then or after. Once a narrow thread of what looked like steam shot up, but not a drop of water was sent into the air. As they looked at the creature it roared savagely, and then drew close up to the side of the schooner, giving them ample time to observe the head, and all agree that it was very board; that it tapered almost to a point, and that it was not very thick through the thickest part. The creature was about 75 to 80 feet in length and had a very broad tail, very different from that of an ordinary whale. In fact, at the time there were three or four whales in sight, and they had no difficulty in noting the points of difference between them and the stranger.

The great creature went down head first, and then made a series of attempts to strike the side of the schooner with its tail. It did not succeed and swam around them, roaring loudly in evident anger. Then it went down and under the schooner.

Captain Crossman, who had watched for this movement, gave orders to be ready to lower the boat, fearing that the whale might come up under them and break them in two. It was very fortunate that they were not forced to lower their boat, as it proved later to be leaking, and would not have carried half their number safely to land.

For more than an hour the whale continued his remarkable acrobatic performance, standing on his head with his tail waving in the air most of the time. It seemed bent on hitting the schooner and it took the best of good seamanship to prevent an encounter.

At last the whale seemed to get tired of what had been fun at first, and it headed for the westward.

Captain Crossman is of the opinion that this strange whale must have been mistaken for a sea serpent, not once, but many times. Seen but a short distance off the head would look more like that of a great serpent than that of a whale.

The creature, while making its long and repeated attempts to hit the schooner, continued its roaring when above water. It would scrape against the sides of the schooner and then would draw off, seeming to be calculating the distance, and then strike. The schooner was kept off at the right moment, and the creature missed the vessel every time. It was an odd experience and for a time there was something resembling a panic, the women being badly frightened.

Miss Houston said last evening that the sight of that great mass standing almost up right in mid-ocean was something not to be forgotten. Captain Crossman is uncertain whether the whale is a natural fighter or whether it was frightened when it came up out of the water, and as a result of its confusion made the repeated attempts it did to sink the schooner. One of the crew hit it with a bolt, and many times Captain Crossman said he could have hit it with a board from the deck. He did not venture to do anything to still further arouse its anger and so let it go in peace.

SEA SERPENT CAUGHT.
The Portland Daily Press – July 4, 1896 – Maine

Monster of the Raging Deep Captured at Tacoma.

Tacoma, Wash., June 21 – Special correspondence of the Chicago Inter-Ocean. The sea serpent has at last been taken alive in his native haunt, or rather from his native haunt, if this, the placid waters of Puget Sound, can be called the haunt of such an animal. A porpoise finds his way into the sound from the Pacific, and occasionally a whale is seen spouting, but the sea serpent was never thought of until two Tacoma fishermen, R.E. McClean and W. J. Kennedy, while fishing for black bass about two miles north of the mouth of the Humi Humi River, which empties into Hood's Canal near this city, made the catch.

They were alongside a ledge where the water drops to 100 to 150 feet deep and were using minnows for bait when their attention was attracted to a commotion in the net. The water becoming agitated was followed immediately by the head of the monster appearing above the surface. This struck terror to the already frightened fishermen, who at once made for the shore, dragging it after them and hauling it upon the beach. The monster was as ferocious as a tiger, and bit and snapped the gaff stick in pieces, and when hauled on the beach rushed back over the sands with the 100 feet of line and swam out to sea as far as it could go.

The reptile was seventeen feet long, and as big around as a man's body, and has every characteristic of the snake, except the head, which is much like that of a pugnacious bull dog. The under jaw is heavy and covered with wrinkled skin, the eyes are as large as a man's, and as bright, and will follow the movements of a person as closely as the eyes of a cat follow a mouse, and without the animal ever moving its head. The general color of the serpent is darkish blue, with spots much like those of a rattlesnake, the spots fading out into lighter blue at the circumference. The skin is smooth, like that of a snake. The monster is finned much like the halibut, having a long dorsal, very thin, running down the back, while underneath there is a similar fin, but only near the caudal extremity. The animal's jaws are set with rows of sharp teeth like those of a cat, and the great strength of the jaw enables it to sink its fangs to the base in a stick of wood.

Immediately on its capture the animal was lariated, and the water was lashed into a foam in its efforts to escape.

McClean and Kennedy say they are positive it is the sea serpent which has so long worried the marine world. In the water they say, the reptile looks larger than it really is, and from this fact lies much of the exaggeration from those who claim to have seen sea serpents. They say that such a monster as they have taken swimming alongside a rowboat with raised head would turn the oldest and bravest fisherman's hair gray.

It has not been fed any since its capture and subsists on whatever it can find within the rope's length. The fishermen have been relieved of their burden by Gilbert Girard, the actor, who is on his way east, and who intends presenting the monster to the Smithsonian Institution.

MAN-EATING PLANTS.

The Kimball Graphic – July 4, 1896 – South Dakota

Vampire vines, flesh and even man-eating plants are products of recent scientific discovery.

In a lecture delivered not long since at the Brooklyn institute by Professor Charles P. Riley, chief of the division of entomology at Washington, attention was called to certain insectivorous plants which "do digest and absorb the fruit they capture, while others absorb the products of decay. For there is a remarkable parallelism between these glands of some of these plants and those of the stomachs of animals in the secretion of their proper acid ferment."

Insect plants that feed on flies and wasps have been known long before the time of Darwin but a man-eating plant like some that have recently been studied in central Africa, Nicaragua or Tasmania is something new. About Lake Nicaragua the vampire vine, which seizes dogs, men and even cattle in its ample tendrils and sucks the life out of them, affords one of the chief obstacles to the exploration of the country.

The following account of a "man-eating plant" is vouched for by an old resident in Tasmania (the scientific name is bauera rubioides; it is a native of Australia and Tasmania and the narrator and a friend have been entangled in its meshes and only escaped with great difficulty): "The bauera is not a creeper or climber but only a plant that is weak in the legs, having a thin, flexible stem, usually supporting itself on its neighbors. A bauera scrub at the outer edge of the patch may be only eighteen inches high but in the thick of it may reach ten to twenty feet; a man may be enveloped even before he is aware of it, and the tangled mass surrounds him till movement is impossible. You cannot cut it with an ax, because it offers no resistance, and if cut with a knife the rope-like stems only fall more closely round you. You cannot see where you are going and only struggle and flounder on to your exhaustion. It usually covers low-lying ground and throws up from the root a number of slender stems, tapering gradually, that become interlaced in all directions and to the solitary bushman or explorer it is formidable. He will perhaps try to wriggle along the damp ground under it and to tear the stems apart and struggle through. Then exhausted with this he perhaps climbs up some old stump and tries to flounder along on the top of the scrub, but he soon sinks helpless into the yielding mass that quickly squeezes out his life."

SCARED BY A PHANTOM GOAT.

The Neihart Herald – July 18, 1896 – Montana

Strange Sights In Mississippi In and Out of the Bock Beer Season.

Three miles west of New Albany the Rocky Ford road crosses a creak which was originally named Big creek but was more appropriately named Hell creek by persons who have been compelled to cross the adjacent bottom in recent years. Just beyond this is another little run called Mud creek, which stream is grown up with thicket and heavy underbrush, and on cloudy nights the blackness that surrounds the travelers could be sliced into chunks and sold for ink. The bottom or lowlands adjacent to the stream is of unusual width for one so small, and at the best is exceedingly uninviting.

Some years ago, a gentleman passing through the bottom at night was almost thrown by his horse shying to one side, and when he looked ahead was confronted by a monster goat of white color rearing upon his hind feet as if to annihilate the animal and rider. One look was sufficient, and, making a sudden turn, he galloped out of the bottom at the risk of his life, swearing that he would drink no more New Albany blind tiger liquor. Not wishing to put himself up as a target for the jeers of the public, he held his counsel and heard or saw nothing more of the apparition for some time.

About a year later his goatship was again on the warpath and confronted a gentleman of known sobriety, who, not daunted, urged his animal forward despite the warlike attitude of the ghostly visitor. The goat kept in the middle of the road and when the small bridge was reached disappeared as mysteriously as he had appeared.

The gentleman related his experience, which became noised abroad and gave courage to the man who first sighted the vapory animal to relate his experience, and the two coincided so well that the people began to give them credit for having seen something to disturb their peace of mind. The story was given enough credence to cause an uneasy feeling to enter the mind of the traveler who crossed the bottom at night and cause a chill to ramble up and down the spinal column as he passed the spot where the ghost had been seen.

Last year Mr. --, who is not a believer in things uncanny at all and has a supreme contempt for a man who has seen spooks, had been beyond the creek harvesting hay and was detained until after nightfall on his return home. The night was intensely dark, and a slight rain was falling. As he drove through the impenetrable gloom, trusting to the instinct of the mules that drew the rake which he was astride to find the road, the misty and uncertain form of the giant goat suddenly appeared in the road ahead of him. The mules reared and plunged, very nearly upsetting the rake. Leaping to the ground, he grasped the bits and was gratified to see the phantom recede as the team moved forward. The mules, trembling in every nerve, carried him along, and when the bridge was reached, he disappeared as on former occasions, much to the relief of the gentleman who did not believe in spirits and unnatural apparitions.

Since that time a number of thoroughly reliable witnesses have been placed in positions to vouch for the truthfulness of the existence of the phantom goat. Persons who travel that road to and from town make their arrangements to pass that spot before nightfall, and very few have the temerity to invade the territory of his goatship after darkness has fallen.

– New Albany (Miss.) Gazette.

A REAL SEA SERPENT.

The Topeka State Journal – August 1, 1896 – Kansas

TACOMA FISHERMEN PROVE THE MONSTER IS NOT A MYTH.
THEY CAUGHT IT ALIVE.

Has a Bulldog's Head, a Tiger's Fangs, a Snake's Body, a Fish's Fins and a Pugilist's Neck.

That the West is rapidly assuming many of the sacred prerogatives of the East was clearly demonstrated the other day by the news from Tacoma, WA., that there had been captured in Hood's Canal, Puget Sound, two sea serpents.

Heretofore the East has monopolized the sea serpent industry, but in its bravest days it never ventured the claim of having seen two sea serpents at the one time, let alone capturing them. In fact, heretofore the East contented itself by thrilling reports from time to time by its sea captains, of the magnitude of the sea serpents which had been sighted. Sometimes these sea serpents were only sixty feet long, and again they reached the stupendous length of 600 feet. One captain of an excursion barge which was kept out all night in Long Island Sound, so that the manager of the bar on board could sell all of his beer to thirsty passengers, reported passing a sea serpent 1,000 feet long, and some of the passengers were quite sure it was 2,000 feet long. It is necessary to state that this sea serpent was sighted after every drop of beer and whisky on board had been consumed.

The Tacoma sea serpents, as far as length go, are very mild in comparison with their Eastern brothers and sisters. One measured ten feet and the other eight feet. This, of course, is disappointing, but their capture proves beyond all peradventure that sea serpents actually exist. A number of scientists have examined them without being able to classify them. One of the sea serpents was killed during the capture, but the other, a female, was alive and well at last accounts.

A COMPOSITE MONSTER

She is not a pretty creature by any means. She has a head like a big bulldog and an extraordinarily thick and long neck measuring about twenty-six inches in circumference. Her body is like that of a huge rattlesnake, striped and spotted and tapering to a point at the tail. A colossal fin runs the entire length of the vertebrae, and a similar fin underneath runs along the stomach to the tail. She has great fangs like those of a tiger and heavy molar teeth. Behind the gills are inside fins, and but for these she would never be recognized as bearing any kinship to the fish family.

If this sea serpent had not been captured the fishermen who first saw it would doubtless be classed with what is generally termed the grand army of sea serpent liars. When the news of its capture reaches all parts of the world it will doubtless cause something of a sensation, as scientists have fought and wrangled over what is called the sea serpent myth for many years. Yet on the books of the United States and British navies are many records furnished by captains of warships of sea serpents which had been seen. Furthermore, it is known, for instance, that monsters exactly corresponding with the descriptions of the sea serpent by people who claim to have seen it existed in past ages. In the museum of Yale College are the skeletons of many of these creatures, dug out of rocks and from the beds of dried-up seas, where they had reposed for ages.

PETERIFIED POINTERS.

Geologists all know that certain strata are almost certain to disclose the skeletons of great sea monsters, hundreds of feet in length, which in far remote ages swam the oceans of the world and bred numerously.

The vertebrae, the ribs, the skull, the jaws of these sea serpents of a bygone age are as well known to scientists as the bones of the megatherium and the mastodon. Coming upon such bones or traces of them in rock formation, the scientist classifies them instantly, knowing that they are the remains of the sea serpent.

AN ANTEDILUVIAN EXAMPLE.

One of these antediluvian sea serpents had a neck at least fifty feet long, according to the scientists of the British Museum, where the skeleton of such a specimen is to be seen. It had a large head, with immense eyes, and it swam through the water something like a giant snake.

Judging from the records on the subject the sea serpent was more plentiful a century ago than he is to-day. For instance: Captain Laurence de Ferry made oath before a magistrate in 1746 that he had chased a sea serpent with a crew of sailors in a rowboat, but that the monster escaped. The captain described the creature as a formidable specimen, fully 600 feet long, whose coils above water looked like a row of hogsheads. It had the head of a horse, with a sort of mane, and it was gray or brown in color.

Eleazer Crabtree, "a man of unimpeachable veracity," who dwelt on Fox Island, in Penobscot Bay, in 1778, said he saw a sea serpent 500 feet long. His description was very much like that of Captain de Ferry's, and the monster he saw had a large black mouth. The same Crabtree saw another sea serpent near Mount Desert in 1793.

AN OFFICIAL SERPENT.

The adventure of Commodore Preble, U.S.N., when he gave chase to a sea serpent took place in 1779. He was then a midshipman, and when the sea serpent was sighted from the deck of the sloop of war, he was placed in command of a boat manned by twelve seamen and sent in pursuit. The monster is said to have been 100 feet long and possessed of a large head. Its motion was so rapid that it could not be overtaken, but it was observed by the officers and men for over an hour.

Captain Little, U.S.N., swore that while in Penobscot Bay, in 1780, on board of a "public armed ship," he saw a sea serpent at sunrise one morning. He had a boat lowered, and took the tiller himself, but before he could get near enough for the marines to shoot, the animal sank out of sight.

Abraham Cummings reported a sea serpent in Penobscot Bay in 1802, and another in 1808. In the same year the Rev. Mr. Maclean, a clergyman, of Eigg, sent a careful description of a sea serpent, with "a head somewhat broad," that swam "with his head above water for about half a mile." He described the creature as about eighty feet long.

In 1817 Captain Tappan, of the schooner Laura, and his whole crew told of seeing a sea serpent off Gloucester. They said it looked like a string of buoys, with a head like a serpent and a long tongue that stuck out of its mouth like a harpoon. Its motion was more rapid than that of a whale.

CAPE ANN'S MONSTER.

Several persons made affidavits in 1818 to having seen a sea monster off Cape Ann. In 1822 the sea serpent was reported from the fjords of Norway, and in 1831 it was seen off Portsmouth, N.H. In 1848 the British ship Daedalus, Captain McQuahae, encountered a sea serpent which was distinctly seen by many of the passengers and afterward described by them with much care. The captain and passengers of the ship Silas Richards reported encountering a monster on June 7, 1826, in latitude 41 and longitude 67, and described the serpent as of a brownish color and seventy feet long.

Three Maine fishermen, "all reliable and God-fearing men," sailed far out to sea one summer's day in 1833 and came across a sea serpent basking near the surface. Two of the fishermen were so badly scared that they went below, leaving the third, a Mr. Gooch, to face the intruder. Mr. Gooch is authority for the statement that the boat passed within fifty feet of the serpent and that he had a good view of it. It raised its head and looked at Mr. Gooch, and then dived out of sight.

There were many kinds of sea serpents in that year. The steamship Connecticut reached port several days overdue and explained the delay by saying that much time had been consumed chasing sea serpents. The passengers and crew were unanimous in their description of the monster, which fled across the sea in spirals. The people on land became very much excited, and three days later the Connecticut put to sea with a hundred excursionists who wanted to get a glimpse of the snake.

Countless other instances could be cited in which mariners belonging to every nation on the globe made solemn, and in some cases sworn, statements of having seen sea serpents, but those already mentioned cover the ground quite fully. It can be seen that in every case the sea serpent escaped, although in some instances the monster was fired at by gun and cannon. Tacoma can justly be proud of the fishermen who made the capture, as the specimen should set at rest forever the disputes which have survived for a century or more.

THE MAN-EATING PLANT.

The Florida Agriculturist – August 12, 1896 – Florida

Strange tales have been told by African travelers about the animal and vegetable life of the Dark Continent. Strangest and weirdest of all are the accounts of the man-eating tree. The following marvelous traveler's tale is told by a German trader. We give the account in his own words:

"I have heard," he says, "of the man-eating tree from the natives. Incredulous at first, I finally grew curious, and got the guide to conduct me to the spot where it stood, in the midst of a small clearing of the dense forest, surrounded by tall, waving grasses. It seemed to be one mass of scarlet and hanging from its branches were delicious looking bunches of ripe, red fruit, swaying hither and thither with the slightest breeze.

"I put it down to fancy at the time, but as I approached, the tree seemed to become suddenly agitated, and the scarlet leaves and fruit to become darker in hue, changing from brilliant scarlet to blood red. I still continued my rapid walk towards it, until I was in some five yards, when I saw the tree suddenly bend towards me. I involuntarily drew back, but too late. From the tree there came a sense-lulling, stupefying perfume, and the leaves seemed to fold over and rub each other in ecstasy. Suddenly I saw dart from behind the branches several tentacles or fangs – for such only could I call them – and before I could retreat, the terrible fangs wrapped themselves like whipcords around my body and drew me toward the tree. Their touch broke the spell of the sense-lulling perfume, and I struggled frantically to free myself. It was in vain. The dread tentacles wound themselves around my left arm and legs, and I was drawn slowly but surely toward the terrible animal vegetable monster. I redoubled my struggles, and in desperation shouted to my guide for aid, but he would not stir to my assistance. A great terror then came over me. It was so awful, this struggle with a monster, half vegetable, and half animal; but, fortunately in my terror, I retained my presence of mind. Once under the branches of the tree, and I knew I was lost; so, drawing my knife with my right hand, I slashed away at the tentacles to release myself. They were hard, and I could not cut through them. The blood red fruits now showed tiny emerald-green spots on their smooth skins, and as I saw this change, the thought flashed through my mind that perhaps the fruit were the arteries of the dread thing. I plunged my knife into the nearest, and a low, faint moan, as of pain, seemed to come from it. A dull, red substance, half juice and half blood, oozed from it, and at the same moment the tentacle grasping my left arm relaxed its grip. In a frenzy of terror, I now slashed away at fruit after fruit, and the tentacles, one after another, loosened their grip, until I shook them from me, and was free. But I did not stop until I had cut to pieces each of the treacherous blood red fruits and killed the dread animal vegetable monster."

— Cultivator and Dixie Farmer.

ROCK LAKE'S MONSTER.

Watertown Republican – September 9, 1896 – Wisconsin

For years it has been known that an immense serpent or water beast of unusual size and peculiar shape made its home in our lake. Numbers of fishermen have reported seeing it, or at least having a fight with it, but always with the result of losing hook and line, as it was always unmanageable.

Week before last Alderman Chapman, of Chicago (Oak Grove house) had a battle with it. He says it had feet and scales somewhat like an alligator.

Fred Seaver, Sr., has for years insisted that there was a "monster" in the lake. That on one occasion several years ago, it seized his trolling hook and pulled his boat after him for several rods and finally raised his slimy head out of the water four feet, shook its homely head at him and disappeared. Mr. Seaver confesses that he was so frightened he immediately made for the shore.

R. Hassam once told the writer that he saw it near the rushes on the west side of the lake. At first, he supposed it to be a large crooked limb of a tree floating. On seeing it move away he struck it with an oar.

Last Sunday Captain Howe, of the boat livery, saw a terrible commotion among the fish a little way off his pier. Pickerel and pike of unusual size were jumping out of the water as if pursued by a demon. Occasionally in the midst of the racket he saw a shape belonging to no fish nor serpent ever seen by him before. The water was soon lashed into a foam. He rowed out to it and soon saw what the disturbance was. A serpent about seven feet long and four or five inches thick and covered with yellow spots and had large projecting eyes. On each side of the head where the gills are located on a fish, was a long fluke through which the serpent spouted large quantities of water while attacking. Captain Howe shot at the monster twice, but his aim was bad under the circumstances; he however succeeded in giving it a mighty blow with an oar. It sank into deep water. The next morning, he found it on the shore dead. It had three fish hooks in its mouth. The animal is a curiosity. It is neither serpent nor fish and cannot be classified by any adept in natural history.

It has been on exhibition for several days at Davis's barber shop, having been embalmed by him.

It is supposed that what Alderman Chapman took for legs on the animal were streams of water thrown out of the beast's flukes. Bathers and timid fisherman may now banish all fear of an attack from the lake monster.

The above appeared in The Lake Mills Leader last week. It is interesting reading to local frequenters of Rock Lake, although many upon first hearing of the capture, were inclined to be skeptical over the matter. There were others, however, who were certain the story was genuine, for they claimed to have had experiences with the monster at different times.

Joe Harvey said he and Henry Bertram nearly caught a whale in Rock Lake twelve years ago; he was sure this was the same animal. George Weber claimed that last summer he, Frank Dickoff and Emil Berg had the monster hooked and alongside their boat but were unable to land it. These confident parties will be somewhat chagrined, however, when they hear the sequel to the story. The whole thing is a stupendous "fake" – a summer resort advertisement.

Mack Henderson, the genial proprietor of the Park Hotel at the Lake, who attended the fair yesterday, gave us the particulars. The "monster" is nothing but a piece of canvas hose, cunningly shaped into a fishy looking and ugly arrangement, the handiwork of a practical joker. It was placed on exhibition and for a time served its purpose well. Hundreds viewed its homely form, and then the delusion became apparent and the fun was over. Our citizens may continue to visit Lake Mills and bathe and fish with the utmost serenity.

CAUGHT IN FLORIDA.

The Iola Register – September 25, 1896 – Kansas

Marine Monster That is Part Fish, Part Bird. Part Animal.

Sea serpents are becoming too common, and when Florida people decided to produce a marine monster the serpent family was ignored and the Diabolus Maris was produced.

The picture which is presented was made from a drawing sent to the Kansas City Journal by Capt. George Bier, of the United States navy. The animal was caught off the coast of Florida, at Malanzas inlet, in 72 feet of water.

It was caught on a hook and line, and when dragged aboard the boat was full of fight. In order to preserve the strange monster, it was found necessary to kill it, for it was so vicious that it could not be handled.

This remarkable relic of the antediluvian monster seemed to be part bird, part fish and part animal. Capt. Bier described it as follows:

"It has no scales, although it can swim. A portion of its body is covered with hair and when it wants to fly it inflates two windbags behind its wings. This inflation is through its gills, which are situated on its breast. It stands upright on its feet, which are shaped like hoofs. Its face and body are more human like than anything else, and its mouth is like that of a raccoon, garnished with two rows of teeth. It stood about 20 inches high and strutted like a rooster."

After its capture the monster was christened Diabolus Maris, and was transferred to Tampa, Fla., where it has since been on exhibition. Naturalists who have seen it can find no other name for it, and its like has never been seen before.

Some fish have fins that resemble wings, and can be used for flying, but fish do not wear hair. The presence of legs argues that it is not a fish, and its ability to live under water and the gills prove it's not a bird.

COLUMBIA RIVER MONSTER.

The San Francisco Call – October 19, 1896 – California

Fisherman Startled by the Appearance of a Hideous Reptile in the Water.

PORTLAND, OR., Oct. 18. – Dominick Bule, a pioneer and very reliable salmon fisherman at Clifton, Clatsop County, reported in Portland this morning that yesterday, while he was out in the middle of the Columbia River in his boat, just about dusk, he saw an immense living object suddenly arise out of the water not twenty feet away from him. It had a head like that of a horse, covered with long hair, and its tusks, four in number, were at least a foot long. It stood out of the water about four feet and remained stationary, as he thought, about two minutes, its large eyes glaring fiercely at him.

Bule was so terrified that he was almost paralyzed. He stopped rowing and gazed at the object. He was not armed, and even had he had a gatling-gun he was too frightened to have used it. Suddenly the stranger opened its immense mouth and gave vent to a roar like that of a maddened bull. Then it began lashing the water, and Bule could see that it was about, as he estimated, twenty-five feet in length. So vigorous were its motions that great waves were created, and Bule's boat came near upsetting. Finally, the monster dove and disappeared from sight.

As honest as Bule is known to be, his story was regarded as a fabrication until to-night, when it was confirmed by Frank Bolton, Henry Schmeer, William Farrell and John Bost, all fishermen. They were out in a boat early this morning, when the monster came to the surface and acted precisely in the same manner as when Bule saw it. It did not attempt to molest the occupants of the boat, but when it disappeared in the water they got to land as quickly as possible.

For the next few days a large party of fishermen on a big raft will watch for the sea serpent, or whatever it may be, to kill it by shooting if possible.

CAPTURED A MERMAN.

The Sun – November 8, 1896 – New York

Pacific Porpoise Hunters Shoot a Strange Marine Monster.

From the Washington Post.

TACOMA, Wash., Oct. 31. – What appears to be a genuine merman was brought into this port last week by a party of Englishmen. They had been porpoise fishing in the Pacific and were more than confused at the extraordinary creature they had captured. They came in with their prize fully convinced that the old stories about merman and mermaids were all true, in spite of the scoffers. The man who deserves the credit of this wonderful discovery is Major W.E. Thorncliff of the British army. The Major was at first rather averse to giving the details of his novel adventure, fearing that he would be classed with the spinners of ordinary fish yarns of Puget Sound, but knowing that his social and official position put his word above question, he finally consented to relate his unique experience and to exhibit his interesting captive, only stipulating that I should repeat the facts exactly as he stated them, and describe the sea monster precisely as it really is.

This is the story of the Major's adventure in his own words:

"Our party, which consisted of several English noblemen, a French statesman, and a Russian prince, left Hokondach, Japan, on a fishing and hunting expedition to the coast, on board Prince Gorenoff's steam yacht Anedamoff, on June 20, and we cruised along the shores of the Aleutian peninsula, calling into many very fine bays and harbors along the coast.

"We shot on shore and fished in the waters of both Behring Sea and the Pacific Ocean, and have as trophies a fine collection of pelts, as well as skeletons of many rare creatures.

"But the climax of all came on the morning of July 26, when we were off the island of Watmoff. Our men sighted a school of porpoises, among which could be seen several white ones.

"Our hunting boat was lowered, and Lord Devonshire, the Earl and I, with the boat's crew, put off from the yacht, determined to capture some of the rare sea pigs. After pulling about four miles we found ourselves in the centre of the school, and Lord Devonshire got a shot at one of the white boys with a large express rifle, which quickly ended its career.

"Just as we were putting our guns away the Earl called out, "See that!" pointing to a most startling looking beast not more than a cable's length away. Picking up his express he fired point blank at it, striking the creature between the eyes. The shot, though it did not kill it, so stunned it that it lay perfectly still on the surface of the sea.

"As our boat hauled alongside, we saw the most hideous and uncanny looking monster probably that human eyes ever looked upon. Although at a distance it might perhaps be mistaken for a porpoise, as we came near, we saw that it could truly be described by no other name than that of 'merman.'

"As we reached over the side of the boat to haul the creature in it regained some of its vitality. It caught the boat by the gunwale amidship, and had it not been for the fact that when the arms came up out of the sea we naturally shrank to the other side of the boat, it would, without doubt, have capsized us. One of the men picked up an ax and quickly dispatched the monster.

"The better way now would be for you to come with me and I will show you the strange creature which I am now taking to England to present to the British Museum. After seeing it you will, I am sure, be inclined to the opinion that one it is placed there it will easily outrank all of the many strange things to be found in that great repository of the world's rarities."

Then the Major led the way to a storeroom on Pacific avenue, where, in the middle of the floor, was a large coffin-shaped box. It was ten feet long, three feet wide, and three feet deep. Taking a screwdriver, the Major unfastened the top. All that could be seen was some ice, covered with a white woolen blanket. Taking the blanket by the end he quickly removed it, and as he did so the sight of the contents of the box almost froze my blood, for right before my eyes was apparently the naked body of a large man.

The Major then removed the cloth which covered the lower part of the body. This is exactly the same as that of an ordinary porpoise. The monster is one of the most remarkable freaks nature ever put together.

The strange monstrosity measures ten feet from its nose to the end of its fluke-shaped tail, and the girth of its human-shaped body was just six feet.

It would weigh, it is estimated, close to 500 pounds. From about the breast bone to a point about where the base of the stomach would be, were it human, it looked exactly like a man. Its arms, quite human in shape and form, are very long and covered completely with long, coarse, dark reddish hair, as is the whole body.

It had or did have at one time four fingers and a thumb on each hand, almost human in shape, except that in place of finger nails there were long, slender claws. But in days long since gone by it had evidently fought some monster that had got the best of it, for the forefinger of the right hand, the little finger of the left, and the left thumb are missing entirely.

Immediately under the right breast is a broad, ugly looking scar, which looked as if some time in the past it had been inflicted by a swordfish. On the sides and body of the monster are numerous other evidences that its life in the ocean had been far from a placid one. There is hardly a space the size of one's hand that does not show evidence of having at some time or other received wounds.

When the hideous body reaches England that country can safely say that it possesses the strangest freak the mysterious waters of the Pacific ever gave up.

"Now mind," was Major Thorncliff's parting salutations, "don't in any way try to embellish what you have seen and heard, but just tell the plain facts, and though this coast may be renowned for strange and weird stories, this story of the merman, simply and truthfully told, will, I am confident, prove the adage, 'Truth is stranger than fiction.'"

Now it only remains for some man as responsible and well known as Major Thorncliff to discover the mate of the merman, and we will be convinced that the old mariners had not, after all, the wonderful powers of imagination and romance so long ascribed to them.

SEA SERPENT SEEN AGAIN.

Kansas City Journal – September 26, 1897 – Missouri

A TERROR WITH SCALES, HORN AND FIERY EYES.

An Officer of a Ship Off the Azores Saw Him as He Sailed By, Horn, Eyes, Scales, Big Wiggle and All.

Officer Prentice, of the steamship Bencliff, reports that he saw when three days from Gibraltar a monster of the deep, the veritable sea serpent.

The day was mild, and the sky was cloudless, he said in describing the appearance of the strange creature. There was just enough air stirring to cause a swell to ripple the surface of the sea. Over the starboard bow he saw a glistening black horn rise out of the sea, something after the manner of the sword mentioned in the King Arthur legend. Then there was a swishing of water, and he beheld abreast of the steamship, and not more than a hundred yards away, a gigantic shape.

The creature was going toward Gibraltar at the rate of about six knots an hour and was evidently propelling itself by its tail. The body was bent up and down in several curves about six feet in depth. The form was that of a serpent. The head was concealed in the water, all save an eye, which seemed to direct its gaze upon the steamship.

Near the head the body was about eight feet in diameter, gradually tapering toward the tail to a diameter of about four feet. The monster was black in color. The body was covered from head to tail with fins, which were about as long as a man's finger and seemed to have the power of motion.

Most remarkable of all, in the estimation of Mr. Prentice, was the horn which the creature carried above its eye. This was about eight feet in height and gradually tapered to a point. About the base of it were the same peculiar fins which covered most of the body. The horn seemed to be solidly braced and was evidently used as a weapon of offense and defense.

"As I live," the captain remarked, "a rhinoceros of the deep!"

"It's a behemoth of Holy Writ," ejaculated the mate, who had been to a circus once.

The creature kept its course for Gibraltar, wriggling like a snake, swimming like a fish and bearing his horned head with stately grace.

The first officer says that he is of the opinion that the head of the monster, be it fish or animal, was about ten feet in length. He can furnish accurate information only with regard to the eye. He was not able to tell what the color of the iris was, for he was not quite close enough for that. The creature seemed to have been attracted to the steamer possibly by curiosity, or possibly by the strong odor of Sulphur.

It swam more slowly in passing, and the first officer was able to get a good view of it. He afterward made a rough sketch of what he is sure he saw.

The sunlight shone upon the glittering horn of the serpent, as it passed in review, like a lieutenant on a dress parade saluting the reviewing officer with his sword. Mr. Prentice, looking over the stern, saw the blade receding from view, and then the horn and its bearer dived into the sea. The first officer estimates that the saw the serpent for a period of about four minutes.

"I do not know," he said, "whether the thing was a fish, animal or devil. I observed it carefully, and I have given an accurate description of it. I am willing to stake my reputation for veracity upon what I have said. I have been at sea many years, yet never have I seen a sea serpent before."

THE UNPLEASANT SERPENT COGGIN DELCARES HE SAW AT LAKE TAHOE.

The San Francisco Call – November 21, 1897 – California

The following is related by a well-known citizen of San Francisco, manager of the Park band. It is presented unaccompanied by affidavits and may be accepted as truth by anybody who chooses to believe it.

The story of a sea serpent comes from so many sources and from people of undoubted veracity that it cannot be doubted that there is living in the Atlantic Ocean a serpent of monstrous size, but it remains for California, with its remains of gigantic monsters scattered all over its surface and where animal life attained its great perfection, to have a serpent now living within its borders much larger than any described by so many witnesses.

It was my fortune to be one of the earliest settlers on the west shore of Lake Tahoe – from June 1861, to 1869. I located a meadow and was engaged in cutting wild hay for the market on Placerville road. In the fall of 1865, in the month of November, I took my gun and, accompanied by a very intelligent setter dog, started out for a hunt for grouse along the shore and in the creek bottoms emptying into the lake.

My attention was called to a very curious state of things happening around me. First, a flock of quail and other birds were flying out of the canyon, uttering cries of alarm; next came some rabbits and coyotes, and soon three deer came running at full speed; last of all, an old bear with one cub came along. All passed close to me, not seeming to notice me, and all running at their best.

All this did not occupy much time, and I began to wonder what was up. My dog kept looking up the canyon and was evidently alarmed, and I began to feel shaky myself. All at once the dog set up a howl and started for home, eight miles away, running as fast as a dog could run, and going under the cabin stayed there two days and nights and no amount of coaxing could get him to come out sooner, and never after would the dog go in the direction of the lake. I began to feel that some unknown danger was near, and looking about me, saw a spruce tree with very thick limbs, standing near a very large pine. I climbed up about sixty feet from the ground and began to look up the canyon. I had not long to wait. I heard a sound as if the dead limbs of trees, willows and alders that grew in the canyon were being broken and crushed. Soon the monster appeared, slowly making his way in the direction where I was hidden in the tree-top, and passed on to the lake within fifty feet of where I was, and as his snakeship got by, and I partly recovered from my fright, I began to look him over and to estimate his immense size. After his head had passed my tree about seventy feet, he halted and reared his head in the air fifty feet or more, and I was thankful that the large pine hid me from his sight, and I dared to breathe again as he lowered his head to the ground and moved on.

His monstrous head was about fourteen feet wide, and the large eyes seemed to be about eight inches in diameter, and shining jet black, and seemed to project more than half his size from the head. The neck was about ten feet, and the body in the largest portion must have been twenty feet in diameter. I had a chance to measure his length, for when he halted his tail reached a fallen tree, and I afterward measured the distance from the tree and it measured 510 feet, and as seventy or eighty feet had passed me, it made his length about 600 feet. The skin was black on the back, turning to a reddish yellow on the side and belly, and must have been very hard and tough, as small trees two and three inches in diameter were crushed and broken without any effect on his tough hide. Even bowlders of 500 or 600 pounds weight lying on the surface of the ground were pushed out of the way. His snakeship slowly made his way to the lake, glided in and swam toward the foot.

This serpent has been seen by several of the old settlers at the lake since that time, but it was generally agreed that it would be useless to tell the world the story, knowing that it would not be believed. I will give a few names of the early settlers that have seen his snakeship at different times since I first saw him. William Pomlin, now living in San Francisco; John McKinney, Ben McCoy and Bill

McMasters, all at that time living on Sugar Pine Point; Homer Burton, now living in Sacramento; Captain Howland of the old steamer Governor Blaisdell, Tony and Burk; fishermen living near Friday's station; Rube Saxton, now at the lake, and several others could be named.

I know many will doubt this story, but sooner or later his snakeship will be seen by so many that all doubt will be removed.

I was induced to write this description by reading an article in THE CALL of last Sunday, stating that there was a living mastodon in Alaska and that it had been seen by the natives. Believing that I have seen a more wonderful sight and, as in time my story is sure to be verified, I venture to give this to the public.

– L.C. Coggin.

FROG RIDES A BIKE.

Waterbury Evening Democrat – February 1, 1898 – Connecticut

His Appearance Caused a Sensation in a Jersey Town.

What looked like an antediluvian monster rode through the town of Haddonfield, N.J., the other day and occasioned great excitement as it scorched along the highway. The monster was unmistakably a frog, but a giant size. He was monstrous, terrible, appalling.

Finally, a wheelman rode up in pursuit, and then another and another. The frog on the bike scared a horse, frightened a cow and almost drew a bullet from the gun of a huntsman in a field. Dogs chased him and small boys stoned him.

The spectators who were in at the finish were then treated to the greatest surprise of all. Instead of throwing the monster from his wheel and fastening him with ropes the pursuers gathered around, laughing and cheering. Then the big frog suddenly opened up and down the center, and out from the interior stepped a man, panting and exhausted.

The idea originated with Mr. G.L. Carr, of Haddonfield, who offered a handsome medal for the winner of the race. The distance covered was 11 miles, and the time was 38 minutes.

The man who caught the frog said: "The frog was allowed five minutes' start, and 17 of us went in pursuit. It was the finest sport ever seen in this vicinity.

"We are arranging for another frog run; this time to take place at night. The frog will be furnished with illuminated eyes and a phosphorescent suit."

MONSTER OF THE DEEP.

The Topeka State Journal – June 22, 1899 – Kansas

Long Island Fishermen Astounded at Their Catch.

Patchogue, L.I., June 22. – Lying on the beach here today is a monster of the deep that is puzzling the oldest of seafaring men in this vicinity. Whether it is fish or reptile not even the most ancient fisherman can say. It is staked on the beach, where hundreds are observing it. Its weight is half a ton; it is 10 feet long, 8 feet wide and 3 feet thick. It has a head and a neck as large as a common barrel and feet and legs that look like the claws of a dragon.

This strange creature, which is still alive and very ugly in disposition, snapping at everything that approaches and hissing like a steam engine, was caught in a fisherman's net four miles from shore.

Weird and thrilling tales are told of the terrible combat between the fisherman's crew and the huge monster when it became enmeshed in the net. The monster is said to have made a noise like that of a thousand bull frogs croaking in unison. It is said to have leaped up against the side of the boat with great ferocity, until it was feared that the craft would be sunk. Great dents and cracks are shown in the boat where the monster is said to have sunk its teeth and used its claws.

John A. Smith of Watch Hill is the owner of the boat, and with him were seven men. They were fishing for sturgeon four miles out. They started to haul up their nets, when they found them apparently caught. They pulled and worked for a time, when suddenly there arose above the surface an apparition that almost froze their blood. A huge head and neck protruded from the water. A rasping sound filled the air and a forked tongue, red and hideous, shot out malignantly towards them. Eyes red and green glared and blinked by turns. Mr. Smith was the first to recover from the fright, and he ordered the men to throw a hawser over the monster's head. This was done and the crew started to tow the catch to shore. Then the immensity of the creature was seen. Half a dozen men could have easily ridden to shore on the creature's back, which, in a way, resembled that of a turtle.

Shore was reached only after long and laborious toil. The creature fought and protested all the way, snarling and hissing and lashing the water to foam.

Finally, when land was reached, a team of horses was procured, and these, together with the aid of the entire fishing crew, dragged the sea monster up on the beach, where it was tied out.

News of the catch soon spread, and the beach has been crowded all day with persons who have been trying to guess what manner of creature the monster is.

214

STORIES FROM THE:
1900's

KILLED LAKE MONSTER.

The Washington Weekly Post – July 31, 1900 –
Washington D.C.

Interesting Hot Weather Tale from New York State – Carcass Lost, of Course.

From the New York Telegraph.

Geneva, N.Y., July 21. – The Otetiani, a sidewheel steamboat belonging to the Seneca Lake Steam Navigation Company, officered by Capt. Carleton C. Herendeen and Pilot Frederick Rose, was between Dresden and Wilkard a few minutes before 7 o'clock last evening when Pilot Rose saw, about 400 yards ahead, what appeared to him to be an overturned boat.

He called Capt. Herendeen, who examined the object with the glass. It appeared to be about fifteen feet long, with a very sharp bow and long, narrow stern. Amidships it was much broader and higher than at either end.

A number of passengers gathered around the pilot house and discussed the supposed boat. Among them were President F.A. Mallette, of the board of public works, editor and publisher of the Sunday Review; Commissioners of Public Works Albert L. Fowler and D.W. Hallenback; Police Commissioner George G. Schell, Fred S. Bronson, manager of the Geneva Telephone Company, and Charles E. Coon, a commercial traveling man of Philadelphia.

When Capt. Herendeen completed his examination of the object the pilot signaled the engineer to slow down. The steamboat approached to within 100 yards and preparations were made to lower a boat. As the davits were swung outward the supposed upturned boat turned and began to move away.

"Full speed ahead!" shouted the captain. The object was moving slowly, and the steamboat gained on it rapidly. The object again turned, this time toward the boat, raised its head, looked in the direction of the boat and opened its mouth, displaying two rows of sharp, white teeth.

The captain said that he would ram the creature, wound it, and take it alive if possible. Otherwise he would kill it and either take it aboard or tow it to Geneva. The boat was turned so that the creature would be approached from the side. The deck was crowded with passengers. These the captain ordered amidships.

The captain cautioned everybody to get a life preserver and keep cool, because he said he did not know what would happen when the boat struck the monster. Some of the women, who were in tears, retired to the cabin, the others showed as much interest and excitement as the men.

The boat fell away some distance and turned to make the attempt to ram the creature. The captain signaled full speed ahead, and in a moment the Otetiani was under way. Everybody on deck was watching the monster and hardly a person was breathing normally.

While the boat was some distance from it the monster again looked at the boat, sank out of sight, and the boat passed over the spot where it had been. Some of the passengers declared that they could see the dark outline of the creature's body.

The streamer prepared to continue her course to this city. "There it is!" suddenly exclaimed one of the women passengers who was standing on the after deck. "The thing has come up."

The passengers, with the captain in advance, ran to the stern of the vessel, and within fifty yards the long body of the monster was lying on the surface in practically the same position as when discovered. The captain ordered the boat put about and the attack was renewed. Instead of trying to strike the creature full in the side the boat was maneuvered so that the starboard paddled wheel would strike it about midway between its head and tail. The boat went ahead under full steam; the monster paid no attention to it, and with a thud which all heard and felt the boat struck the mark at which it aimed. The force of the impact threw every one off his feet, and the vessel careened violently to port, but quickly righted.

For an instant, in which everybody wondered what would happen next, there was not a sound on board except the engine. Then the men on board cheered and some of them recovered from their fright. Lying beside the steamer with a gap in its side was the monster. It raised its head, gave what sounded like a gasp, and lay quiet. Its spinal column had been broken and it was dead. The lifeboats were quickly lowered and rowed to its side, and with the aid of boat hooks ropes were passed around the carcass. Other ropes which were fastened on board the steamer were then passed down and attached to the improvised swings. All helped to haul the monster in.

The carcass was clear of the water when the rope near the tail slipped off and the tail dropped into the water. The weight on the other rope then became so great that it began to slip through the hands of those holding it. They were compelled to let go or go overboard. As soon as the body struck the water it began to sink and disappeared. At the point where the carcass was lost the lake is over 600 feet deep, and, as is well known, bodies of persons who have been drowned in that part of the lake never again rise or are recovered.

When the steamer arrived in the city, shortly after midnight, the stories told were about the same and the length of the monster was estimated at from twenty-five to fifty feet. The most careful and perhaps the most trustworthy account was given by Prof. G.R. Ellwood, a geologist, who lives at Guelph, Ont., who was in one of the lifeboats that made a rope fast around the carcass.

"Do you know what a clidastes is?" the professor asked the reporter. "Well, that is exactly what the creature we saw last night seemed to be. It was about twenty-five feet long, with a long tail, which tapered until with about five feet from the end, when it broadened out and looked much like that of a whale.

"The creature weighed about 1,000 pounds. Its head was perhaps four feet long and triangular in shape. Its mouth was very long and was armed with two rows of triangular white teeth as sharp as those of a shark, but in shape more like those of a sperm whale. Its body was covered with a horny substance, which was as much like the carapace of a terrapin as anything else of which I know.

"This horny substance was brown in color and of a greenish tinge. The belly of the creature, which I saw after the rope slipped and the carcass was going down, was cream white. Its eyes were round like those of a fish and it did not wink."

SEE A SEA MONSTER.

New Ulm Review – August 29, 1900 – Minnesota

Visitors to Michigan Resort Tell a Hair-Raising Tale.

Attacked by a Hideous Sea Serpent and Barely Escape – Had Bulging Eyes, Large Mouth and Vicious Looking Teeth.

A hair-raising sleep destroying sea serpent story has spread terror among the visitors at Allendale on Gull Lake, near Kalamazoo, Mich. Bathers no longer go into the water and boating parties venture out only when heavily armed. The marine monster was discovered by Harry Kemper and Miss Carrie Wirthin, of Cincinnati, who were out fishing just before dusk.

Mr. Kemper describes the serpent as having short, thick forelegs and a head as large as that of a calf, with bulging eyes, large mouth and vicious looking teeth. On its forehead was a thick growth of a hairy-like substance and its body was covered with scales that gave forth a phosphorescent glow in the twilight. Kemper says the thing had a face almost human in its expression and that it reminded him more than anything else of pictures he had seen of Aguinaldo.

Mr. Kemper and his companion say their suspicions were first aroused when they lost a half dozen spoon hooks and lines, then their minnow pail, trailing behind in the water. Noticing the water strangely agitated nearby, Mr. Kemper started to row to shore. He says something grabbed one of his oars and the blade came up with a piece torn out. Then he says there appeared above the water a hideous head that swayed from side to side and emitted a hissing sound. Some 20 or 25 feet away the tip of the reptile's tail could be seen lashing the water to foam. Kemper rowed for his life toward shore, with his companion in a state of collapse, with the monster pursuing them. When about 20 rods from shore he beat it off with his oar and in doing so capsized the boat. The couple were rescued by a passing launch.

Kemper came to Kalamazoo and purchased a large quantity of dynamite, which he is going to explode on the spot where the monster disappeared. In 1893 a strange water nondescript was said to have appeared at Gull lake and killed calves, sheep and fowls along the shores.

A TERRIBLE MONSTER.

The Weekly Messenger – November 17, 1900 – Louisiana

In the vicinity of Whitestone Landing, New York, according to that veracious newspaper, the New York Sun, a frightful aquatic animal recently made its appearance and terrified the whole of the countryside. It has been seen, it is stated, by a dozen persons, each of whom gave a horrifying description of the monster's aspect. Combining their accounts, the new animal is a bird, reptile and fish, all in one, with a high voltage of electricity to boot.

A 13-year old boy describes it as a dark object with eyes like two red balls of fire which give off a green vapor. Its mouth is like that of a catfish, the lips tricking blue flame. It walks with a feline tread and seems to have webbed feet. As the boy watched, too fascinated to move, the creature stood upon its hind feet, shot in and out a fiery tongue three times, which in the flash of an eye, with a great sizzling and whirring noise, shot up in the air like a skyrocket shrouded in a thin yellowish mist."

Two boatmen who saw it swimming toward them thus report: "A trail of purple fire and effervescing sprays of sparks marked its progress. Two feet from the bow of the boat it dived, whereupon a geyser flaming with blood-red particles shot up twenty feet in the air."

An elderly man, much respected in the community, saw it go up a tree like a squirrel. As it climbed, little clusters of sparks – snapping and cracking – shot off the end of its tail. A young woman saw it turning handsprings along the roadway and three boys saw it running, walking, crawling, and flying.

This accords very well with the descriptions which the Republican spell-binders in the recent campaign gave of the calamity demon that Mr. Bryan carried about with him in his gripsack.

– States.

FOUGHT WITH AN EAGLE.

Freeland Tribune – April 8, 1901 – Pennsylvania

A woman named Callahan, living at Carmel, Penn., had a desperate fight with an eagle which was trying to carry away her two-year-old child. The child's face and hands were torn by the bird's talons and Mrs. Callahan was seriously pecked before she succeeded in driving off the big bird.

The child had wandered into a clearing near the house, and soon afterward Mrs. Callahan heard her screaming. From the door of her home the frightened mother beheld the monster bird pecking, clawing and flapping the little one who, with her hands and arms was trying to break away from her antagonist.

Once the bird caught the child's dress in its talons and prepared to bear it aloft, but the child's struggles compelled the bird to let go. The frightened mother secured a rifle and ran to the rescue of her child. She dared not shoot, but with the butt of the gun she ran screaming toward the eagle. It was not to be driven off without a struggle.

It let go of the child and turned its attention to the parent. The bird flew into the woman's face and pecked her eyes and nose, but with a well directed blow from the club the eagle dropped to the ground, and after a moment's scrambling took to the air and went flying away. It is said that during the past summer this eagle has carried away several pigs and that once before it had made an attack upon a child. Mrs. Callahan says that the bird was five or six feet from tip to tip of wing, and that its talons were almost razor-like in their sharpness.

STRANGE MARINE MONSTER CAUGHT.

Tazewell Republican – April 18, 1901 – Virginia

Expert Who Has Seen It Says it is a Mermaid Toad.

Newport News, Va., April 15. – Captain Buck Wyatt, who has a number of fish ponds along the beach near Bay View, captured a day or two ago one of the most peculiar marine monsters ever seen in this section. The Rev. C.B. Bryan, rector of Old St. John's church, Hampton, who is an authority on such matters, pronounced the catch a "Mermaid Toad," which is found only in waters south of the thirty-seventh meridian.

The fish was a complete mystery to the fishermen of this section, who had never seen one of a similar kind before. It was shaped something like a tadpole but was four feet in length and about two feet broad. Its mouth was shaped like that of a toad and was of the same proportion to the size of its body as is the mouth of a toad. It weighed in the neighborhood of seventy-five pounds, and when held up by the lips the whole ventral cavity could be seen. Whole fish of considerable size were in its stomach in the process of digestion. The monster had wings on both sides of its body and there were claws on its stomach resembling the hand of a ten-year-old boy – having five jointed fingers.

The freak was regarded with interest and curiosity by all who had the good fortune to see it, and there is much speculation as to how a "mermaid toad" lost its bearing so far as to be caught in these waters.

A BATTLE WITH A SEA MONSTER.

The Minneapolis Journal – June 26, 1901 – Minnesota

NEW YORK JOURNAL.

One of the strangest sea fights on record is that which the crew of the British warship had lately with a sea elephant near the Falkland Islands, off the sea coast of Patagonia.

As actual proof of the tremendous size of this little known marine monster, its head, trunk and ribs have been sent to the British museum in London, where they will shortly be put on exhibition.

H.M.S. Flora is a second-class protected cruiser. She had just arrived at Port Stanley, in the Falkland Islands, and the commander, desiring to go ashore, ordered the gig to be lowered and manned.

The sea was comparatively smooth, and the boat shot along rapidly, propelled by six stalwart blue jackets. On nearing the shore, however, they saw a strange creature in the water. What it was they did not know. It churned and beat the water in the whiteness of snow within a few fathoms of the boat.

Then the splashing and beating ceased, and from the hissing foam arose what seemed to be the dark head and trunk of an infuriated elephant. For a second the creature glared at the astonished boat's crew; then, with an ear-splitting scream, lowered its head, and like an arrow came for the boat.

There was no time to do anything, to jump or even think. Crash! And the frail craft rose bodily into the air, while the bruised and half-stunned occupants were thrown violently into the sea. Fortunately for them, the monster's attention seemed exclusively riveted upon the boat, the fragments of which it literally smashed into matchwood.

Neither the commander nor his men seem to know very well how they reached land, so exhausted and unstrung had the experience left them.

Returning later to the cruiser on a shore boat, the commander determined pluckily to organize a party for the hunting down and, if possible, the capture of their assailant. On the following day nine boats went forth, each containing the full complement of men armed with rifles, and among whom were several harpooners.

Advancing in a semi-circle, the boats drew across the small bay which had been the scene of the previous day's incident. Till within fifty yards from the shore nothing unusual occurred. Then suddenly a huge black mass rose threateningly in a circle of foam and quite close to the center boats. Two harpooners poised their weapons, which in another instant stuck quivering in the monster's body, while a shower of bullets followed in a volley.

With angry snorts of pain, the creature darted toward the nearest boat, only to be met by another deadly volley, fired at very close range, which ripped and tore it unmercifully. Dazed by such a reception, the monster appeared to hesitate. Another volley followed, and when the smoke cleared there was nothing visible on the surface save a streaking of blood-red foam. Whir! went the harpoon lines, while the men sat excitedly waiting a reappearance of the foe.

"He's making in for the shore now, sir!" shouted one of the officers to the commander, and the boats were signaled to close in. For nearly two minutes the brute remained below, swimming slowly back and forward; then, on reappearing, it lay quietly, as though exhausted. The boats approached cautiously, and when quite close five more harpoons were transfixed; then instantly dividing, the boats pulled rapidly for the shore.

Now commenced the tug of war lasting for nearly three hours, till at last, weak with struggling and loss of blood, the huge monster was hauled into shallow water to await the receding tide. Not one of the party, from the commander down to the little middy, but was thankful for the rest.

In about an hour's time the tide had gone out sufficiently, and the battle began again, but now all the advantage lay with the sailors. After a vicious struggle in which several blue jackets were severely injured by fragments of rock hurled about by the monster in its death throes, it lay battered, silent and motionless.

This gigantic specimen of sea life is macrobinus elephantinus or proboscideous, measuring just under forty feet long, and weighing over thirteen tons. It has a trunk four feet long, and a general conformation closely resembling that of the ordinary elephant, save that there are huge fins in place of legs. It is found only in Antarctic waters.

HUMAN MONSTER SEEN IN IDAHO.

The Morning Astorian – January 28, 1902 – Oregon

Residents of Chesterfield Excited Over Appearance of Eight-Foot Hairy Man.

WAS FIRST SEEN BY SKATERS.
Started to Attack Party Which Managed to Escape in Wagons – Twenty Men Sent in Pursuit.

SALT LAKE, Jan. 27. – According to the Pocatello (Idaho) correspondent of the Desert News, a terrible monster has made its appearance in the Saw-tooth mountain district, and the presence of the thing has terrorized the inhabitants of a whole town. The Saw-tooth mountains are said to be the home of various types of monsters, but this latest discovery is described as the most terrible of all.

The monster is human, eight feet in height and covered with long hair, and the residents of the little town of Chesterfield, Bannock county, are greatly excited over his appearance. He was first seen on January 14, when he appeared among a party of young people skating on the Portneuf river. The creature, flourishing a great club and uttering blood-curdling yells, started to attack the skaters, but the latter managed to reach their wagons and drove at breakneck speed from the river.

Those who saw the monster say it is eight feet high and of a terrorizing appearance, with the form of a giant and the actions of a wild beast. A party of armed citizens that returned from the river found the creature's tracks in the snow. Measurements showed the tracks to be 22 inches long and seven inches broad. People living in the neighborhood have sent 20 armed men to affect the capture of the monster, pending which the community is terror-stricken.

The district in which the human monster has made its appearance is that in which bald-faced bears are said to live. These animals are reported to be very ferocious, and it is related that they follow the tracks of man or domestic beast until they run down their prey.

STRANGE MONSTER IN FLORIDA.

Republican News Item – February 13, 1902 – Pennsylvania

Reptile Formerly Thought to Be a Creature of Indian Imagination.

An enormous reptile, more like the extinct brontosaurus, or fabled sea-serpent than any living creature, has just been killed by a hunter in the lower Florida Everglades. He means to send the skeleton to the Smithsonian Institution at Washington.

It has for 100 years not only been a tradition among the Seminole Indians who inhabited the borders of Lake Okeechobee, but it is stated as a fact within the knowledge of some of the Indians now living that an immense serpent made its home in the Everglades and has carried off at least two Indians.

The Indians reported the animal to be snakelike in appearance, with ears like a deer; that it had only been seen in the Everglades, and that it was very wild. They said that when it traveled it frequently stopped, raised its head high above the sawgrass to take a view of its surroundings to discover enemies or to locate victims, a deer, bear, hog or some other animal. If frightened, the Indians asserted that it glided off at immense speed.

These stories have kept the venturesome hunter and trapper on his guard and in a state of more or less anxiety, notwithstanding they did not give credence to these Indian stories. Recently Buster Ferrel, one of the boldest and most noted of the hunters of Okeechobee, who for 20 years has made the border of the lake and the Everglades his home on one of his periodical expeditions noted what he supposed to be the pathway of an immense alligator.

For several days he visited the locality with the hope of killing the saurian but was unsuccessful in finding him. His pride as a hunter was piqued, and his desire to obtain the hide of what he felt sure to be one of the largest alligators ever seen in this section, where alligators are noted for their immense size, grew daily. He studied some plan to outwit it. A large cypress stood near its pathway, and he concluded to climb the tree and take a stand for his game. He accordingly took his position in the tree. For two days he stood watch with his rifle ready. Nothing appeared. He was becoming discouraged but determined to give one more day to the effort.

On the third day, before he had been on his perch an hour, he saw what looked to him like an immense serpent gliding along the supposed alligator track. He estimated it to be anywhere from 25 to 30 feet long and fully 10 to 12 inches in diameter where the head joined the body and as large around as a barrel 10 feet further back. The creature stopped within easy range of his gun and raised high its head. As it did Ferrel shot at its head. Taken by surprise the serpent dashed into the marsh at tremendous speed, while Ferrel kept up firing until he had emptied the magazine of his rifle.

About four days afterward he ventured back into the neighborhood and about a mile from where he first saw the monster he saw a large flock of buzzards, and went to see what they were after, and there he found the creature dead, and its body so badly torn by the buzzards that it was impossible to save the skin.

He, however, secured the head, and has it now in his home on the Kissimmee river. It is truly a frightful looking object, fully 10 inches from jaw to jaw, and ugly, razor-like teeth. He described the animal as dark colored on its back and a dingy white beneath, with feelers around its mouth similar to a catfish.

He has gone back into the swamp with the invention of obtaining the skeleton and bringing it back, after which he will send it to the Smithsonian Institution in Washington.

— New York Times.

THE DISMAL SWAMP "MONSTER".

Richmond Dispatch – February 18, 1902 – Virginia

L. Frank Ames, a merchant at Benet's Creek, thirteen miles from Suffolk, on Thursday night had an experience with the Dismal Swamp monster, which earlier this week killed seven of Edward Smith's dogs, ate two of them, and attacked smith himself. Ames says he shot at the strange animal several times without effect. Six of his dogs were sent after it, but they fled in terror and hid. The monster escaped. Later it appeared at the home of Henry Jordan (colored) and set defiantly on the curbing of a well. Superstitious persons are much upset over the strange visits, and farmers are fearing for the safety of their stock. The thing is described as of long, gaunt form, vicious eyes, and shaggy, yellow hair. – Exchange.

This monster may be the same that followed the Norfolk boat to this city, and which has caused no little apprehension among many of the colored population. – Alexandria Gazette.

Perhaps it may be another "Hanover lion." About ten or fifteen years ago the people of Hanover and Henrico, living between Atlee's Station and the Broad-Street road, were in a tumult of excitement and dread by reason of a widely circulated report that a lion or tiger had escaped from a menagerie and was prowling through the country.

Several reliable gentlemen informed the newspapers that they themselves had seen the great, ferocious beast. His tracks were measured and were shown to be enormously large.

The people soon rose in arms against the invader, and he was killed one night in a carriage-house, or stable, where he had taken shelter. The gentlemen who discovered his hiding-place poked their guns through knot holes or cracks in the planks and fired a volley at him with deadly effect. There was some dispute as to whether he was a lion or a tiger; but in the course of the inquest – not "crowners 'quest" exactly – it was discovered that he was a huge mastiff, a dog not as common in these parts then as now.

It further appeared that the dog in question belonged to a foreign gentleman who was visiting these parts and who was at that very moment diligently searching for his missing and much-loved mastiff, and whose imprecations upon a people who did not know how to distinguish between a lion and a dog, were both loud and deep.

The truth is that the country folk in question are both intelligent and courageous, but they never stopped to investigate.

The Dismal Swamp "monster" seems to be a dog-eating beast; which would almost exclude the idea that it is a dog. However, we believe it was rumored that he "Hanover lion" was eating up horses and dogs and was getting ready for human blood.

We do not wish to imperil the lives of any of our brethren of the press – they are all valuable citizens – but what is wanted to run down the Dismal Swamp "monster" is a reporter with "a nose for news" and a lead pencil and pad of paper. Be it panther or wolf, dog or demon, he would be brought to taw in a few days by such a reporter.

IT HAS THEM GUESSING.

The Newberry Herald and News – August 29, 1902 – South Carolina

A CURIOUS CREATURE, HALF MAN, HALF FROG.

It is Alleged to Have Come Out of Colonial Lake and Negroes and Superstitious Persons are Much Disturbed – Expert Opinions, Including Some by Mr. Beeswax.

Negroes and superstitious folk are much concerned over the story that a hideous monster, half man and half frog, appeared on the bank of Colonial Lake a few minutes before 12 o'clock Thursday night and uttered strange and distressing cries. The frog man, as it has been dubbed, came out of the waters of Colonial Lake and remained on land probably a half hour before plunging again beneath the rippling wavelets. A fairly good view of the repulsive creature was obtained by William Harper, a colored truck driver and J.H. Thompson, a carpenter who lives on Smith street. There were others who could have enjoyed the pleasure of a close inspection of the frog man had they not excused themselves and gone away hurriedly when the saurian, or whatever you may choose to call it, crawled out of the lake.

"I was sitting on a bench on the east side of the lake," said Mr. Thompson yesterday to a Reporter for The Courier, "when I heard a mighty splashing in the water and a noise that sounded like this: Oough! O-o-o ugh! O-o-o ugh-how-ow! I wasn't' scured exactly, but I began to perspire. I watched the thing awhile, although I was prepared at any moment to go somewhere else. Finally, to my great surprise and – err, regret, the monster came ashore and laid down with another long o-o-o ugh! It was too horrible looking to describe. The head resembled that of a huge frog, the wide, protruding eyes burning with a lurid light. It had arms and shoulders like a man, but the body tapered down like a serpent. It was covered with large, greenish scales, and I should say it was at least eight feet long from head to tail. Its mouth was filled with crooked fangs, which it snapped together with a vicious click. I do not like to remain out late at night, so I started for home soon after the thing came ashore. I can't imagine what it is, where it came from, or whether it will ever show up again. But I'm entirely satisfied with the little knowledge I have of it. I wish now I'd never seen it. I'm afraid it's going to trespass on my dreams."

"Boss, I cayn't give you no particlers about dat frog man," said Harper, the colored truck driver, to a Reporter for The News and Courier. "I didn't wait for no particlers. I was des sittin' and coolin' myself at Colonial Lake Thursday night, when I heard a mighty thrashing in de water. What in de debbil is dat, sez I to myself. My heart began to confabulate with mo' than its usual swiftness, when suddenly de horriblest lookin' critter I ever seen lunged out of de water and de nex' thing I knew I waz runnin.' Down Broad street I went a clippin', and I didn't have sense enough to stop until I collided wid de old Postoffice building. I thought I wuz both killed and injured, but when I got more calmer I realized that, while I wuz safe, it wuzn't necessary for me to go to Colonial Lake no more. Yas, sir, dat's all I kno' about dat owdacious critter. See dis bruise on my head? I got dat when I tried to run over de old Postoffice building."

Scientists are ever interested in these infrequent visitations to various seaports in divers parts of the world of monsters from the deep that defy classification and offer the widest latitude for speculation and imagination. Naturally, the frog-man of Colonial Lake will come in for a share of local interest of the speculative sort. What is its mission? A Charleston man, whose knowledge is of sufficient scope to enable him to discuss the Colonial Lake mystery from the view point of a scientist, was seen by a Reporter for The News and Courier. After listening to a description of the frog-man he said:

"It is probably a megalosauria."

"What is a megalosauria?" asked the reporter, respectfully.

"A megalosauria is a sub order of dinosaurian reptiles," he replied, "having the brain case unossified in front and no ossified alisphenoids. It has a short abdomen and an external chin. It also has deciduous scales which indicate that it is akin to the family of symbranchiate fishes. The megalosauria is almost extinct, although, according to science, it was very common in these waters forty-two million years ago."

Not being wholly convinced that the frog-man was a megalosauria, the reporter sought Mr. Nathan Beeswax and asked for an expression of opinion from him.

"Megalosauria! Bah!" exclaimed Mr. Beeswax, contemptuously. "Listen to me. This frog-man is nothing more nor less than a chilliandae, which is of the genus basommotophorous gastradods. Now hold that down if you have to choke it, and I'll tell you something about it. It has a bulimiform shell and a moveable lip that continues without interruption from the nose. These are the main characteristics of the chillinidea and they fit the frog-man exactly. No, it is not dangerous, but I don't think it will be given an ovation in Charleston."

The colored folks were excitedly discussing the frog-man yesterday and Colonial Lake, as the place of resort, has ceased to attract them.

IS IT A REAL HODAG?

The Minneapolis Journal – April 20, 1903 – Minnesota

A Most Uncanny Nocturnal Brute at Minnetonka Reported by A.H. Opsahl.

He Says It Has Spines and Its Scaly Coat Turns Shot.

A.H. Opsahl asserts excitedly that it is a surviving representative of a supposedly extinct saurian that looks like a cross between an iguana and a rocking horse and offers to produce witnesses to the strange nocturnal proclivities of the uncanny brute that haunts the woods about his Minnetonka place, Ruritania.

The hodag is supposed to be dead. As a matter of fact, "there weren't no such animal." A lot of lumbermen over in Michigan faked up a hideous looking reptile and had a picture taken of him, which the Northwestern Lumbermen printed, but somebody blew the game and the hodag, hideous as an inhabitant of Dante's dread picture, proved to be a stuffed nothing in particular.

But Mr. Opsahl swears that the Michiganders builded better than they knew. If Mr. Opsahl has not discovered a hodag he certainly has turned up some awful creature that bellows like an elephant in a rage, wallows in the swamp and grunts, jumps stiff legged from the dead grass and brush of dark nights with its spinal projections all standing, and generally keeps people at Orono Point wondering what sort of horror has invaded their sylvan retreat.

To come down to cases, there is a determined hunt going on from Ruritania and surrounding estates after some strange creature that has been seen and shot at a dozen times in the past winter, but which seems to bear a charmed life. Opsahl himself emptied a double load of BB shot at the beast or reptile, the range being less than thirty yards in the moonlight. The shots were heard to rattle like hail on the scaly coat of the creature, which promptly emitted a sound that resembled, roughly speaking, a cross between the laugh of a hyena and the bawl of an indignant cow.

Several parties have visited the locality during the winter in an effort to round up the strange visitor to Ruritania, but without success, the animal making its appearance only at night and preferably, it seems on dark nights.

"I don't know what breed this creature belongs to," said Mr. Opsahl to-day, "but what I do know is that there is nothing in the books describing him. He is scaly all over like a big fish. I have seen his scales shining in the moonlight and taken a steady shot over the bough of a tree at him. He is not in the least injured by being shot at with any sort of small arm. I tried a Winchester on him twice and know that he was hit, because he jumped and scuttled for the woods as hard as he could go, bellowing fiercely. When he runs, his tail is held high above his back and it has spines sticking out all along its length like an iguana. I never could get a good look at the creature's head, but I've got a picture of it in my mind. I should like to get a photograph of this thing with a good sized camera, but its habits are nocturnal and the only picture we shall ever get will be taken after its dead."

The prevailing opinion is that the creature which has created so much discussion at the point is an escaped specimen from some circus or side show. No report of such an escape is remembered, but the people who witnessed the latest "hodag" refuse to be laughed out of countenance. Mr. Opsahl takes a walk around his place every night in an effort to get another shot at the animal. He has provided himself with a 45-90 Winchester and hopes to report results within a few days.

MADE BIG TRACKS.

The Corvallis Times – September 16, 1903– Oregon

BELIEF THAT A MASTADON STILL SURVIVES IN ALASKAN VALLEY.

Its Track, Twenty Inches Long – Followed by Portland Man Until They Entered Cave and Disappeared.

Portland, Sept. 11. – The Portland Journal says: Dr. John P. Frizzell is organizing an expedition in Portland to bring back to this city the body of a mastodon which he firmly believes exists upon Unimak island, off the western coast of Alaska.

Dr. Frizzell, while employed as a United States surgeon on that island, on July 4, 1903, saw tracks which were 20 inches long by 19 ½ wide, followed them for two miles inland, and traced the course of the monster into a cave that makes into the side of a volcano. Dr. Frizzell was accompanied by James Nugent, James Geary and S.F. Smith sailors from the Nellie Coleman, a San Francisco ship. These sailors corroborate Dr. Frizzell's statements. Geary himself measured the tracks, and all of the party agree regarding the evidences of the presence there of an animal the like of which has never been known to naturalists as living in the modern times. So tangible are these evidences that prominent citizens of Portland propose to back him in an expedition to hunt and kill that mastodon.

When Dr. Frizzell and the three sailors discovered the track, they had gone in the ship's dory 16 miles to the north end of the island. They were on a caraboo hunt, and seven miles inland toward Sheshalda mountain and Pomgronni mountain, in a valley between the two, the doctor saw the imprints in the earth, to which he called the attention of his companions.

"Up there on Unimak island, where I was stationed as surgeon for the government," said Dr. Frizzell yesterday, "is a region so fascinating that I propose to return. I have hunted in New Zealand, Van Dieman's land, Mexico, Florida, Canada, and in other countries.

My father was one of the famous rifle shots of Ireland. I have hunted since I was 8 years old. Yet I know of no country in which are such marvels as are found in the Far North within the limits of the United States possessions.

"When we found those enormous tracks, they were several feet apart and looked as though one had made them with a stable bucket turned upside down on the earth. On the outer rim in front was the mark of what was apparently a horny substance, while inside were smaller marks as though of numerous toes running around the inside of the rim. The tracks are larger than those of an elephant. We followed them for two miles and established the fact that the monster inhabited a cave in the side of a volcano. This volcano is active, emitting every five minutes smoke and ashes, which showed for two miles down the mountain side.

"The valley of which I speak is between Mount Sheshalda, 9,500 feet high, and Pomgronni, 6,000 feet high. One the sides of these mountains grow luxuriantly beautiful specimens of the lupen, violets with stocks a foot long and blossoms two inches across, strawberries luscious and of immense size, and various flora. Even so early as June the flowers come out with wonderful brilliancy. The ground at that time of year is warm from the heat of the underground fires, which accounts for the marvelous early advancement of all blooming. The strawberries are found in tracts acres in extent.

MONSTER IN THE LAKE.

Jamestown Weekly Alert – September 24, 1903 – North Dakota

Kensal News: Wright Marks and Plummer Purington went down to Airwood Lake last Monday night hunting ducks and had an adventure which they will long remember. The fact that both of them had their heads shaved a short time ago is all that saved their hair from turning gray. They had found a good place to lie down in the grass on the west side of the lake and were waiting for the ducks to come and be killed, when they were suddenly startled by a roaring and hissing and a terrific splashing of water. They started to their feet and the sight that met their gaze almost froze the blood in their veins. There, not a hundred feet away, wallowing about in the lake, was a ferocious looking monster about fifteen feet long with a horrible looking alligator-like head covered with scales and the jaws armed with long, curved tusks. The body was also covered with huge scales of a dirty yellow color. The creature had four legs and two long arms terminating in cruel looking claws that looked as though they were sharpened up for business.

As the boys leaped from their place of concealment the monster spied them and immediately disappeared in the water only to appear in a few minutes close to the shore. Two guns were immediately leveled and fired at the monster, but he did not pause a second. Emitting terrible bloodcurdling roars, he made for the boys and they were obliged to turn and fly for their lives. After a chase of half of a mile the monster gave up and returned to the lake while the boys made the best of their way home. There is talk of organizing a party to thoroughly search the lake for the monster and capture him if possible.

Airwood Lake is about seven miles southwest of Kensal and is quite a popular resort for picnic parties during the summer.

A WINGED MONSTER.

The Saint Paul Globe – October 11, 1903 – Minnesota

Creature Emitting a Dazzling Light Terrifies Hawkeyes.

DES MOINES, Iowa, Oct. 10. – The town of Van Meter, containing 1,000 persons, is terribly wrought up by what is described as a horrible monster. Every man, woman and child in the town is in a state of terror, and fully half of them fail to close their eyes in slumber except in broad daylight.

The monster put in its appearance Monday night. U.G. Griffith, and implement dealer, drove into town at 1 a.m. and saw what seemed to be an electric searchlight on Maher & Grigg's store. While he gazed, it sailed across to another building and then disappeared.

His story was not believed the next day. But the following night Dr. A.C. Olcott, who sleeps in his office on the principal street, was awakened by a bright light shining in his face.

He grabbed a shotgun and ran outside the building, where he saw a monster, seemingly half human and half beast, with great bat-like wings. A dazzling light that fairly blinded him came from a blunt, horn-like protuberance in the middle of the animal's forehead, and it gave off a stupefying odor that almost overcame him. The doctor discharged his weapon and fled into his office, barring doors and windows, and remained there in abject terror until morning.

Peter Dunn, cashier of the only bank in the town, fearing bank robbers, loaded a repeating shotgun with shells filled with buckshot and prepared to guard his funds next night. At 2 o'clock he was blinded by the presence of a light of great intensity.

Eventually he recovered his senses sufficiently to distinguish the monster and fired through the window. The plate glass and sash were torn out and the monster disappeared. Next morning imprints of great three-toed feet were discernible in the soft earth. Plaster casts of them were taken.

That night Dr. O.W. White saw the monster climbing down a telephone pole, using a beak much in the manner of a parrot. As it struck the ground it seemed to travel in leaps, like a kangaroo, using its huge, featherless wings to assist. It gave off no light. He fired at it, and he believes he wounded it. The shot was followed by an overpowering odor. Sidney Gregg, attracted by the shot, saw the monster flying away.

But the climax came last night. The whole town was aroused by this time. Prof. Martin, principal of the schools, decided that upon the description it was an antediluvian animal. Shortly after midnight J.L. Platt, foreman of the brick plant, heard a peculiar sound in an abandoned coal mine, and, as the men had reported a similar sound before, a body of volunteers, started an investigation. Presently the monster emerged from the shaft, accompanied by a smaller one. A score of shots were fired without effect.

The whole town was aroused, and vigil was maintained the rest of the night, but without result, until just at dawn, when the two monsters returned and disappeared down the shaft.

A PRIZE YARN ABOUT A MIXED SEA MONSTER.

The Star – January 6, 1904 – Pennsylvania

Combination of Fish, Alligator and Bat Found.

Throws the Old Sea Serpent into the Shade – Gigantic Survivor of Prehistoric Ages is Over Sixty-five Feet Long, and Equally at Home in Air or Sea.

Salt Lake, Utah. – A terrible, nameless, unclassified creature of the animal world is exciting the curiosity, wonder and fear of occasional visitors to Stansbury Island, in the southern portion of Great Salt Lake.

This monster, so strange and unnatural in appearance, has lately, it is said, been seen by several persons, but the best account of its characteristics and movement is given by Martin Gilbert and John Barry, two hunters who this week returned from an expedition over the island, in the course of which they studied the habits of this hitherto unheard of creature for three days.

The monster, which appears to be almost equally at home in the air, on the beach, or submerged in the briny waters of Salt Lake, is probably the sole survivor of a prehistoric species. It is doubtless the last representative of a family whose other members, dead ages since, have left the testimony of their existence in the primeval rocks of the mountains.

Arranging in concise from the description of this incredible relic of the animal world, from the accounts given by those who have observed it at close range, it seems in plain, unscientific language, a combination of fish, alligator, and bat.

DESCRIPTION OF THE BEAST.

In size it is simply tremendous. Gilbert places its length at sixty feet, while Barry, who is an amateur scientist, says that an examination of its tracks demonstrates that the monster must be sixty-five feet from head to tail.

The head is like that of an alligator, the eyes fiercely glowing, the jaws, capable of opening to a distance of ten feet from the top of the upper to the lower, are provided with a fearful array of sharp saw-edged teeth; the body, so far as observation goes, is encased with heavy horny scales. As to this Gilbert and Barry are not positive, as the constant diving of the beast, if such it may be called, into the strong brine of the lake has incrusted it with a thick coating of salt, which, save near the wings, completely hides the body.

According to their account they first sighted it at a distance of between one and a half and two miles. The day was clear, the sun intensely bright. Gilbert's own words of the discovery are:

"We were walking westward from the east shore of the island about 9 o'clock in the morning, when suddenly to the northwest there appeared a thing, I don't know what to call it; it looked to me like a brilliant rainbow folded into a compact mass, moving rapidly through the air.

"I was so astounded that for a few moments I doubted the evidence of my own senses. The object came nearer, but the colors were so dazzling that it was some time before it assumed definite form. No one who has not witnessed the sight can conceive its strangeness. The mass of color was glowing, flaming, radiant. I spoke to Barry, saying:

"'For God's sake, man can you see that?' and he was no less astonished than myself.

"In three or four minutes the monster's position was such that it no longer reflected the sunlight directly toward us, and we could then discern the outline of the form. Its wings were bat like, stretching out over a great expanse, I should say at least one hundred feet from tip to tip. The tail was proportionately short and resembled that of a huge fish. We were not close enough at this time to tell much about the head, only we saw that the jaws were very long. In shape the head was like that of a crocodile."

Gilbert gave a long account of how he and Barry watched the monster, which supported its enormous wings, swung round and round in immense circles through the air, gradually descending and approaching nearer to them. He declares that it was not more than 300 yards above their heads, when, now convinced that the awful creature was about to attack them, he fired at the monster with his rifle, a 44-calibre gun loaded with a steel cased bullet.

The missile, he believes, struck fair, but inflicted no apparent wound. The monster gave utterance to a strange, fear-inspiring cry, half snort, half roar, and, rising rapidly in the air, veered quickly to the west, and after three miles of flight settled down and disappeared beyond the crest of the hills.

BULLET HAD NO EFFECT.

A few seconds after the shot was fired, while the hunters were watching the flight of the dragon-like beast, some small lumps of salt fell almost at their feet. They were more than ever mystified by this, but not until the next day were they able to ascertain its source.

Determined to learn more of the monster, Gilbert and Barry hastened in the direction of its flight, and after surmounting the range of hills to the westward, found with little trouble the tracks the beast had left in the soil after ceasing its flight. These led the hunters to an immense cave, near the head of a narrow gulch.

They approached to within three rods of the opening in the rocks but finding that the freshest footprints led into the gloomy cavern feared at that time to make any closer inspection.

"These tracks," said Barry, "were five-toed, almost exactly like the imprint of a gigantic hand, if you can imagine a hand nearly four feet across the palm."

Gilbert and Barry constructed a barricade for themselves of the largest rocks they were able to handle and lay down to await the results.

The day wore on and the men were weary and almost despairing of success in their vigil, when, just at dusk, the horrible creature crawled slowly from the cave, and, pausing at its mouth to take flight, gave them their first view at close range.

Barry says that the hackneyed phrase of exaggeration, "made his blood run cold," is none too strong for the sight they saw.

"The monster slowly moved his great jaws," declared the hunter, in speaking of his experience, "until it seemed as if he could have swallowed a large horse in one mouthful. He gave a snort that might have been heard a mile, and then slowly spread his huge wings. We now saw that the huge body was coated with salt, apparently nearly a foot in thickness. This explained why the salt lumps dropped at our feet when the bullet struck the monster. By this we knew that the creature must spend much of its time in the waters of the lake.

"The great beast made a short run before taking flight, taking long jumps upon its hind legs and tail. The forelegs were comparatively short and appeared to be used only when it crawled flat upon the ground.

"The frightful head was not more than ten feet from us when it rose in the air, but so well were we screened by our shelter of rocks that we were unobserved. The large, fiercely gleaming eyes, the sharp serrated teeth, the wide expanse of wings that began to move rapidly as the horrible beast rose from the ground and passed directly over our heads, combined to make a terrible sight – one that I shall never forget.

"We watched it disappear in the gathering gloom of night, but were for a long time paralyzed with fear, not knowing when it might return. It was probably an hour later when it did come back.

"We heard the swish of the mighty wings before it could be seen, but as it drew nearer, by the light of the young moon in the west, we saw that carried in its great jaws was a large horse, which I suppose it had swooped down upon while feeding. The horse was badly crushed and mangled.

FEASTED ON THE HORSE.

"The monster carried its burden into the cave, and we could hear the crunching of its jaws and the cracking of the horse's bones as the beast devoured its victim. After an hour or so all was still, and we then slipped quietly away in the darkness and returned to our camp on the eastern shore of the island.

"Had it not been for a bad break in our boat we would have fled the island that night. As it was, we worked all night to repair the craft, although the task might have been accomplished in two hours except that we feared to build a fire to afford light.

"It was just dawn and we were preparing to launch, when Gilbert said: "There it comes again!" In an instant we turned the boat bottom up and crawled under it. One end was lifted about a foot above the end by a rock, and we were able to watch the monster's actions.

"It settled down on the beach less than fifty yards to the north and dived quickly into the lake. From its actions while nearly buried under the waves I judged that the creature was gathering and feeding upon the salt water shrimps which abound along the coast there. When the monster came up it was very close to us, and we were particularly impressed by the fact that the strong brine had no effect upon its eyes, which appeared lidless. Evidently the animal's food in the water was found by the sense of sight.

"Although of such gigantic size, there was nothing sluggish in the movements of the monster. It swam and dived as rapidly as any large fish.

"We watched it for perhaps half an hour as it gradually worked its way northward and finally disappeared."

— *Philadelphia Record.*

ENEMY OF WHALES.

The Mt. Sterling Advocate – January 6, 1904 – Kentucky

Strange Creature Said to Exist in Alaskan Waters.

While operating a fishery on Admiralty island, Alaska, last summer, says a writer, my attention and the attention of my fishing crew was almost daily attracted to a large marine creature that would appear in the main channel of Seymour canal and our immediate vicinity. There are large numbers of whales of the species rorqual there, and the monster seemed to be their natural enemy. The whales generally travel in schools, and while at the surface to blow one would be singled out and attacked by the fish, and a battle was soon in order.

It is the nature of the rorqual to make three blows at intervals of from two to three minutes each, and then sound deep and stay beneath the surface for 30 or 40 minutes. As a whale would come to the surface, there would appear always at the whale's right side and just above where his head would connect with the body, a great, long tail or fin, "judged by five fishermen and a number of Indians after seeing about 15 times at various distances," to be about 24 feet long, 2 ½ feet wide at the end, and tapering down to the water, when it seemed to be about 18 inches in diameter, looking very much like the blade of a fan of an old-fashioned Dutch windmill.

The great club was used on the back of the unfortunate whale in such a manner that it was a wonder to me that every whale attacked was not instantly killed. Its operator seemed to have perfect control of its movements, and would bend it back till the end would touch the water forming a horseshoe loop, then with a sweep it would be straightened and brought over and down on the back of the whale with a whack that could be heard for several miles. If the whale was fortunate enough to submerge his body before the blows came, the spray would fly to a distance of 100 feet from the effect of the strike, making a report as loud as a yacht's signal gun.

What seemed most remarkable to me was that no matter which way the attacked whale went, or how fast (the usual speed is about 14 knots) that great club would follow right along by its side and deliver those tremendous blows at intervals of about four or five seconds. It would always get in from three to five blows at each of the three times the whale would come to the surface to blow. The whale would generally rid itself of the enemy when it took its deep sound, especially if the water was 40 fathoms or more deep. During the day the attack was always off shore, but at night the whales would be attacked in the bay and within 400 yards of the fishery.

"I do not know of any whales being killed, but there were several that had great holes and sores on their backs. Questioning the Indians about it, I was told that there was only one, that it had been there for many years, and that it once attacked an Indian canoe and with one stroke of the great club smashed the canoe into splinters, killing and drowning several of its occupants."

QUEER LOOKING MONSTER DUG OUT OF ROCKS.

The Evening World – April 29, 1905 – New York

Long, Hairy Animal Scared Workmen After a Blast on West Side.

Whether it was a jabberwock, a Bandersnatch, a jub-jub bird or a snark that emerged from the bowels of the earth in this city to-day, causing thirty workmen to drop their tools of trade and take to the highest points in sight is a moted question. That it was something fully as bad as any beast in the late Mr. Carroll's menagerie, there can be no doubt. Zoologists are cordially invited to the saloon at Sixty-fourth street and Amsterdam avenue to view it and pass an opinion on genus and habitat.

What happened was this: Thirty workmen, honest Irish sons of toil, with an Italian scattered here and there among them, were busily engaged to-day in making deeper the hole on Sixty-third street near Eleventh avenue, where the foundation for the first of Henry Philipps's model tenements is to be laid, when out from between the ruins of a giant rock which had just crumbled from blasting powder, came a queer hairy animal, as long as a man, with legs like those of an orangutan and a head the size of an orange.

A creature so ridiculously out of proportion according to modern standards could only be of some prehistoric monster, and however interesting such may be to naturalists, they are not the least bit so to the knights of the pick and the spade.

The little cluster of whiskers in the centre of old Terence McManus's throat stood out at a fearful angle when his eyes lighted on the creature. Then down went Terry's pick into the earth and up when his voice to the heavens in a shriek that fair froze the blood in the veins of his comrades.

"Howly mither! Luk at it, luk at it!" wailed Terry, and, of course, everybody took a look.

Then there was quick action, and in less than thirty seconds the monster had the hole to itself. Along the edges, scared, white faces peered over at it. They saw a long, sinuous body and muscular legs, with three fierce talons at the end of each foot. They saw a foolish little head in the centre of it, two beady black eyes. They saw a tail that curled at the end and a body full of irregular bumps.

Leisurely around the hole went the monster. Then it decided to climb out. There was a scattering of citizens at once. Big Pat Coughlin didn't get out of the way in time, and before he knew it the monster was close to him. Pat didn't wait to learn whether or not its intentions were hostile. He just swung the spade which he had clung to around at it and landed on the top of its little head. There was a crack and the monster rolled over for the count. Before he could get up again some of the others landed on him with rocks and he gave up the ghost.

Then he was carried into the saloon where Big Pat sold him as a curiosity, the gang taking the price out in mixed ale. The only animal expert around Eleventh avenue gave it as his opinion, that the beast was a South American sloth.

"I was down there once," he said, "and seen them hanging to trees by them talons. It's a sloth, that's what it is."

No one could explain how a South American sloth could get from his habitat on the Amazon river to an Eleventh avenue excavation, but there he was, and he is on view for the skeptical.

MONSTER ANIMAL.

The Hartford Republican – July 7, 1905 – Oregon

Sighted and Photographed in Minnesota.

Only Specimen of its Kind in the World – Resembles the Hippopotamus.

Conductor Smith, in a descriptive letter to the dispatch correspondent says: "The monster hogag, which has for years past been the terror of the Cass Lake and Bemidji small boys, and which I recently succeeded in securing a picture of after several weeks of patient work at the customary lair of the brute, is a long lanky, ungained bodied monster, with a head similar to that of a hippopotamus, only horned. The back of the hogag is ribbed on lined with protruding spikes about 14 inches in length, which extend clear to the tip of the long broomstick tail. Two monster horns, about eight inches in diameter at their base and sharp as needle points at their tips, some 18 inches from the head of the animal, lend a ferocious aspect to the brute's appearance, which is awful to behold when angry the hogag shakes the head savagely, and shrubs and trees within range of the ugly horns are slashed to shreds. When in motion the hogag assumes a gait somewhat similar to the lope of a kangaroo.

The rear feet have three protruding claws some six inches in length and as sharp as an eagles talons. The fore feet are also equipped with talon-like claws, but the joint is somewhat shorter, and the first joint is higher upon the limb than it is in the rear portion of the beast's anatomy. One very peculiar feature of the hogag's physique is a lack of one eye. There are two sockets, and when the beast is dozing it would appear as if two eyes served usual purpose. When aroused, however, the right orb does not open, and it is thought that in some battle with beasts of the forest or with man that the animal has lost the member. The one eye which serves is about the size of a quart dipper bottom and of a deep red during the day time and a glowing green at night. So far as can be ascertained, it is believed that the animal is of neither sex and that it is the only one in existence of its particular species. In habits and diet, it much resembles a rhinoceros and makes its appearance in the open but twice a year, once in the fall and again in the spring. People who have seen the animal at night and told of its horrible appearance have been believed insane and never before has the story of the beast's existence been actually credited by reasoning people of Cass Lake and Bemidji. Long stories have been written about the supposed myth, but my picture secured after weeks of vigil at the animal's customary haunts, has set at rest all doubt as to the reality of the yarn and the existence of the hogag."

A company may be organized at Cass Lake for the purpose of eradicating the community of the presence of the beast and as well capture one of the biggest amusement and sideshow freaks ever heard of in the world. Certainly, if the hogag is captured and placed upon exhibition there will be no better freak of nature in the museums of the country. The ferocious nature of the beast, however, will make the undertaking extremely hazardous, and, if the project is undertaken, lives will be risked in the capture. So far as known the hogag contented itself with a diet of fruits, grain, grasses and fish and has not molested cattle or human beings unless aggravated.

BAY RIDGE SEA MONSTER HAS FOUR SETS OF TEETH.

The Evening World – July 21, 1905 – New York

But the Blooming Beast Is Now Shy Two Broken Fangs that It Fastened in the Foot of a Dare-Devil Englishman, Who Fancies He May Will Them to the British Museum – My Word!

The world of science is going to be agitated over two slivers of bone which are now regarded by their possessor as the fangs of a sea monster. They are also offered to the universe as testimony of the fact that Bay Ridge was visited by a sea creature of uncanny appearance and queer conduct.

Theophilus Ralley, a young Englishman, who is sojourning at Ninety-third street and the Shore road, Bay Ridge, secured the teeth in a rather unusual manner. "I got them in a deucedly lucky fashion," he says, and when his story is pondered on, his observation does not seem so far wrong.

A HUSKY HERO

Mr. Ralley is an athlete. Huge in bulk, he is all sinew and muscle and has the Liverpool record for lifting weights, having once lifted with both hands a bale of cotton that weighted a little short of a ton. He is very fond of sea bathing and other outdoor sports, though he has not decided when he will take his net plunge at Bay Ridge.

His last entrance into the waters of the Narrows was in the dark of the night – the hottest night of the year. Because of the rocks on the shore he wore a pair of rubber soled canvas shoes, but when he had waded out some distance, he struck out bravely for the float anchored in the bay. The rest of the story is best told in his own language, for he was the only one there when the singular thing happened.

"Really, it was all very annoying. I had been hot and angry at the climate all day and the water was very cooling. It was very dark though, and pretty soon I began to see little wriggling things in the water. If I hadn't been a teetotaler, I would have thought I had 'em, though when I think it all over I grant it may have been the light filtering through the trees that made the wriggles.

"But I was getting a bit squeamish when suddenly I felt something heavy jar against my right foot, which was dangling in the water from the raft. I jumped up, trembling in every blooming limb of my body.

"I had hardly got in the middle of the raft when there was a rare commotion in the water about the float. A great object was whirling around in a circle like a fool dog after its tail. Suddenly a great head, surely as big as the dome of St. Paul's, rose out of the water and leaned over me.

AN AWFUL MONSTER

"I shivered all over with terror, for it was a most horrible sight. The thing had four rows of teeth in each jaw and fully a half dozen eyes. Around its long neck were a lot of fiery hooples that looked like rings of gold, and from the collar down it had eight legs that it waved at me like so many flappers.

"I was right frightened, you may be sure, and stood rooted to the centre of the raft. But the thing didn't do anything but stand there with its mouth open, making a noise that sounded like a chuckle. Then quite suddenly it dropped down into the water again and disappeared.

"I was sure the thing wanted to eat me, and just as sure that I didn't want to be eaten, don't you know. I should judge, from the look of its head and neck, that it was several hundred feet long and had hundreds of feet. There was only one thing for me to do, to dive into the water and give it battle., unless I preferred it to come up and nibble at me with its four sets of teeth.

CAUGHT HIM BY THE FOOT

"I was so desperate that I decided to die hard, devilishly hard. I dove with my eyes open and swam all around but could see nothing of the monster. I swam back to the raft and pulled myself up. I had drawn up one foot when I felt something seize the other. I turned around and there was the head of the thing. It had my right foot in its first set of teeth.

"Dash it all, but I was angry, and I struck the monster in the face with my doubled-up first. With a cry of pain it let go and sped off in the water. It made great waves as it went, overturning a number of rowboats. When I saw that it had got far off I swam ashore and in taking off my canvas shoes I found two teeth stuck fast in the rubber sole. I will keep them as testimony of my rare experience, by Jove, and perchance when I die, I will leave them to the British Museum."

RED SEA SERPENTS.

The Jackson Herald – October 12, 1905 – Missouri

DESCRIBED BY MEN OF VERACITY AND SOBRIETY.

Photographs of Curious Monsters of the Deep – Scientific Men Discuss Form and Habits of Sea Serpents – Where Seen and When.

(Special Correspondence.)

There is a popular tendency to insist that sea serpents are only the creatures of the humorists or of sailors with distorted imaginations, but the learned societies of the world have lent a kindly ear to tales of these monsters of the seas, and while modern zoologists express a belief in "the great unknown," it is expected that photographic proof will soon be added to the ever-increasing number of declarations of its existence.

The latest learned society to practically admit the existence of the mysterious leviathan is the French Academy of Sciences. At a recent meeting the Academy discussed the subject, owing to the presentation of testimony of two French naval officers who claimed to have seen the monster. The officers attempted to photograph the serpent, but had no success, and the Academy, while not doubting that the sea serpent is a fact, did not feel like putting itself on record until either a specimen is captured or until a photograph is produced in verification.

WELL AUTHENTICATED.

Perhaps the only joke that has enjoyed a longer term of popularity than the allusions to the sea serpent and the summer hotel is the so-called mother-in-law joke, and that only because the mother-in-law has longer been a recognized force in the world. However, there are at least a score of well-authenticated reports of sea serpents, and several species of the genera Pelamys, Hydrophics and Platurus, inhabiting the Pacific and Indian Oceans, that are true ocean snakes and more or less venomous, have been on exhibition in zoological gardens at times.

The persistence of Norwegian claims for the sea serpent certainly prove that some immense denizen of the deep must frequent the Scandinavian coast. In 1847 the Zoologist, a scientific journal, noted the appearance of sea serpents that year in the Norwegian fiords. The following year Captain McIuhae, of H.M.S. Daedalus, made an official report to the British Admiralty describing a sea serpent observed by the officers and crew of the warship.

AT LEAST SIXTY FEET LONG.

This sea serpent was seen off the southwest coast of Africa. The captain was measuring the quarter deck and the ship's company were at supper, but night had not yet fallen. The monster was rapidly approaching the vessel before the beam. It was "an enormous serpent, with head and shoulders kept about four feet constantly above the surface of the sea, and, as nearly as could be approximated by comparing it with the length of what the main top-sail yard would show in the water, there was at the very least sixty feet of the animal a fleur d'eau, no portion of which was, apparently, used in propelling it through the water, either by vertical or horizontal undulation."

The captain in his report adds: "It passed rapidly, but so close that, had it been a man of my acquaintance, I should have easily recognized his features with the naked eye, and it did not, either in approaching the ship or after it had passed our wake, deviate in the slightest degree from its course to the southwest, which it held on at the pace of from twelve to fifteen miles an hour, apparently on some determined purpose. The diameter of the serpent just behind the head was about fifteen or sixteen inches. The head was without doubt that of a snake, and it was never, during the twenty minutes that it continued in sight of our glasses, once below the surface of the water; its color, a dark brown, with yellowish white about the throat. It had no fins, but something like the mane of a horse, or rather a bunch of seaweed, washed about its back."

Not long after this report was published another report, that of the master of the American brig Daphne, stated that in twenty degrees of latitude further south a sea serpent had been seen soon after it had been observed by the Daedalus.

A very different looking sea serpent was reported by Captain W.H. Nelson, of the American ship Sacramento, in 1877. This animal was seen in the north Atlantic and resembled from the drawings made by the mate the ancient ichthyosaurus. About forty feet of this specimen appeared out of water, and its girth was described as "about that of a flour barrel."

One of the most extraordinary sea serpent stories of modern times, and one which makes old Olaus Magnus's picture seem authentic, was that told by Captain Drevor and his crew of the bark Pauline. On July 8, 1875, at 11 o'clock a.m., while the ship was off Cape St. Roque, northeast corner of Brazil, the weather clear and wind and sea moderate, captain and crew "observed some black spots on the water and a whitish pillar, about thirty-five feet high, above them.

SERPENT KILLS A WHALE.

"At first," he reported, "I took it all to be breakers, as the sea was splashing up fountain-like about them, and the pillar a pinnacle rock bleached with the sun; but the pillar fell with a splash and a similar one rose. They rose and fell alternately in quick succession, and good glasses showed me it was a monster sea serpent coiled twice around a large sperm whale. The head and tail parts, each about thirty feet long, were acting as levers, twisting itself and victim around with great velocity. They sank out of sight about every two minutes, coming to the surface still revolving, and the struggles of the whale and two other whales that were near, frantic with excitement, made the sea in this vicinity like a boiling cauldron.

"This strange occurrence lasted some fifteen minutes, and finished with the tail portion of the whale being elevated straight in the air, then waving backward and forward and lashing the water furiously in the last death struggle, when the whole body disappeared from our view, going down head foremost to the bottom, where, no doubt, it was gorged at the serpent's leisure. Then two of the largest sperm whales that I have ever seen moved slowly thence toward the vessel, their bodies more than usually elevated out of water, and not spouting or making the least noise, but seeming quite paralyzed with fear."

MONSTER SEEN OFF BRAZIL.

This monster serpent was said to be about 160 to 170 feet long and between 7 and 8 feet in circumference. Five days later, in the same latitude and about 80 miles off the Brazil coast, the captain saw either the same one or a similar monster. This time the sea serpent elevated itself about 60 feet above the water and gazed calmly at the ship. The captain in his report also stated that a ship in the Indian Ocean, about three years before this occurrence, "was dragged over by some sea monster."

There are numerous creditable reports which might be added, including that of the celebrated sea serpent which in 1819 was seen off Nahant. Hundreds of persons saw this monster, and all along the beach parties followed its course for miles in coaches, on horseback and running on foot. All New England was alive with the subject, and while it may be admitted that one person may be easily deceived by the falseness of eyesight, it is difficult to believe that hundreds of persons would be similarly deceived at the same time. The only proof which appears to be needed to establish unqualifiedly the existence of the sea serpent – beyond, of course – the capture of one dead or alive – is photographic evidence. Up to the present time that evidence is not in existence.

SEE WILD MAN IN HIS CAVE.

The Evening Statesman – February 12, 1906 – Washington

James McLay, While Hunting, Encounters Mysterious Creature.

NANAIMO, B.C., - Feb. 12. – James McLay, of Gabriola island, the rediscoverer of Malispina Gallery, has made another remarkable discovery on the island. The Vancouver island wild man, strange and weird tales of whom have been reported from different parts of the island from time to time, has been seen by Mr. McLay. Several days ago, in company with a trapper, Mr. McLay was hunting in the northeast end of the island. Hearing noises and mumblings, as if proceeding from strange animal, they started to investigate.

A few feet up the side of a precipice they perceived a cave, from which the noises seemed to emanate. Creeping carefully up, they were rooted to the ground with astonishment to perceive the wild man in the cave rocking himself to and fro with folded arms and mumbling in a strange language, in which the trapper recognized broken phrases of French, which, translated ran something like this:

"Damn! Damn Jonnie Bull and Wolfe. They kill me people in Quebec."

The description they give of the wild man's appearance is practically the same as that told by Mike King, of Victoria, and others who have seen this strange creature, different only in this particular – that on this occasion the "mowgli" had a gridle of leaves around him. When seen before he was always absolutely naked. He is a giant in size, very powerful looking, and covered with long hair all over his body many inches in length. From the fact that the only intelligible words he uttered are French, it is presumed that he is a French Canadian. What connection there is between "Johnnie Bull" and Wolfe, in Quebec, and the man is hard to say. Wolfe captured Quebec in 1754, and it may be possible that some of his ancestors fell while defending the city at that time.

While the two were gazing at him he suddenly looked up, discovering their presence. For a few seconds not a movement was made on either side, until the trapper reached to lean his gun up against a rock, which action the wild man evidently interpreted as a hostile movement, for, giving vent to his usual half man-like, half wild-beast-like shrieks, he leaped fully 10 feet from the cave into the water and swam outwards, using a stick rudely paddle shaped at either end to help him in his progress, kicking his feet and paddling at the same time, progressing through the water with the speed of an average canoe. Going up the shoreline a short way, where Mr. McLay and his badly frightened companion could not follow him, the wild man made for the shore and disappeared with the alacrity of a deer through the dense underbrush. Although vigilant search has been made by different parties since he was seen last week, no more sight or tidings have been received of the wild man.

ADVENTURE OF AN OCTOPUS.

The Chickasha Daily Express – March 7, 1906 – Oklahoma

True Story of Eight-Armed Beast – Arms of Monster Measure 25 Feet in Length.

Here is a true story of an octopus, not the kind that has its headquarters in New Jersey.

"Two fishermen were plying their vocation off Great Bell island, Conception bay, off the Newfoundland coast. Suddenly they discovered at a short distance from them a dark, shapeless mass, floating on the surface of the water. Concluding that it was probably part of the cargo of some wrecked vessel, they approached it, anticipating a valuable prize, and one of them struck the object with his boathook.

Upon receiving the shock the dark heap became suddenly animated, and, spreading out, discovered a head, with a pair of large, prominent, staring eyes, which seemed to gleam with intense ferocity, the creature at the same time exposing to view and opening its parrot-like beak with an apparently hostile and malignant purpose. The men were petrified with terror and for a moment so fascinated by the horrible sight that they were powerless to make a move to defend themselves.

"Before they had time to recover their presence of mind the monster, now but a few feet from the boat, suddenly shot out from around its head several long, fleshy arms, grappling with them for the boat, and seeking to envelop it in their folds. Only the two longest of the arms reached the craft, and, owing to their great length, went completely over and beyond it. Seizing his hatchet, with a desperate effort one of the men succeeded in severing these limbs with a single well-delivered blow, and the creature, finding itself worsted, immediately disappeared beneath the waters, leaving in the boat its amputated members as a trophy of the encounter.

"One of the arms was, unfortunately, destroyed before its value was known, but the other, when brought to St. John's and examined by Rev. M. Harvey, was found to measure no less than 19 feet. The fisherman who acted as surgeon declares there must have been at least six feet more left attached to the monster's body. The story is preserved in the proceedings of the British Zoological society."

FOUR-FOOTED BEAST RAVAGES DUCK HOUSE.

The Pacific Commercial Advertiser — July 9, 1906 — Hawaii

Kaimuki poultry-raisers are again suffering from the depredations of the strange beast which wrought such havoc in the chicken-houses of the district a year ago.

The latest ravages by the four-footed intruder occurred in the depression between the Leahi Home and Diamond Head. One lady lost 53 young chickens one night, the wounds being made in the neck and the blood sucked.

Early yesterday morning another lady was awakened by a disturbance in her duck-house, where were roosting seven full-grown Pekin ducks.

Her husband went out into the yard to investigate and saw a lithe form slinking away in the moonlight from the duck-house. It was more than twice as big as a full-grown mongoose and disappeared in the lantana thicket.

Inspection of the ducks' abode revealed three of the Pekins lying stark dead, a fourth dying, and the remaining two badly bitten in the neck. The slayer of the bird had eaten a neat hole from a little beyond the base of the skull into the brain.

It is improbable that the blood-thirsty midnight marauder is a mongoose, for this pestiferous little animal seldom hunts by night and an instance of it attacking a bird as large as a Pekin duck is almost unknown. A mongoose that would attack, kill or maim seven big ducks at one sitting would have to be a veritable monster.

The opinion of the afflicted neighborhood is that the murderer is an animal which has made its escape from a zoological collection.

FRIGHTENS LONG ISLAND LOVERS.

The Evening Statesman – July 20, 1906 – Washington

Strange Creature Roosts In Trees – Big Man Hunt Is Planned.

BALDWIN, L.I., July 29. – That a wild man lurks in the woods by this village there can be no possible doubt. Constable Stephen Petit led a posse into the haunts of this creature but was able to find only a few deserted nests in the trees where the unwelcome visitor had lodged. Residents of the section are in a state bordering on terror. They bar and bolt their doors at night and two or three of the inhabitants have set spring guns on their front porches.

Because the creature has been seen perched like a wild turkey the story has gained circulation that he has wings. Miss Sempronia Jenkins, principal of the Freeport high school, has called him Dracula, after the principal character in one of Bram Stoker's novels, and the watchword of all Nassau is "Dracula alive or dead."

Dracula has been wandering near the pumping station, which is used to supply a portion of Brooklyn. He has also appeared at dawn to Mr. Simpkin, who was gathering the products of his Plymouth Rocks. The wild man seized the rubber dating stamp with which Mr. Simpkin was about to imprint an egg, and with a fiendish cry tore across the railroad track and disappeared in a clump of blackberry bushes.

Haunts the Kissing Bridge.

Young persons who are accustomed to visit the kissing bridge at twilight now shun it, for the unpleasant experience of a Freeport couple there has alarmed the community. They were leaning against the rail when the wild man approached and laid a rough, heavy hand on the youth's shoulder, and then laughing in his face suddenly swung himself into the branches of a weeping willow which was on the overhanging bank of the stream.

Miss Conway, who lives at Oakview avenue, outside the main portion of this village declares that last Monday afternoon she saw a tall man emerge from the woods. His clothing, which was torn and threadbare, was black. His hair was intensely black, and he also wore a black mustache.

His eyes had a wild and restless expression, and she noted also that his feet, which were incased in patent leather shoes, seemed small and that he apparently had little or no toes. The wild man looked about him in every direction, and catching sight of an automobile, gave vent to ribald laughter and receded into the underbrush.

Wild men have been seen from time to time in this vicinity, for several sanatoriums for the weak-minded are with a radius of ten miles, but this is the first one who goes to roost. Rude platforms of branches on which he has been in the habit of sleeping are in evidence.

Unless Dracula is treed by the end of this week, preparations will be made for a man hunt next Sunday, and the woods will be filled with determined sportsmen.

HAS LEGS OF DOG AND BODY OF FISH.

Watertown Weekly Leader – August 10, 1906 – Wisconsin

STRANGE CREATURE FOUND ON BANKS OF LAKE.

Head and Four Legs Like Dog. Also Fins and Gills – Scientists Have Known of Them – Verification of Theory That All Mammal Life Evolved from Water Species.

Oconomowoc, Wis., Aug. 9. – When is a fish not a fish? The answer is in the possession of Dr. A.S. Bleyer of St. Louis, at present living at the Woodlands hotel here.

A creature with head and four legs like a bulldog, and the body of a fish, with fins and gills, was captured Tuesday upon the banks of the lake, where it had evidently come to die. Although scientists have known that such an animal existed in the Wisconsin lakes, and at one time a delegation of French and German professors came to this country to get a look at one of these strange water dogs, but few of them have ever been seen.

"The discovery of these animals or fishes or whatever one may term them is a living verification of the theory that all animal life has evolved from water species," said Dr. Bleyer. "This creature has been named the Nocturis by scientists. He is probably the only animal in existence today that is undergoing the transformation from a fish to a land animal. In short period the Nocturis will probably quit the water, taking up his home on land like other mammals. At present, however, he is still a fish and cannot live for any length of time out of his natural environment.

CALLS IT NOCTURIS.

"This specimen in my possession was wounded when I found him on the shore, either by some natural enemy or by the propeller of a launch. He made no attempt to escape when he saw me. I do not think he is poisonous or at all dangerous."

Dr. Blyer's Nocturis is one of the most perfect specimens of the strange animal ever caught. Its length is something over thirteen inches. The body is covered with a smooth, soft skin of a dark brown color.

The head is strangely like that of a bulldog with heavy jaws, deep set eyes and a blunt snout. Its teeth are small, although well formed. The tail is like that of a perch and is proportionate to the rest of the body, while rudimentary fins grow from the back.

The Nocturis possesses two complete sets of respiratory organs – the gills of a fish and the lungs and nostrils of a mammal. When on shore breathing is performed through the nose, the air entering the lungs and the blood in this manner, and the gills remain closed. If the animal is placed in water the gills immediately begin to perform their usual functions. The gills are arranged in sets of three on each side of the head and protrude like wings.

RESEMBLES A DOG.

Although the four legs are boneless, they have a startling resemblance to those of a dog. In the present stage of the development of the Nocturis he is unable to do more than crawl over the ground, but as the transformation continues, the cartilage of the legs will harden and become bone, the heavy tail will decrease in size, the nostrils and teeth will become larger and the gills will entirely disappear. Then nature will probably provide fur or hair and a new species of land animal will begin its existence.

Dr. Blyer will present his Nocturis to Washington university at St. Louis.

GREAT SERPENT LEAVES ITS LAIR.

Los Angeles Herald – August 26, 1906 – California

SAN GABRIEL RIVER HARBORS MONSTER.

Campers Above Azusa Fire Hundreds of Shots at Strange Ophidian, Which Comes from Fissure in Mountains.

Special to The Herald.

AZUSA, Aug. 25. – With wings extended so that they rested on the water like a web, covering the surface for a distance of ten feet on either side, a water monster swept down the San Gabriel river near Azusa this morning, and while more than a dozen campers pumped shot at the creature from Winchester rifles the great snake slowly disappeared in the water and was finally lost from sight at a sudden turn of the stream.

As a result of the monster's appearance campers and tourists in the vicinity are spending much of their time following the river trails in the hope of catching sight of the dread beast again, but thus far no damage from settlements in the neighborhood have been reported, and aside from the lucky ones who thronged the river bank on the hour of the snake's appearance, and by reports brought in by two prospectors of the lower hills who saw the monster in the waters of the river, nothing has been heard from it.

The camps in the neighborhood of Azusa have been unusually well populated this season because of the fact that huge fissures have appeared in the Sierra Madres, probably caused by recent earthquakes. These places have been curiously examined by students and by the usual number of campers, and one theory as to the water monster's appearance is that he came from some subterranean passage of the San Gabriel river, and losing his way continued down the stream until he again entered one of the fissures.

Saurian or Ophidian?

At any rate, about three miles above the spot where the monster was first seen the San Gabriel swings within 100 feet of an unusually deep fissure. From the depths of the cut can be heard the rush of subterranean waters, but no light penetrates far enough to show the hidden caverns.

The monster, according to the statements of those who not only saw it but shot at it, was about the size of a pony in the body, with wings about twenty feet wide, from tip to tip. The head resembled the head of a snake, while the color was of a grayish white, common to the subterranean creatures. The entire body was covered with slime. The eyes were white and distended, and apparently the beast could not see, but was gliding himself by a sense of direction. The first camper who saw it gave a yell of surprise, and with others began firing. It is thought that one of the shots took effect in the animal's neck, as the great tail lashed the water in a fury and the body quickly began to disappear under water. A thousand feet farther down stream the campers again beheld the monster as it waved its head high above the waters, and then the great wings, closed over the back of the water, became submerged and the campers lost sight of it. Ripples on the water showed for some distance down stream until all trace of the monster was lost.

A careful watch is being kept on the river by forest rangers and campers, and if the creature appears again some of the eastern institutes may have a remarkably good specimen of a strange ophidian or saurian.

Harry Morse and Bill Brown, the ferrymen at Austin's crossing, have announced their determination to capture the monster, and they are constructing a net made of a section of Page wire fence. The ferrymen say their net is horse-high, hog-tight and bull-strong. They believe it will hold the winged horror.

The efforts of these river men are watched with great interest.

UPSETS IDEAS OF SCIENTISTS.

Los Angeles Herald – September 9, 1906– California

MAN CAPTURES A STRANGE ANIMAL.

Monster Swims About in Great Salt Lake – Resembles Both Fish and Saurian – Imitates the Human Voice.

Special to The Herald.

MURRAY, Utah, Sept. 8. – James Franson of this village recently made one of the most remarkable discoveries of the century – one which will keep the learned men busy for months to come in explaining what they have always declared was an impossibility, namely, that no living thing could exist in the salty waters of the inland sea – Great Salt lake.

Until a week ago Mr. Franson was of the same opinion as the professors who have written so much about the briny waters of the lake, but today you couldn't make him believe that any animal resembling a cross between a monster fish and an alligator does not thrive where nothing else can sustain life.

Mr. Franson's discovery came about in this way: While camped on Antelope island one day last week Franson, his wife and two sons were sitting on the shore of the lake. While they were looking out across the water toward Salt Lake City the father beheld an animal swimming lazily on the surface of the lake and not more than 100 feet from shore. Without taking his eyes from the spot he called to his wife and sons to look where he was pointing.

As they did so the queer looking object raised itself from the water and sent forth a shriek that was the nearest approach to the wail of a human being that could be imagined. As the terrifying sound ceased the animal dropped back into the water and continued its journey toward the shore.

Almost instantly the Franson's were again startled to see several smaller members of the same family swimming ten or fifteen feet behind the great Salt Lake Monster.

Captures Strange Saurian.

For a few seconds the Murrayites kept their eyes on the strange appearing group of animals (or whatever you are pleased to call them), but as the importance of the discovery revealed itself to the elder Franson he jumped to his feet and set about to effect a capture.

In his early days, as everyone hereabout knows, Mr. Franson was one of the best steer punchers that Montana boasted, and quick as a flash he ran to the tent and returned with a rope some fifty feet in length and prepared to take a try at lassoing the strange animal.

By this time, it had approached to within twenty feet of the shore, closely followed by the smaller members of its family. Circling the rope above his head, Franson made a swift and accurate throw and caught the wriggling monster about two feet below its head. Then, like a flash, he made a half hitch of the other end of the rope around a limb of a tree and the capture was complete.

For fully an hour the monster wriggled and twisted, straining so hard at times that Franson feared the half inch rope would be snapped, but slowly the animal lost its strength and eventually was hauled ashore.

By actual measurement the monster was thirty-three feet long. Its head resembled that of an alligator, but the tail and body were of a slate colored hue, and it looked more like a man-eating shark than anything else.

After securing the "fish-alligator" with other ropes and making sure that it could not escape, Franson got into his launch and made a hasty trip to Saltair and thence to Salt Lake City, where several well-known men who knew Franson would not concoct such a story for the purpose of playing a joke on them were induced to return with him and transport the monster to Salt Lake.

Taken to Saltair.

The trip was naturally a dangerous one, for the instant that the monster recovered its strength it lashed the water into a white foam and more than once succeeded in taking the launch a mile or more out of its course.

A huge tank was secured at Saltair and eventually the strange monster was landed in the Salt palace, where a special aquarium was erected for its home.

The palace has been crowded with visitors every day since the doors were thrown open to the public, more than 10,000 people having already paid 25 cents each to behold the only animal of its kind ever captured, and, so far as known, the only one (with the exception of the other member of the same family which promptly disappeared when Franson lassoed the mother) that has ever been seen.

As the waters of Salt Lake are more than one-third salt it seems impossible that anything could live in it, but the evidence furnished by Mr. Franson is indisputable.

What seems all the more remarkable concerning the monster is that it comes nearer imitating the human voice than a parrot. Many who have watched the gigantic "fish-alligator" declare that it all but talks, and the attendant who never leaves the Salt palace goes further and declares it does talk.

"I don't care how much fun you make of me," he said the other day, "that thing can talk as plainly as a man can, for I have heard it say things when there was no one but myself anywhere near the building. Why, just last night, shortly after the doors had been locked and I was preparing to go to bed, that great whale of a fish raised its head out of the water and said:

"Say, Bill, what has become of my old friend Brigham Young? I heard indirectly that he was dead."

The attendant also declares that the monster can sing, and he would not be much surprised if some enterprising theatrical manager tried to secure it as an attraction. The attendant has figured it out that the blamed thing could even be taught to play piano, there seemingly being no limit to its powers of imitating the human voice and doing what it sees or hears human beings doing. Scientists from Bingham Junction declare that the monster is 44,000 years old at least, and possibly older.

STRANGE MONSTER SCARES CITIZENS.

Barbour County Index – January 2, 1907 – Kansas

WEIRD BABOON-LIKE CREATURE SEEN NEAR DARBY, PA.

MAY BE PRACTICAL JOKE.
Belated Wayfarer of Delaware County Frightened by Mysterious Thing and Many Residents Are Arming Themselves.

Darby, PA. – All Delaware County is stirred up over the supposed antics of an alleged wild animal which is asserted to look like a gorilla and to have frightened belated wayfarers almost out of their wits in various parts of the county. While it is believed by most persons that the whole thing is a practical joke on the part of someone who is literally making a monkey out of himself, still many of the more timid class are thoroughly alarmed and fully believe all the tales that are told about the mysterious creature.

Those professing to have seen the wonderful animal, assert that it sometimes goes upright like a man and then dashes along on all fours with marvelous speed, maintaining a queer galloping gait. They furthermore feel certain that it has a coat of dark hair, but that is not considered remarkable, as the weather is cool. Their stories of how they almost encountered the strange beast have been so thrilling that many of the negroes in the county cannot be induced to pass the spots where it is said to have been seen. Others have purchased pistols and go about armed, fully resolved to sell their lives dearly should they encounter the mythical monster in any of its hypothetical haunts.

Others take the thing seriously without being unduly alarmed and they try to explain the matter. That it is an ape escaped from zoological collection is the most commonly accepted theory. This was strengthened by a rumor that the authorities of the Zoological Gardens of Philadelphia were out looking for a lost Simian in

Delaware County. But a telephone message to the zoo exploded the story. All the Philadelphia monkeys are safe in their cages. Their keeper respectfully suggested that the animal down by Darby is probably a monkey of native Delaware County stock.

Nevertheless, several persons in Springfield township are so convinced that there is a strange animal prowling about that they have set traps for it. Frank Carr is one of them, and he set a number of traps in an enclosure in the rear of his house near some woods where the reputed creature was reported to have been seen. It is now stated that the traps were found broken, the bait devoured and all evidences on hand of a struggle made by some animal.

The practical joker who is working the scare, if such is the case, has succeeded to an extent which may work his own harm. For there are a number of Delaware County citizens who, while not getting in hysterics about the matter, have quietly placed big guns in their hip pockets and are waiting for a chance to pot anything that looks like a baboon.

YOUNG BOY ATTACKED BY BIG GRAY EAGLE.

The Idaho Recorder – February 7, 1907 – Idaho

Monster Bird Swoops Down on Child, Carries Him 50 Yards, Then Releases Him.

Coweta, J.T. – The five-year old son of Nero Charles, a farmer living near Coweta, was attacked by a large gray eagle a few days ago, and narrowly escaped with his life after being carried 50 yards by the fierce bird. So far as known, this is the first time in the history of Indian Territory that a child has actually been picked up and carried by an eagle.

The child, with others, was playing in a field on his father's farm, near Jackson Ferry, on Verdigris river, eight miles northeast of Coweta, when the eagle swooped down upon him, catching the child's clothing with its talons and starting off. The screams of the other children apparently frightened the eagle, and, finding that it could not make much progress with the child, it dropped him 50 yards from the place where he was picked up.

The child weighs 50 pounds, and at no time did the eagle succeed in getting more than eight or ten feet above the ground with him. The child was not injured save for a few bruises and scratches when his parents found him. The eagle made no attempt to strike its talons into the child nor beat him with its wings.

It has been known for some time that there were two gray eagles nesting on the Verdigris river not far from Jackson's Ferry. About ten days ago a farmer named Kirkbride, who lives near the ferry, killed one of the eagles with a rifle. They were very cunning, and it was impossible to get close enough to kill them with a shotgun. When this eagle was shot it was devouring a pig which it had killed. Since the child was attacked by the eagle another one has been killed, and it is believed that these two are the only ones on the river that are large and fierce enough to cause trouble. Each of the two killed measured over seven feet from tip to tip of wings.

THE OSAGE MONSTER.

Clarke Courier – July 10, 1907 – Virginia

How a Steamboat Whistle Affected Missouri Pioneers.

STORY OF A HISTORIC HUNT.
Armed for the Fray, the Frightened but Determined Old Settlers Sought the Ferocious Beast with the Fearful, Screeching Voice.

The first steamboat that ever turned her prow against the muddy Osage waters was the Flora Jones in the spring of 1844. There was no commercial club in those days to stimulate river traffic, no telegraph or telephone to her aid to the hardy pioneers the approach of the boat – only the unearthly shrill screech of the banshee-like whistle, enough to blanch the cheek of the simple minded folk who had lived far from the world's progress.

The little boat went up as far as Harmony, MO., in Bates county. History records the fact that when the Flora Jones puffed her way along the St. Clair county shores and the wail of her siren was tossed back and forth by the limestone bluffs many of the old settlers were not only frightened figuratively out of their boots, but literally out of their homes. Matthew Arbuckle, a pioneer, tradition tells us, was plowing his field about a mile from the river when the wail of that whistle struck his ear. He unhitched his horse from the plow, managed to get on its back and, wild with terror, struck for the hills. In one hour, he was at Papinville, fifteen miles distant, the horse white with foam, the rider white with terror. He had barely strength to tell of "an awful animal" from which he had made his escape. He had not seen the fearful beast, he confessed, but he had heard its voice, by which he knew it to be a monster of terrific proportions.

Arbuckle's neighbors were brave and, though much disturbed by his account, determined upon a campaign of extermination. They had defended their homes against Indians, and they reasoned that no wild animal, however ferocious, could withstand their rifles. They gathered at Uncle John Whitley's. He had seen service under Jackson at New Orleans. His home was up the tortuous stream from Arbuckle's farm.

The next morning a crowd of hardy pioneers, with guns and dogs, were ready at Uncle John's. The gallant band numbered among its members Uncle John Whitley, James Breckenridge, Benjamin Morris, William Bacon, Hamilton Morris, Benjamin Burch, William Roark, Frank Roark, Benjamin Snyder, Snowden Morris and Matthew Arbuckle.

They were agreed that there should be undertaken a quest for the mysterious monster threatening their homes and families.

Just before the signal to start was given Mattie, a daughter of Whitley's, went down to the river, 300 yards distant, for water. In her absence the Flora Jones, which had tied up for the night at a bend in the river below, again sounded the terror inspiring whistle.

"Charge, men!" roared Whitley, seizing his gun. "Mattie went to the river for water, and I reckon she's dead afore now!"

The crowd rushed to the river, determined to rescue the girl if she was yet alive. But Mattie, it is hardly necessary to state, was met on the way. She was headed homeward, her hair streaming behind and her face blanched with fear.

With their weapons ready for instant action the determined hunters continued riverward. The crew of the Flora Jones, proud of her whistle, continued to sound it at frequent intervals, and its reverberations rang from bluff to bluff unceasingly. Each fresh blast added to the uneasiness of the band of settlers. Frequent councils were held. The failure of the dogs to take the scent nonplused them.

The hunters scoured the Osage thickets all day. Breckenridge lost faith in hounds and declared that he would go to St. Louis for Newfoundlands. Meanwhile the Flora Jones had proceeded up the river to Harmony, and her whistle was no longer heard. As night came on a storm broke, and the hunters took refuge in a cave.

With the return of dawn there began again the hideous wail of the mysterious monster. The Flora Jones was making an early start on her return trip down the river. Nearer and nearer sounded the whistle, until the hunters, who had tumbled hastily from their cave, could distinguish a puffing and blowing, supposed to be the snorts of the advancing foe.

The moment of decisive action seemed at hand. The hunters rushed to the river bank. Each selected a tree to stand behind and looked to the priming of his gun.

An instant later the Flora Jones rounded a bend and loomed into view. Upon her deck was a gay crowd of passengers watching the early sunrise flooding the water with rosy light. Uncle John Whitley, Jimmy Breckenridge and their band of heroes were too astonished to answer the friendly hails as the boat swept down to the next bend, her whistle mocking their past fears.

Little was said as the hunters tracked homeward. Unostentatiously each sought out his home. And so ended the historic hunt for the monster of the Osage valley.

— Kansas City Star.

BIG SNAKE BELLOWED LIKE AN ANGRY BULL.

The Hartford Herald – July 31, 1907 – Kentucky

When the Monster Threw a Man Twenty Feet, Breaking His Ribs.

Valley, Neb., July 26. – A monster snake, 50 feet long with a head like a bushel basket, is causing terror to the farmers east of this town, where it has been seen several times and where yesterday it picked up Joseph Anderson, a farmer, and threw him 20 feet, breaking two of his ribs in doing this.

The farmers have organized a grand snake hunt for next week, and every man for miles around will take part.

For 25 years reports have been circulated about a big snake which lived near Agees Lake, and which occasionally caught and swallowed a pig or a calf. Twice this year the snake has been seen.

Yesterday, while Joseph Anderson and W. Nightengale, both farmers, were en route to the lake to go in bathing, and were walking through high grass, the monster snake suddenly rose up right under Anderson.

He attempted to step over it, thinking it a log. The force of the head threw Anderson 20 feet. Then, with its head raised six feet above the ground and bellowing like a bull, the snake made for the lake, which it entered in sight of the men.

Anderson and Nightengale say the snake was 40 feet long, one foot thick, and hissed like a locomotive letting off steam. When it rushed through the woods to the lake it broke off limbs of trees three and four inches thick.

The country around Agees Lake is wild over the report, and none of the farmers will venture out of the house after dark.

BEAR LAKE MONSTER APPEARS.

The Logan Republican — September 18, 1907 — Kansas

Leviathan Comes from Lake and Devours Horse While Men Shoot at It.

The Bear Lake Monster, a combination of dragon, bear, and fish, measuring twenty feet in length and possessing the roar of a lion is again agitating the people over the mountains. According to the Republican's informant, this monster made its appearance on the lake front a few nights ago and killed a horse tied near a campfire, the owners Messrs. T. R. Mooney and Fred Horne, firing a number of shots at the peculiar looking dragon without effective results.

Several years ago, this prehistoric leviathan made its appearance at the lake quite frequently and the people of that valley were in a continuous state of excitement as a result. Camping parties on the lake were few and far between and people about the lake were afraid to go to sleep at nights for fear of having their homes and themselves eaten up by this ferocious monster of the big lake. To those who remember the excitement of the earlier days, the following will come with special interest:

BEAR LAKE, Idaho, Sept. 12. – Editor Logan Republican: We camped on the eastern shore of Bear Lake just after sundown. After getting our horses tied to a large tree near the water's edge, and fed, we started to prepare our supper. My partner, Mr. Horne, called my attention to something out in the lake about half a mile. As we watched, it would sink into the water for a second then out again. The lake being perfectly calm we couldn't account for the strange object, but it came nearer to us and still going down and out of the water. Had it not been for this we would have thought it a gasoline launch or some other vessel. It now was close enough for us to see that it was some water monster. We grabbed our 30-30 rifles, and each fired at it, but could not see that we hit him, although he turned slightly to the south. Before we had time to fire again, he turned towards us.

Our horses were now very frightened, one of which broke loose. We stepped back into the trees a few feet and both fired, and my God, for the growl that beast let then stated in towards us like a mad elephant. We ran up the hillside a few rods to a slift of rocks and then began to shoot as rapidly as possible. With every shot he seemed to get more strength and growl more devilish. The animal was now so close to shore that we couldn't see it for the trees. We thought of our horse that was tied to the tree and after re-loading our guns we ran down to protect him, if possible. Just as we reached our campfire, which was blazing up pretty well, we could see that ugly monster raise his front paw and strike the horse to the ground. Then he turned and started for deep water. In our excitement we began to pour lead at him again, and then with a terrific growl made a terrible swish in the water and sprang towards us. Before we could move, he grabbed the horse with his two front paws, opened its monstrous mouth and crashed its teeth into it like a bull terrier would a mouse. After tearing the horse badly, he made an awful howl and then was gone, plowing through the water. But the sight I'll never forget. It seemed to be all head, two large staring eyes as large as a front wagon wheel, nose and mouth like a great large fish. Its arms seemed to come out on either side of its head where the ears naturally would be. The hind legs were long and bent like that of a kangaroo. Then the hind end was like the tip end of a monster fish.

We walked to a ranch up the shore, a quarter of a mile and staid till morning. When we went back in the morning, we found the animal had come back again in the night and carried the dead horse off. He also broke off trees four and five inches through. Also tore large holes in the beach, and its tracks were like those of a bear, but measuring three feet long and nearly two feet wide. We could not tell if our bullets would go through his hide or not but noticed some of them would glance off and hum like they had struck one of his teeth, which always seemed to show. As there was so much blood from the mangled horse, we could not tell whether the beast of the lake was bleeding.   Yours respectfully, T.R. MOONEY, FRED HORNE.

HALF WOMAN AND SNAKE.

The Caucasian – September 19, 1907 – Louisiana

Peculiar Creature Which Party Seeks to Capture.

Jamestown, Va., Sept. 19. – An expedition has started from this city, headed by several veteran mountaineers, having for its object the investigation of a weird tale regarding a snake woman who, it is alleged, frequents the wild parts of the moonshine country.

This strange creature who, several witnesses have declared, resembles a reptile as much as a woman, will be captured if it is possible for the members of the expedition to catch a glimpse of her. A mountaineer on a visit to Jamestown brought the first story of the snake woman and claimed to be one of the very few people who had actually seen her.

For years, he stated, tales of a wild woman with the skin of a snake, who traveled upon the ground like a reptile and subsisted upon living prey, have been told, but these tales were generally regarded as idle rumors. Stone Colby, a grizzled mountaineer who visited the exposition, however, declares that the stories, instead of being exaggerated, only tell half the truth about the strange woman. It was he who made the offer to lead an expedition to the place where the woman lives.

Covered with the scaly skin of a snake and shedding it regularly once a year in one piece, the snake woman glides among the trees and rocks in search of small animals, mice, frogs, ground squirrels and other forest and swamp prey, which Stone has seen her eat alive, swallowing them like a reptile, without mastication.

WHAT GOT THE HOOK?

New-York Tribune – December 23, 1907 – New York

THINK IT A 'SQUARE DEAL'.

Deep Sea Monster Baffled Captain Johansson, F.M.

The Swedish barkentine Elise got in yesterday after a long passage from Bristol, England, whither she had sailed from the Dutch Antilles with a cargo of hides and dye stuffs. The trip was uneventful as far as weather went, but the Elise came abeam of a sea monster off the Azores that will no doubt make piscatorial wizards sit up and take notice when the tale of the Elise's skipper finds its way to the public ear.

Captain Peter A. Johansson, who has sailed the barkentine over the seven seas, holds the world's record for shark killing, and although he has the degree of M.F. (master fisherman) he is content to omit it when writing his signature. The skipper is a man who has seen about thirty-seven summers, and his knowledge of the monsters of the deep that occasionally come to the surface and bark or hiss at the barkentine is the talk of the waterfront.

He is a close student of the fish and its ways, and apart from keeping the Elise on her course and the sailors in their places the captain finds time to troll for shark and read from Shakespeare. When the Elise was visited yesterday at her pier over in South Brooklyn the skipper was reading "Hamlet." He laid the book aside to talk of the sea monsters, but suggested later as a preface to his story of the freak fish off the Azores that Hamlet's remark to Horatio might have been written to read, "There are more things in heaven and earth (and in the sea), Horatio, than there are dreamt of in your philosophy."

Mr. Johansson showed a varied fishing tackle, which included an adequate supply of nitro-glycerine bombs with time fuses attached, which he frequently tucks away deceptively into a fine fresh piece of porpoise meat and throws to a hungry shark that chances to follow the wake of the Elise. "Sharks are the enemy of man," said the captain, "and for that reason I am the enemy for the sharks. I have harpooned them and blown them up with dynamite. No, I am not afraid they will blow up under the barkentine. I have studied the ways of the shark and know that he always sheers off either to port or to starboard after he has gulped the bait. I have fed hundreds of sharks with my little explosive pill, and only one exceptionally bright fellow came under my ship to let himself explode. It did not bother me, because the Elise is built of iron."

After showing his fishing paraphernalia and the special line made of insulated wire that explodes a bomb in the shark's stomach through a battery from the deck, the skipper of the Elise told of a sea monster that he played for and lost while the barkentine was running along at about two knots to the southward of the Azores.

It was believed at first that the skipper was about to describe an amphibious manifestation of the proverbial "square deal," when he said the monster was about twelve feet long and twelve feet deep. It was not a manatee, because the skipper had seen that mammal before, and it was not peculiar to the waters of the Azores. The captain said briefly that the monster was first discovered when about two ship's lengths dead ahead. It was of a bluish-gray color, with a dorsal fin that appeared above the water, resembling the conning tower of a submarine. The fin served to propel the monster when the latter submerged himself and its swishing sound attracted the crew of the Elise.

Fearing the monster would get away, Captain Johansson got his "ever baited" hooks ready and threw a few out to the "square deal." Instead of plunging to windward, the creature came alongside and stuck up a head which looked like that usually carried by an ostrich, and, if the skipper's memory serves him well, the mouth was much like that of a camel; and the fish could go as long without a drink as the ship of the desert, but probably never had to. There were no teeth visible, but there must have been a row or two in his stomach, for the bait was literally absorbed by the camel-like mouth much as the jellyfish takes its nutriment, and a smile of thanks seemed to be manifest about the lips. There was no attempt at line snapping, but, notwithstanding this, the skipper always pulled in his wire line sans hook and bait.

Harpooning was the last resort. The monster thrived too well on the hooks and porpoise flesh, and a more effective means of capture must be applied. The peculiar gases in the creature's stomach evidently made a peculiar chemical reaction which destroyed the effectiveness of either the time fuse or the dynamite. The first mate threw the first stone – or, more correctly, the first harpoon. It struck a point aft the conning tower dorsal fin and bent. The skipper threw a second shaft, and it sank into a soft tissue abaft amidships, but did not hold. The "square deal," or whatever it was, submerged, and was never seen again.

"The sea holds many strange creatures," observed the skipper, and although no one doubted the encounter with the monster to the southward of the Azores, he reached over to a rack and showed the twisted harpoon.

CAUGHT STRANGE BEAST.

The Mena Weekly Star – February 20, 1908 – Arkansas

An Animal Resembling Monkey and Otter Captured on Stillwell Heights – Has Been in Captivity.

After an exciting chase James Lacy and several of his children assisted by John Beavers and his son captured an animal which as of yet no one has been able to name.

Mr. Lacy lives on South De Queen street at the edge of town just beyond George Petty's home. Several times in the last few weeks a strange animal has been seen prowling around in that neighborhood, often seen by Mr. Lacy's children.

Tuesday one of the boys came upon the animal in W.E. Watkins' pasture, a half mile south of their home. Other members of the family were summoned, and a chase taken up with a view of taking the animal alive if possible.

After a lively chase the animal ran into the buggy shed of John Beavers on Stilwell Heights where it was captured by Mr. Beavers and his son and turned over to Mr. Lacy, who carried it home and placed it in a cage.

Mr. Lacy described the beast as weighing about 25 pounds, with a body over two feet long. It has a tail of about equal length. Its body and tail are covered with heavy coat of brown fur which turns to almost a grey on its neck and head. Its legs are short, the hind legs and feet resembling in shape those of a bear. It runs with its back humped up like a monkey and resembles one in many ways, but the head would put it more in the class of an opossum, having a very long pointed nose and ears.

It evidently is not a native of this portion of the country and has probably escaped from captivity as the fur is worn off a streak around its neck, apparently by a collar. While it was quite wild and made fierce fight before being captured, it has become very submissive since placed in its cage. It eats bread and meat and seems perfectly at home.

Mr. Lacy is anxious to have someone tell him what kind of a beast he has captured.

BIG SEA SERPENT GLOWED LIKE FIRE.

The Barre Daily Times – March 18, 1908 – Vermont

Phosphorescent Monster 120 Feet Long Ate Bananas from Admiral Farragut.

New York, March 18. – A sea monster 120 feet long that glowed with phosphorescent so that it could be seen miles away was reported by Capt. Mader of the fruit steamer Admiral Farragut, which arrived from Port Antonio. This is the way the Farragut's log records it:

"March 13 – At 8 p.m. Thursday, March 12, latitude 22.06 north, longitude 74.21 west. One-half mile off starboard bow sighted strange marine monster. It approached and followed ship all night. Friday, at 9 a.m., monster crossed our bows. Passengers in a panic. Reduced speed to five knots."

Capt. Mader said:

"We picked the sea serpent up – or rather the monster picked us up – late Thursday night. I was on the bridge, when one of the passengers rushed up and excitedly called my attention to a phosphorescent light several miles astern. As it came nearer, we placed the searchlight on it and could see that it was some strange sea monster.

"It seemed about 120 feet long and threshed its way through the rough sea at a fearful speed. All night long it followed the vessel. The phosphorescent glow of the monster lighted up the sea within a radius of 50 feet.

"On Friday morning the serpent swam within 30 feet of the starboard side. The creature resembled a huge boa-constrictor, with the exception that its body was green. From its sides streamed seaweed and other marine growth.

"The monster raised its head several feet above the water. It had huge eyes projecting from the top of its head, and two green horns that projected upward nearly five feet. The horns resembled large antennae and moved about continuously.

"We threw overboard several sacks of peanuts and a few bunches of bananas.

"When we were 100 miles north of Watling island, we sighted a floating island about two miles long, and the trees were filled with monkeys.

"You notice how the Admiral Farragust is listed to port. There are over 1,000 sea turtles in the hold. As soon as we tied up all these turtles crawled over on the port side. If several stevedores hadn't rushed some of the freight over on the starboard side, I am afraid the steamer would have turned turtle."

ENGLISH NOBLEMAN ON A SECRET EXPEDITION TO ALASKA.

Evening Star – May 9, 1908 – Washington D.C.

Duke of Westminster to Hunt the Keratosaurus of the Arctic Circle, the Partridge Creek Monster, Guided by Sporting French Explorer.

Animal Is Alive and Its Capture Is Hoped For – New Testimony From a Jesuit Father Who Saw It Twice – James Lewis Butler, San Francisco Banker, and His Friend, Georges Dupuy, Add Their Testimony – Fitting Out Large German Vessel for the Voyage – Peculiar Formation and Great Size of the Prehistoric Creature, Which Carries a Live Cariboo in Its Mouth With Perfect Ease and Makes Footprints of Amazing Size.

Special Correspondence of The Star.

Paris, May 1, 1908.

The antediluvian keratosaurus of the arctic circle is alive and may be captured. This is why the millionaire young Duke of Westminster is now in conference in Paris. This explains why he will visit the United States in June.

In London they say vaguely that the duke and fair young duchess are to "spend a long American vacation." "Just what are their plans, nobody seems to know," admit the cables; "but undoubtedly the richest peer and peeress in England will receive unusual social attentions; while the duke will take a hunting trip in the Rockies."

In Paris we know the sensational secret motive of the Rocky mountain expedition – which will quietly extend away up to the McQuesten river in the Yukon, where the Klayakuk tribe of the Snow Indians wait, close-mouthed and patient, around the Canadian post of Armstrong creek till the good Jesuit father Lavagneux shall give the word: "They come!"

In San Francisco, too, there is a man who knows, the banker, James L. Butler. Long before the duke's party comes, he will be strangely busy at the railway and the water-front, receiving stores and Hamburg cablegrams and testing silent, fearless men who take cash in advance and ask no questions.

And there is a miner of the Yukon, Tom Leemore, who, with Georges Dupuy and James Butler and the Jesuit father, saw the Keratosaurus in its range and photographed it in its rampage when it flicked an avalanche of great rocks down around their heads.

Who has seen the photographs of the Partridge creek monster? Not the Dawson authorities, who refused to lend a hundred mules and fifty armed men to go hunt it. Not the editor of the Daily Nugget, who dubbed Georges Dupuy "a rival of Edgar Poe."

Duke Become Interested.

The miner, Leemore, who remained at Armstrong creek, pig headedly confided them to Father Lavagneux alone – "to interest some rich and serious French or English sport"; and now that Georges Dupuy is back in Paris with the Duke of Westminster behind him, one of the most extraordinary photographs on earth is in the young duke's pocket; while Dupuy has in his pocket a liberal contract to indemnify all those concerned and fit an expedition that must include a 4,000-ton tramp steamer – to bring straight to London the live monster weighing eighty tons and more!

The Duke of Westminster has also in his pocket the following letter from the Jesuit missionary to Georges Dupuy after his return to Paris. It enclosed the photograph.

"Armstrong Creek Canadian Post.

"January 1, 1908.

"My Dear Boy: The McQuesten trader has arrived, with sledge and dogs. He will make the hard trip to Dawson by the Barlow, Flat creek and Dominion. On his return I shall have fresh food and news from the world – I hope from your dear self, with a word for Leemore, who, you will see by the precious photograph herewith, deems the time ripe for your best effort.

"What joy will it not give me to receive you again under my roof, here at the world's end! Because I will not believe you could permit your friend of the Great North to give up his old carcass to the branch coffins of the Stewart Indians without visiting him once more!

"I have your book; its reading captivated me incredibly; but you err as to poor John Spitz – he is no longer mail carrier. He died at Eagle Camp from the wounds given him by the "bald-face" (grizzly) you know of.

Priest Sees the Monster!

"And now, would you believe, in the name of our Lord, that I and ten of my Indians again saw, Christmas afternoon, Leemore's terrible monster?

"It passed like a hurricane across the frozen river, smashing, dashing, crashing immense blocks of broken ice into the air behind it. All its long bristles were covered with hoar frost, and its red eyes flamed in the twilight.

"The monster held in its mouth a cariboo that weighed at least 700 pounds, while it careered along at twenty miles per hour. At the corner of the cut-off it disappeared.

"In company with Chief Stineshane and two of his sons, I took prints of its tracks, exactly as you, Butler, Leemore and I did that last day in the moose lake."

The present writer has copied the letter; there may be omissions; added words, of course (it is a translation) also; but as to the substantial accuracy of everything touching the existence of the monster, I am positive there is no error of copying or translation.

The positive good faith of Georges Dupuy is also beyond doubt in Paris, where he is so well known. His place as a writer and sporting explorer is quite fixed. When the New York-Paris automobile race was being organized his mere word convinced Parisians of the impossibility of crossing Bering strait upon the ice – which doesn't exist. Three times in the last eight years Dupuy has made long visits to the Klondike, always as a sport with money.

James Lewis Butler, his friend and his San Francisco banker, being up at Dawson buying gold claims last July, sent word to Dupuy he would meet him at McQuesten post for a week's hunting. Taking his coffee on the porch of Father Lavagneux's house, the French sport perceived Butler hurrying to him from the birch-bark canoe and two

Indians Father Lavagneux had sent to meet him. Butler was much agitated.

"Do you know that there are prehistoric monsters alive up here?" were his first words.

Laughing, Dupuy led the banker inside to the Jesuit; but when he saw Father Lavagneux receive the story with grave faith he laughed no longer.

"From Gravel lake, my last camp, was to be the mouth of Clear creek, where I would meet your men," said Butler. "It was terrible going – forty miles of swamp. At night, therefore, I joyfully perceived Grant's cabin lights. He gave me a good supper.

"At 5 a.m. Grant came, announcing, in his furtive way, three big moose back of Partridge creek. He, your two Indians and I saw the moose. They had been quietly feeding. Suddenly the male let out the bellow that means fright, and off they went at breakneck speed. What could it be?

"We hurried up to the moose lake and found that fresh in the mud was the print of a monster body. The belly had made a gully two feet deep, thirty long and twelve feet wide. Four gigantic feet – a yard by half a yard, and claws twelve inches long – had made a lot of prints."

"Grant and Butler followed the tracks three miles to 'the gulf,' a dark and rocky ravine, where they disappeared.

"What do you think of that?" concluded Butler.

"At 5 o'clock the next morning Father Lavagneux, Dupuy, Butler and Leemore – the only miner, except Grant (who refused to join the hunt) – went to the tracks, accompanied by the five Indians. Neither the sergeant of the mounted police nor the traded would have anything to do with it.

"We tramped the flats of Partridge Creek in vain that morning," says Dupuy. "At noon we built a fire in a big rocky ravine. We had almost given up expecting anything. Then, as the tea was boiling, down came crashing an avalanche of bowlders, amid roarings, snortings, rumblings, and thunderous wind-breakings that made the earth tremble.

"The thing was upon us in an instant. The monster, black, gigantic, its chops dripping bloody slather, with a sickening noise of mastication, punctuated by the deafening claps of a Titanic colic, lurched down the ravine – beyond us – sweeping rocks aside like pebbles.

"Father Lavagneux and I were petrified. The Indians lay upon their bellies.

"A keratosaurus! The keratosaurus of the arctic circle alive!" babbled Father Lavagneux, as the outrageous thing stopped and stared at us with disdainful curiosity.

Guide Gets Three Snapshots.

"For ten long minutes, nailed to the spot, we stared at the prehistoric creature. It stared at us. In full daylight. You have seen the Eiffel Tower? In the same manner, I have seen the keratosaurus. Its withers stood twenty-five feet high. Its entire body – from rhinoceros horn to tail tip – must have measured seventy feet. Its hide was like that of the wild boar, covered with two-foot long bristles, gray black. From its hairy belly hung clods of mud as big as a ten-year-old child!

"The noise of its mastication – crackling bones – was like the grinding of ice in a debacle. That of its indigestion was like when a hurricane tears the shrouds out of a big schooner. Its stench overpowered us.

"Then, suddenly, it raised its head, shook the hills with a long roar, and romped down the ravine in gigantic bounds at forty miles per hours. Its head, held forty feet above the ground, was the last thing I saw in the whirlwind of rocks hell-racketing behind it.

"No use to shoot at such a fellow," Dupuy heard a casual voice behind him monologuing. "But I got three snapshots at him with my faithful kodak, the sun well upon my back. Just my luck to have only three films in it!"

It was Leemore, the most phlegmatic temperament Dupuy has ever run across. While others were transfixed with horror, Leemore was already calculating what he could make from his snapshots.

"If I take them in to Dawson," he said, later, in reply to all appeals for proofs, those smart-Alecs will give us the laugh for faking photos, or there's just a possibility the whole town will turn out to hunt the ker-at-"

"O-saurus."

Details of Expedition.

"Thanks. Where will we be? No, we'll keep quiet about it. Father Lavagneux and Dupuy-sport will use the photographs to interest one of those game English earls with millions, who'll be glad to fit a proper expedition and square us in a proper lordly manner."

These are the facts that are leading up to the Duke of Westminster's "American vacation" that beings next June.

Leemore was right in his surmise, from first to last.

"On the 24th of the month," says Dupuy, "Butler and I went down to Dawson." (Evidently their excitement got the better of them and they talked.) "We asked the governor for fifty mules and 100 armed men. For thirty days we were the laughingstock of Dawson City, and the Nugget published on myself the flattering editorial that had for title, 'A Rival of Edgar Poe.'"

At this hour, even while they fit the expedition out, neither Dupuy nor the young duke will be disturbed that I have told the bare outlines of their great project.

"No one will believe it," said the duke, last night, while dining at Paillard's.

No one will believe that they are chartering a German tramp at Hamburg, with the privilege of tearing out of it a central steel-grilled space sixty feet long, twenty-five feet wide, and thirty deep. What for? What do you think? To bring back gold?

— AN AMERICAN IN PARIS.

SPLITS NIGHT AIR WITH ITS SHRIEKS.

The Plymouth Tribune – May 28, 1908 – Indiana

Strange Wild Beast Terrorizing Farmers and Others Near Akron, Indiana.

A strange wild beast, with a cry that resembles the shriek of a frightened woman and with eyes that shine in the darkness as if they were balls of fire, is causing terror among the farmers who live near the woods and swamps northwest of Akron, Ind.

The beast was first heard by the farmers ten days ago. Its cry was described as weird and piercing. One man said he first thought it was the shriek of a woman, but as the cry came from a swampy woods, he concluded that he was mistaken. Next day he investigated and found tracks large and broad enough for a bear. Several men procured dogs and guns and trailed the beast along the roads and across fields, but finally lost its tracks in a swamp.

Another search was made last Saturday, but without avail. On Monday night scores of people heard the cry in the woods a quarter of a mile west of town, and on Tuesday morning fresh tracks were found.

No one seems to have heard the beast on Tuesday night, but on Wednesday about dusk, Miss Clara Orr, who lives one mile north, heard a commotion in the pigpen. When she went out to learn the cause of the disturbance, she was startled by seeing a strange animal with eyes glowing like coals of fire among the hogs. She screamed and ran to a neighbor's, Jacob Saygers. He and his hired man armed with shotguns, at once went to the pen. The strange beast was still there. Both men fired at the same time.

There was a screech and a snarl, and a dark mass leaped the side of the pen. The men fired again, but the beast went on toward the woods apparently not crippled. The pellets in the cartridges were small and probably only stung the animal.

Tracks were found later leading from the pen to the woods, but although a party of hunters searched diligently until dark the "varmint" could not be found.

Inquiry has been sent to several circuses, in the belief that the beast has escaped from a menagerie. One man who got a glimpse of the animal said it was as large as a leopard, another believed it was a huge Canada lynx, but his belief was discredited by examination of the tracks. Some people are of the opinion that the "shrieker" is the same animal that was seen in the "Hell's Neck" part of southern Indiana several months ago, and that it has worked northward in the woods on the banks of the Wabash and other streams. It is about 250 miles from the "Pocket" to Akron.

The whole neighborhood is excited over the strange animal, and timid people will not go near the swamps or woods at night.

TERROR OF GREEN TOOTHED MONSTER.

The Enterprise – June 17, 1908 – Montana

THE CUCUPIRA OF AMAZON WOODS IS BULLET PROOF, BUT NOT INTELLIGENT.

IS FOND OF HUMAN HEARTS.

Brazilian Explorer of Wilds Tells of Peculiarities of Demon of Wilderness of Which Natives Are Deathly Afraid.

Washington. – "I had not been in Brazil for 24 hours before I heard of the Cucupira," says a man who has been in out-of-the-way parts of Brazil. "At Para you can enter the primeval forests in a three-minutes' walk from our hotel, and so it happens that one may lie in bed and hear the prowling denizens of the woods giving their nightly concert. I was told, even while there, that any particularly frightful cry was made by the cucupira.

"Just what the Cucupira was no one pretended to know. I was going up the river 600 miles to visit an old friend, and before going I read up about it.

"Prof. C.F. Hartt of Cornell, in 'The Mythology of Brazil,' wrote: 'One of the most important among the myths of the Indians of Brazil is called in the Tupi language the Cucupira. In all parts of the country one hears of this evil spirit of the woods, but no good and exact description of it exists.'

"C.B.F. De Souza, in Valle de Amazonas,' wrote in 1873: 'I believe it is certain that the Indians believe in the existence of a spirit or demon which appears in the woods and is called the Cucupira.'

"Mr. Bates, the naturalist, is quoted as saying: 'The Cucupira are both sexes and have children.'

"At the plantation of my friend, Capt. Manuel Valdez, I heard the same vague accounts of the creature. Almost every night at sunset, when the nightly concert begins, some one among his 30 employees would smilingly say, as he heard some particularly unearthly cry: 'That is a Cucupira.'

"To do justice to these people one must forget the impressions of tropical forests which he got from school geographies. Along the outskirts of the streams birds, butterflies and flowers are everywhere, and there is an incessant chatter and chirp of small birds. Go but a short distance and all is changed.

"One may walk for hours without seeing a living creature, and the silence is only broken by the harsh cries of macaws and parrots as they fly over or feed on the surface of the canopy of green, nearly 200 feet overhead. The forest is like a deserted cathedral and until sunset the silence is oppressive.

"But the moment the sun drops this silence is broken by sounds like the crash of a great orchestra. Even an educated man will feel that hidden all about him are creatures of which he can form no conception save by their frightful cries.

"In these solitudes, when the light is beginning to fall, and remembering the nightly pandemonium, it is not so hard to understand the origin and influence of the most absurd stories one has heard. For instance, a lost Indian hunter who had shot a large monkey lay down to rest and fell asleep. He was awakened by a strange creature, who proved to be a Cucupira.

"'What is the matter, brother?' the Cucupira asked, and sitting down beside him added: 'I am hungry, give me a piece of your heart to eat?"

"Secretly reaching behind him, the hunter gave him the monkey's heart.

"'That is good, now give your liver,' said the hungry demon.

"This was eaten also. Then the hunter said:

"'I, too, am hungry: give me your heart and liver."

"The Cucupira, seeing that the man was uninjured, and not wishing to be outdone, took the hunter's knife and slashed out his two organs and fell down dead.

"Another hunter found a curious skeleton at the foot of a hollow tree. From the skull he removed one of the teeth, which were green, for a souvenir."

MONSTER ANIMAL IN DEVILS LAKE.

Devils Lake Inter-Ocean – July 10, 1908 – North Dakota

People of the Chautauqua Have Been Thrown into Horrors.

There is truly some horrible monster animal inhabiting Devils Lake. It was seen Thursday evening just as the sun was going down and those enjoying the cool breezes from the lake that evening were thrown int a fit and ran wild in horror of the fearful beast as it shot half of its body out of the water and then sank out of sight.

So quickly had it risen and again gone down that those on the shore of the lake were unable to describe the fierceness and size of the animal. It was in the shape of a large fish only much larger and those who saw it estimate the size as the same as that of a good size shark, only it did not resemble a shark in the least, as its head was much larger and on each side of the head there were sort of sharp horns projecting several inches.

It was black from all appearances and as it shot out of the water it let a terrible sort of a scream which sent a chill over those witnessing the affair, and the noise was heard by several parties in various parts of the park. For the last week the inhabitants of the Chautauqua have heard these strange noises but were unable to locate just where they came from and it is probable that this wild animal of the sea has been the cause of the annoyance. It is strange, but every evening about 8:30 these strange noises have been heard coming from the same direction and the people have wondered what they were and this evening there is a large crowd going to the spot from which this animal was seen and try to get a glimpse of it.

A great many years ago the lake was inhabited by a great many strange animals and fishes and a number of the wild Indians fell prey to the deadly jaws of these monster creatures and it is safe to say that the one seen Thursday is one of the many that was in the lake a number of years ago. We are unable at this late hour to give an accurate description of the monster, but from what we can learn it was about twelve feet long and was of a black appearance, with a huge mouth and large horns on either side of its head. From the actions of the beast during its short stay out of the water those witnessing the sight claim that it is human, while others say that it was in the shape of a serpent.

BEAR MAN CAPTURED.

Devils Lake Inter-Ocean – July 24, 1908 – North Dakota

Two Young Farmers Have Terrible Experience Wednesday.

While driving home from the city Wednesday evening about ten-thirty, D. Haye and G. Grass, who reside about eleven miles south of the city had a terrible experience which threw a terrible scare into them and had it not been for the thoughtfulness of the two might perhaps cost them their lives.

When about five miles from the city and slowly driving along their horses were suddenly frightened by the appearance of a man in the road ahead of them. The two parties in the carriage drove steadily along not heeding the man in front, thinking perhaps he would vacate the road as the team and carriage approached.

When near the man the horses became more frightened and almost stopped in the road and the driver took the whip and attempted to urge them on, whereupon the man turned and grabbed hold of the bridles of the horses and attempted to bring them to a standstill. Seeing that he was out of the ordinary looking they urged their horses harder and with careful driving managed to urge them ahead of the party. After passing the man he gave chase for about a mile, but the driver hit up a merry clip with the team and outdistanced him and he made his way across the prairie.

After arriving home, they informed their folks about what had happened and they were advised to take firearms and drive back and if they were molested by this party to fire upon him. Taking the advice of their friends they drove back to the scene and on nearing the place saw this same man creeping stealthily along the ground until he neared the road and as they came opposite him he made a leap and grappled frantically for the reins of the horses, whereupon one of the occupants of the carriage leveled a shot gun upon him and discharged the full contents into his body and he fell backwards in a swoon. They alighted from the carriage and upon examination they saw that they had wounded if not killed a terrible looking creature human in appearance but wild from the way that he was dressed and as his terrible eyes glared upon them they felt that they had captured a terrible creature, not knowing to what danger they had put their lives in. He was perhaps seven feet tall and scarcely had anything to cover the nudeness of his body and from all appearance he had never been shaved and was a dweller of the wilds about the country.

As the body which was entirely covered with long black hair lay helplessly upon the ground they did not wish to go away and leave the being to die in agony so they loaded the body into the carriage and drove to the city. And it was a terrible drive. All the way to the city one of the parties had the struggle of his life holding the wild creature in the carriage and keeping him from strangling the two of them. He pawed frantically in the air and foamed at the mouth and several times the two occupants of the carriage were tempted to throw the man from the buggy and flee. They arrived in the city at an early hour in the morning and he was turned over to the authorities and placed in jail. He refused medical aid to the extent that he would not allow any one in the cell with him and although wounded from the discharge of the gun he fought terrible with the authorities upon being locked up. After being tightly secured in the cell he pranced up and down and pulled and twisted upon the iron bars and it was feared that he would release himself from captivity. He raved so terribly that it was necessary for several of those who were present to enter the cell and do something to quiet him and, in the morning, make an examination as to what he really was. They forced their way into the cell, and he was chloroformed and he dropped helplessly to the floor. Examination will be held today and arrangements will be made as to what will be done with the beast.

– Buenos Aires S.A. Lyre.

THRILLING TIME IN A DARK CAVE.

Times-Promoter – January 15, 1909 – Mississippi

MEMBERS OF EXPLORING PARTY ENCOUNTER STRANGE BEAST WHICH ATTACKS THEM.

LIKE PREHISTORIC MONSTER.

Emits Howl Like Enraged Bull – Eyeless Fish and Rivers with Opposite Currents Among Wonders at Mammoth Spring, Ark.

Little Rock, Ark. – A thrilling experience in a dark cave of unknown dimensions and origin, which is a natural curiosity in the vicinity of Mammoth Spring, Ark., is being told by a party of pleasure seekers.

Finding of eyeless fish and an encounter with a strange animal which roared like an enraged bull and which, according to the description of the men who saw it, resembled one of the prehistoric monsters, were among the incidents of the subterranean visit.

In the party which ventured to explore the mysteries of the cave were Mr. and Mrs. Albert Eshom of Medon, Ill.; H.E. Corey and wife of Ursa, Ill.; Mrs. C.W. Curtis of North Vernon, Ind., and John Ryan, a liveryman of Mammoth Spring.

"On entering the tunnel we walked through it for about six hundred feet and found that it continued of the same size as at the entrance and that it had several turnings, so that after the first 100 feet daylight was entirely shut out," said Mr. Eshom in telling of his experience. "Suddenly we came to an abrupt cul-de-sac of solid rock. The bottom was covered with soft mud two inches in depth. By the use of a bicycle lamp we discovered an opening in the rocky wall of the tunnel at the side and low down, about ten feet high and as much in depth. This orifice was filled with water as clear as crystal, coming to within four feet of the top of the hole.

"With Mr. Corey I decided to enter the second cavern. A raft was constructed from some two-inch planks which had been left near the entrance to the first tunnel by some former visitors, and on this raft we two, with camera, gun and the lamp, crouched and were pushed through the opening in the rocky wall, leaving the remainder of the party with a fire of sticks at the edge of the pool of water.

"Mr. Corey set up his camera to make a third flashlight picture, after which we intended to return to the outer cavern. He had scarcely fired the flash, when there was a tremendous splashing in the water ahead, followed by the roaring howl something like that of an enraged bull. In that confined space it was deafening. From the water there arose an animal which, by the light of the lamp in our hands, seemed to be of immense size. It was larger than a bull and had a long neck and the head of a horse without ears. It charged toward us. The jaws were armed with long teeth.

"I fired one barrel of my gun into the creature's face and as it hesitated, I gave it the contents of the other barrel. The animal continued its bellowing but thrashed around and headed for the opening in the wall. It had a sort of flipper on each side like those of a seal or the wings of a bat.

"While we were having our experience with the strange animals our wives had heard the shots and roars of the injured animal. One of them was prevented with difficulty form plunging into the water, while the other fainted.

"Whether the animal seen by us was one of the prehistoric monsters, some of which, it is asserted, were seen in the far north last summer, is a puzzle to us."

HIST! JOBBERWOCK HERE, SPITS FIRE!

Evening Journal – January 22, 1909 – Delaware

Creature Attacks Night Officer, who Says It Screams Like a Lion. Down State Citizens See "It"; Many Alarmed.

The uncanny creature known variously as the "air hoss," the "Leeds devil," "Jobbernosk" and the "Grosswauk" that has started all New Jersey and Pennsylvania has come into Delaware. Last night it was reported to have been seen in Brandywine Village, Elsmere, duPont's Banks, Holly Oak, Hillcrest and Claymont. It is believed the monster came from Philadelphia, where it has been scaring people for several nights.

It was first seen last night at Brandywine Village. Big Policeman Frank Kane was walking along Concord avenue at midnight when he saw something that looked like an open umbrella squeezed against a fence. His curiosity excited, the portly officer walked forward to examine it more closely when there was a peculiar screech of anger and the object sprang at him. There was but a brief struggle for Officer Kane is one of the strongest men on the force and the creature was being rapidly subdued. Just when it appeared that Kane had the creature under control, however, it gave a wrench, tore from his grasp and disappeared up West street. Mrs. Jane Maguire who lives in the street, says she saw the "devil" pass her door.

The policeman is now recovering from his chilly experience. He is unable to describe the animal accurately, owing to the darkness, but he declares it had blazing green eyes, screeched like a loon and had a pelt like a horse. The creature was as large as a calf he says.

Reports from the suburbs tell of the creature's visit to many places during the night. This morning there were numerous phone calls to THE EVENING JOURNAL announcing that the monstrous thing had been seen in many parts of Brandywine hundred. Mrs. Smith Jones, of Elsmere, was one of those who excitedly called up THE

JOURNAL. The "Thing" had left a single footmark in the snow in front of her front door. This confirms the reports from New Jersey that the creature has but one leg. The footprint is like that of a horse, Mrs. Jones says.

At Holly Oak and Hillcrest, it is reported that during the night the "devil" devoured several garbage cans. It also has a tooth for front doorsteps, chickens, dogs, ash barrels, tool chests and beer and coffee, according to many who have suffered by its ravages.

Dr. Mynhaur Beeskobe, Belgian scientist, who is visiting friends in the city, was interviewed by an EVENING JOURNAL reporter this morning concerning the freak. The doctor very kindly left a very large dinner of sauerkraut and wurst to talk to the reporter. It is his belief that the unknown creature is a relic of a very rare specimen of the Cos Ingeniorum and is closely related to the Copia Verborum, which although practically extinct, is found occasionally in his own country.

"If the papeer will but bring me zee animal I weel tell you more. It woel be veer, veer simple," he said.

THE EVENING JOURNAL has dispatched its office boy to Brandywine hundred in search of the beast. He is armed with a huge net and a squirt gun. The boy will appreciate the assistance of public-spirited citizens in his efforts to corral the bug.

Dr. Albert Robin gives no credence to a suggested theory that the mysterious animal-bird is a Brandywine water bacteria that has fled because of a fear of being corralled in the proposed new filter, nor does he think it one of the microbes he says were walking in an alley near Twelfth street recently.

LEFT TRACKS LIKE A PONY.

The creature must have paid a visit to the rear yard of the home of S.S. Harris, at No. 8 West Nineteenth street on Wednesday night. Its footprints were found in the yard yesterday morning. Mr. Harris and his son came to the conclusion that a Shetland pony had been in the yard. The prints in the snow were just like those which would be made by a horse.

The tracks of the animal lead from one end of the yard to the other and it must have crawled under the fence for there is no evidence of it having jumped over it. The tracks lead on beyond the fence, but the Harris' did not follow them.

PTERNADON! SO SAYS PROFESSOR BUGG.

Special to THE EVENING JOURNAL.

NEWARK, Jan. 22. – Professor Harry Hayward of the Agricultural Experimental Stations was away today and his views as to the Leeds Devil could not be obtained. Professor Hayward, it was stated, had gone to Pennsylvania, but officials at the experimental station denied that he was searching for the "Jobberwock."

Professor Bugg, an authority of this town, consented to talk of the strange bird-animal. "In my opinion it is a pternadon," he said. "You know the pternadon was a strange creature of the air that figured in mythology. Who knows but that this prehistoric creature has not become reality? I have grave fears for the safety of our citizens if this should be so, for the pternadon was a monster vampire, with feet of peculiar formation. No other animal or beast had such feet, and it always left a trail that could be traced readily, only to end in nothingness, for the pternadon could fly even more rapidly than it could traverse the earth. So speedy was its flight that the sound of the terrible whirr of its wings was followed in an instant by an attack, and with one blow of its sword-like beak and a ripping with its talons its victim was left lifeless, mangled, torn worse than by an bloodthirsty cannibal. I hardly credit, though, that the pternadon has become a reality, even in this day of startling things."

MAY USE AIR SHOVEL AS CANAL DIGGER.

Special to THE EVENING JOURNAL.

LEWES, Del., Jan. 22. – Congressman Hiram R. Burton is much interested in the stories of the peregrinations of the Leeds Devil about Philadelphia. He hopes the singular monster of air and land will develop the qualities of uprooting the earth, and if it does, he is in favor of raising many of the animals for use in digging out the Chesapeake and Delaware Canal.

MILFORD NOT SEEING THINGS.

MILFORD, Del., Jan. 22. – Colonel Theodore Townsend says no apparition like the Leeds Devil has been seen about Milford. "Folks down here don't see such things" said the Colonel. "You know Milford is now 'dry' and there is not the inspiration to see things." Colonel Townsend says he had heard of not movement to call out Company B of the militia to guard against a visitation of the air-devil.

FIGHTS BIG EAGLE TO SAVE BABY BOY.

The Spanish Fork Press – April 29, 1909 – Utah

ILLINOIS FARMER IN DESPERATE CONFLICT WITH MONSTER MONARCH OF THE AIR.

STRUGGLE LASTS TWO HOURS.
Giant Bird's Wings Are Broken and It Is Finally Overcome with Help of Neighbors – Measures Twelve Feet.

St. Charles, Ill. – Fighting desperately for two hours with a monster eagle to keep his baby from the menacing talons of the great bird, Peter Johnson, a farmer, with the aid of neighbors, finally captured the king of the air.

Fully a score of persons participated in the conflict with the eagle, and pitchforks, clubs and stones were brought into service before the bird, exhausted from his efforts, gave up the battle. Johnson was terribly scratched in the encounter, although his son was unhurt.

The Johnson boy, a sturdy child of three years, was playing on his father's farm near St. Charles the other morning when the eagle was first observed.

The great bird circled about the vicinity at a great height for several minutes. Suddenly, with the speed of a lightning flash, it darted down, and its steel-like talons caught in the child's dress.

The child's surprise for a second struck him dumb, and the eagle, using every ounce of its strength, bore the boy upward. Surprise gave way to alarm. The child screamed for aid and struggled vigorously to free himself from the eagle's clutches.

The boy is a stockily built lad, weighing about 35 pounds, and the bird was unable to make great progress.

The father heard the screams of his child and hurried from his home. He saw the boy in the bird's clutches and ran toward the scene of the struggle.

With all his strength he threw himself on the eagle and bore it to the ground. The child was saved and ran shrieking for assistance for his father. The man and the bird were locked in a death grip, the eagle using his claws, while Johnson struck out with his free hand as he held the bird with the other.

Neighbors were soon on the scene. From the start they were determined, if possible, to capture the eagle alive. Sticks and stones fell on his monster body, while both wings were immediately crippled.

The breaking of the wings made escape of the eagle impossible, but for two hours he fluttered along the ground fiercely repelling every attack until, completely exhausted, he was pinioned to the earth by two pitchforks.

The eagle when measured proved to be 12 feet from tip to tip of his wings and a perfect specimen of its kind. It is believed he will speedily recover from the injuries in its struggle with the men, and Johnson plans to present it to some zoological garden.

Although Johnson is suffering intense pain as a result of the scratches received in the fight, none of his hurts are regarded as dangerous, the worst wound being an immense gash torn in his left shoulder. He was greatly weakened from loss of blood.

The boy is none the worse for his experience and takes great delight in watching the imprisoned bird.

SEA SERPENT RACED SHIP.

Judith Gap Journal – June 25, 1909 – Montana

The Monster Gave Sailors the Greatest Scare of Their Lives.

From the Boston Herald:

Entered in the permanent log of the British steamship Mereddio, Captain Clark, is a record of a sea monster sighted while the ship was on a passage between Penarth and Santos. Chief Officer Neil S. Murray was in charge of the bridge at the time and a Greek quartermaster was at the wheel. The quartermaster, who first sighted the monster, was almost petrified with fear and was at the point of permitting the big freighter to take her own course.

"It was like this," explained the chief officer, when Mereddio docked at East Boston. "The ship was 500 miles from Santos. I saw the Greek acting strangely and followed the direction he was looking.

"My hair nearly stood on end at the sight. Swimming parallel to the ship was a monster lizard. It was big as a whale. The ocean fairly seethed as it propelled itself with enormous dragon's claws. A head as big as pilot house and one coil of the beast's neck were above water.

"For a distance of nearly 300 feet the sea heaved and was lashed into foam. I think the lizard was fully the Mereddio's length, and I feared for the safety of the steamship as the creature, mailed in huge, bony scales of a dark green color, swerved as if to come alongside. It had a saw-like ridge on its back and its girth was fully as great as that of a whale.

"After the serpent had raced the ship several minutes it humped its back and sounded. The swash from its commotion shook the ship and sent the spray over the starboard rail.

"I have followed the sea many years and, mind you, I am not given to fancies. That creature so impressed me that I entered the incident in the scrap log, and later made a permanent record of it."

The Mereddio's crew substantiates Officer Murray, while the Greek quartermaster admits he did not recover from the shock for several days.

QUEER CREATURE CAUSES ALARM.

The Bisbee Daily Review – August 3, 1909 – Arizona

Devil Horse Roams Abut Frightening People in Vicinity of Philadelphia.

Search Made by Armed Men.
Hunt for Strange Animal That Makes Odd Footprints and Runs Through Deep Snow on Only Two Legs.

Philadelphia – Clearly defined in the crust of the snow, the footprints of a two-legged beast or bird, shoed with steel, are creating a tremendous sensation in this city and the South Jersey towns. People who read this narrative may form their own opinions as to the cause of these manifestations.

It was originally intended to treat this subject with a light and scoffing touch; to make merry over the mystery of the "Leed's Devil" that has transformed scores of towns and hamlets of Camden, Gloucester and Burlington counties, into settlements of timid folk, where women and children fear to walk abroad at night, and armed men make nocturnal searches.

Before noon, however, the telephone wires were hot with messages from persons who had seen the hoofprints. Two men declared they had seen the marks in their own yards in this city. They were William L. Smith and William Heimbold, and their neighbors know them for sober truthful men.

Of course, practical people scoff at these reports, but none has yet offered an explanation that will meet the situation. Then comes Nelson Evans, a paper hanger of Gloucester City, with the declaration that he and his wife saw the "devil" early in the morning as he sat on the roof of their back shed.

White-faced and trembling, Evans entered police headquarters there the other morning and leaned up against the wall.

"I saw it," he whispered, round-eyed with recollection.

"You did!" exclaimed the chief. "What did it look like?"

"About two o'clock," said the paper hanger, "my wife and I were aroused by a noise on our shed roof. I went to the window and looked out and then I called her. We saw the strangest beast or bird, I don't know which, you ever heard of.

It was about three and a half feet high, with a head like a collie dog and a face like a horse. It had a long neck, wings about two feet long, and its back legs were like those of a crane, and it had horse's hoofs. It walked on its back legs and held up two short front legs with paws on them.

As far as I could tell, the thing seemed to be trying to get into the shed. My wife and I were scared, I tell you, but I managed to open the window and say 'Shoo!' and it turned around, barked at me, and then flew away."

The tracks were first seen after the heavy snowfall, but at first nothing was said about them, as they were believed to be the work of some practical joker. Then it was noticed that the mysterious creature left hoof prints in farm yards and on roofs of buildings as well.

Marks of the beast were found in Gloucester, Mount Holly, Clayton, Woodbury, Wenonah, Mantua, Paulsboro, Lumberton, Ayerstown, Vincetown, Almonessen, Mount Ephraim, and other towns within a radius of twenty miles or more. This nearly upset the theory that it was the work of a joker and the oldest inhabitant got busy.

He remembered that as far back as 1869 that part of South Jersey was visited by a creature that was known as "Leed's Devil," because it was supposed to emerge from Leed's point, on Brigantine beach. The "devil" reappeared in 1874 and 1879 and even as recently as 1904.

Early in the morning there came a report that the monstrosity had crossed the river and was disporting himself in the yards of residents of Sansom street, above Forty-fifth street.

A young man who gave his name as Harry L. Smith, said that in the yard of his home there were marks like the footprints of a two-legged horse.

DEAD 'JERSEY DEVIL' FOUND IN WOODS.

The Citizen – November 10, 1909 – Pennsylvania

Body of Strange Animal Explains Puzzling Hoofprints Left in the Snow.

SENT TO THE STATE MUSEUM.
The Spinal Column Extends Six Inches Behind Junction with Hind Legs, Somewhat After the Manner of the Tail of a Kangaroo.

Burlington, N.J. – If anybody ever doubted that a "Jersey Devil" left its strange and puzzling hoofprints in the snow of this and adjoining States last winter, proof was produced here that the scare was never due to highballs. There is on exhibit in this city the carcass of the queerest animal ever seen about here, a beast not on the schedule of any natural history ever read by any one of this section.

The animal's body, still in good condition, as though it had been dead only a short while, was found by Morris Cabinsky of this city, and Charles Malsbury of Kinkora, in the woods near Kinkora, and was brought to this city, where hundreds have seen and marveled. Photographs have been made of the beast and Prof. Henry Morse, curator of the State Museum, will be asked to give the animal a name and place it where it belongs – if he is able to do so.

The boys thought at first they had come upon the carcass of a big wildcat, but it looked so queer to them that they decided to carry it into town.

The body of the animal is about twenty inches long and thin. The spinal column extends six inches behind the junction with the hind legs like the tail of a kangaroo, but this again is tipped with nine inches of tail like a squirrel's, but of reddish-brown fur. The strangest feature of all and that which would seem to convict it of last winter's famous hoofprints, is found in the fore legs and feet. The legs are fifteen inches long, consisting of four joins and socketed to these are feet, which take the form of a broad, flat bone with a distinct heel. The foot bones are two and a half inches long and over and inch broad in a solid piece.

If the animal traveled by leaps bending the two fore feet down together, he would land after each long spring with the feet forming the puzzling effect of the hoofprints in the snow last winter. The rear feet would explain the finding of "cat" prints near the hoof marks. What looks like the framework of a pair of short wings rises from the animal's back, just above its short hind legs.

The big mouth is set with sharp teeth three quarters of an inch long, while the head is adorned with long, lance-like ears and whiskers four inches long.

STORIES FROM THE:
1910's

WHAT WOULD ST. GEORGE DO?
The Pacific Commercial Advertiser – April 7, 1910 – Hawaii

African Hunter Face to Face with Monster Unknown to This Day Scientists.

The latest terror to be added to those which travelers describe as haunting the African jungle is the dragon. It may come as a shock to find that the awful apparition conjured up in our childhood by fairy tales and myths is a living reality of the present day but no less an authority than Edgar Beecher Bronson tells about the creature in his new book "In Closed Territory." Its appearance on the Maggori River was vividly described to him by John Alfred Jordan, an English hunter who has made his home in the wilderness. The story, however, does not rest on one narrator's word alone as Mr. Bronson gives strong corroborative testimony as to its truth.

"We were on the march," the English hunter narrated, "approaching the Maggori, and I had stayed back with the porters and sheep and had sent the Lumbwa ahead to look for a drift we could cross – river was up and booming and chances poor. Presently I heard the bush smashing and up raced by Lumbwa, wide-eyed and grey as their black skins could get, with the yarn that they had seen a frightful strange beast on the river bank, which at sight of them had plunged into the water – as they described it, some sort of cross between a sea-serpent, a leopard, and a whale. Thinking they had gone crazy or were pulling my leg, I told them I'd believe them if they could show me but not before. After a long shauri (palaver) among themselves they finally ventured, returning in half an hour to say that it lay full length exposed on the water in midstream.

"Down to the Maggori I hurried and there their 'bounder' lay, right-ho!"

"Holy saints but he was a sight – fourteen or fifteen feet long, head as big as that of a lioness but shaped or marked like a leopard, two long white fangs sticking down straight out of his upper jaw, back broad as a hippo, scaled like an armadillo, but colored and marked like a leopard, and a broad fin tail, with slow, lazy swishes of which he was easily holding himself level in the swift current, headed up stream.

"Gad, but he was a hideous old haunter of a nightmare, was that beast-fish, that made you want an aeroplane to feel safe of him; for while he lay up stream of me, I had been brought back to the river bank precisely where he had taken water, and there all about me in the soft mud and loam were imprints of feed wide of a diameter as a hippo's but clawed like a reptile's, feet you knew could carry him ashore and claws you could be bally well, sure no man could ever get loose from, once they had nipped him.

"Blast that blighter's fangs, but they looked long enough to go clean through a man.

"He had not seen or heard me, and how long I stood and watched him I don't know. Anyway, when I began to fear he would shift or turn and see me, I gave him a .303 hard nose behind leopard ear — and then hell split for fair!

"Straight out of the water he sprang, straight as if standing on his blooming tail – must have jumped off it, I fancy...

"His legs? What were they like? Blest if I know! The same second that he stood up on his tail, I got too busy with my own legs to study his.

"Gory wonder was that fellow; a .303 where placed, should have killed anything for he was less than ten yards from me when I shot, but though we watched waters and shores over a range of several miles for two days, no sight did we get of him or his tracks."

HUNTING A LIVE PREHISTORIC MONSTER.

Charlevoix County Herald – October 8, 1910 – Michigan

One of the most remarkable scientific discoveries ever made has just been reported by an expedition of British scientists.

In the wilds of New Guinea, the great unexplored island just north of Australia, these scientists have run across a marvelous race of pigmies whose average height is about four feet three inches, and a monster mammal, considerably larger than an elephant, which they have named the gazeka, and which has seemingly wrought great havoc amongst the pigmies.

Just what species the gazeka belongs to has not yet been determined, but in the description given by the explorers, Dr. W.D. Matthew of Natural History, sees a strong resemblance to a prehistoric monster known as the diprodont, fossil remains of which have been found at different times throughout Australia.

The expedition was sent out by a committee appointed by the British Ornithologist's union to explore the great Snow mountains in Dutch New Guinea, and consists of several famous scientists, headed by Walter Goodfellow, the naturalist.

The expedition landed at the mouth of the Mimika river, on the south coast of Dutch New Guinea, in the early part of the year, and at once pushed into the interior. While ascending the Snow mountains, at an elevation of about 2,000 feet, the explorers came upon the tribe of pigmies, which are said to belong to that division of the human race known as Negritos.

The importance of this discovery to anthropologists can hardly be overestimated, because it has always been a subject of controversy among the scientists as to whether Negritos existed in the Papuan islands.

The New Guinea savages, or Papuans, as they are called, are comparatively well known, but they are a very different kind of men to the pigmies just discovered. The typical Papuan is much taller than the average European, often attaining a height of seven feet, and is strongly built. The color of the skin varies from deep chocolate to nearly black. The nose is large and prominent, and a nose bar of shell, bone or wood is usually thrust through it. Both men and women go about entirely naked. Their houses are generally built on piles, and, as in Borneo, are often communal and of a very large size, many families occupying one building, which may be as much as 700 feet long. Then there are the remarkable houses built in trees and known as "dobbos," but these are used only to escape their enemies. Cannibalism prevails among the Papuans, although it is by no means universal.

The Negritos, on the other hand, which heretofore have been thought to occupy only the Andaman islands, in the Bay of Bengal, the northern portion of the Malay peninsula and the Philippine islands, are characteristically short, no adult standing over four feet six inches, while the women rarely exceed four feet. The average height is about four feet three inches.

The main features of this peculiar human type, apart from the diminutiveness, are the extraordinarily dark color of their skin, which approaches the color of a newly blackleaded stove, the extremely broad nose, the breadth of which is about equal to the height, and the frizzy hair, which grows in isolated peppercorn tufts all over the scalp. Their arms are unusually long, like those of the man-ape, and their mental qualities are sadly undeveloped, not one of them being able to express a higher numerical idea than three.

How these little people have been able to protect themselves against the many dangerous animals that infest the section, particularly the gigantic gazeka, which has just been discovered, is still a mystery, although they have shown remarkable ingenuity in the invention of weapons. One, for instance, is a variety of "spring gun" which might prove effective against almost any living enemy. It is made by setting a flattened bamboo spear attached to a bent sapling which is fastened to a trigger in such a way that it is released by the passerby stumbling against an invisible string stretched across the track. The spears are poisoned, either with the famous "upas" or some other similar vegetable poison, and a wound form one of them means almost instant death.

Whether such primitive defensive methods avail them against the huge gazeka is not known, but the chances are that they find safety in retreat.

According to the official reports, the gazeka is of gigantic size and fearsome aspect. It is black and white striped, has the nose of a tapir and "a face like the devil." Among the English inhabitants of the island, the animal is known as Monckton's gazeka, in honor of Mr. C.A.W. Monckton, a former explorer in New Guinea, who first reported its presence in the mountains.

Mr. Monckton, during his ascent of Mount Albert Edward, in the west of British New Guinea, discovered the huge footprints and other indications of the very recent presence of some tremendous monster that had evidently been prowling on the grassy plains surrounding the lakes on the summit at an elevation of about 12,500 feet. He followed the trail all day, and came upon the monster at dusk, just as it was devastating a settlement of pigmies. The little natives were screaming and running for their lives, although they turned every now and again to aim their poisoned arrows at the brute.

Monckton let fire as soon as he was able to get in a proper position, and the huge gazeka at once turned upon him. As it reared upon its hind legs and pawed the air it looked to the hunter as big as a house, standing fully 25 feet high. Two of Monckton's bullets seemed to take effect, as a stream of blood flowed freely from the animal's shoulder, but before Monckton was able to reload the animal turned and fled. By that time, it was too dark to follow him, and Monckton never had another opportunity to renew his pursuit.

None of the inhabitants was brave enough to repeat Monckton's attempt to capture the brute, and until the British expedition reached New Guinea he has prowled around with impunity, occasionally descending upon the rudimentary huts of the pigmies and destroying those who failed to fly in time.

The British explorers were aware of Monckton's experience, and in fact, it is believed that one of the principal objects of the expedition was to secure a specimen of the strange monster. It has long been known that there were many mammals in New Guinea still to be discovered, but just what they expected to find the scientists themselves could not tell.

New Guinea lies to the east of what is known as Wallace's line, an imaginary line defined by A.R. Wallace, on one side of which only placenta animals are found, while on the other only marsupials exist. No tapirs or rhinoceroses exist to the east of Wallace's line, which includes Australia and New Guinea, but about the period when the mastodon and the mammoth flourished in America a huge marsupial known as the diprodont is known to have existed in Australia. Fossil remains recently discovered leave no doubt as to its gigantic size, and, although there is, of course, no means of ascertaining its appearance in life, as it has been extinct for several thousands of years, the gazeka appears to bear a marked resemblance in form to this ancient monster.

That a few diprodonts could have survived to this day despite the extinction of the main part of the type, is not considered unlikely by the scientists, who point out that nature does not usually blot out a whole class of animals suddenly, but that, on the contrary, it is sometimes thousands of years before the last individual member of the type succumbs to the conditions which destroyed his fellows.

The British explorers are enduing many hardships in their scientific expedition. In New Guinea the temperature is never less than 114 degrees in the shade, and water is not always accessible. But if these ardent explorers really capture a living diprodont they will consider their labors well rewarded.

MAMMOTH SNAKE CAPTURED ALIVE.

The Chickasha Daily Express – January 10, 1911 – Oklahoma

HUGE MONTANA MONSTER MEASURES OVER EIGHTEEN FEET IN LENGTH.

TERRORIZES A WHOLE TOWN.
For Years the Village of Laurel, in Little Pryor Mountains Has Suffered from the Depredations of This Reptile.

Butte, Mont. – The story of an extraordinary battle between two sheepmen and a mammoth snake, coming from Laurel, a removed section of Montana, in the Little Pryor mountains, has caused great excitement among naturalists and others. The huge reptile, declared to be larger than any ever heard of before located in this region and of a species as yet unidentified, was taken alive after a thrilling hunt in a wild mountain ravine whither L.N. O'Dell and J.W. Vaught had been guided by a number of terror-stricken Indians whose superstitious fright sent them fleeing from the neighborhood long before the actual capture of the snake was accomplished. The reptile is 18 feet in length and weighs 200 pounds. Around the body it measures more than eighteen inches.

At different times in recent years, O'Dell had heard from the Indians of the strange monster that made its home in a wild canyon a few miles from Laurel, but until three braves returned terror-stricken recently from the vicinity, he took it for granted that the story had its birth in the superstitious imagination of the redskins. He then became impressed with the remarkable tale and, after enlisting the aid of Vaught, started forth with a party of Indians as guides.

At the entrance to the canyon the swarthy guides deserted precipitately and the two men ventured into the narrow ravine, where a large hole entering near the top of a ledge covered with slippery shale rock and innumerable trails leading in all directions from its mouth gave unmistakable evidence that the opening was a lair. Cutting a square hole several feet back from the entrance to this wild abode, they discovered the coils of a monster even larger than they had been led to expect.

Stirred to wrath by the disturbance, the snake began to make a great noise and the few remaining redskins, who had retired thirty or forty rods, scampered off on their fleet-footed ponies at a gallop. As the monster started to leave the entrance, O'Dell threw a gunny sack over its head and clasped his arms around its throat. Then once of the weirdest struggles ever recorded in Montana history was on. Back and forth over the narrow ledge the huge snake writhed and twisted, finally tightening itself about O'Dell's hips until he was lifted from the ground.

Vaught seized the snake by the tail and forced it to release its hold upon O'Dell. The strange contest continued upon the yielding floor of the little ravine for almost three-quarters of an hour before the two men succeeded in tiring the snake, when they bundled it into a sack and took it alive, struggling, to Laurel, as living proof of their strange story.

The reptile is marked with large, dark mahogany spots, outlined with lighter color, and extending across its back. Its method of killing prey is apparently by constriction, but the spots are not the shape and color of a boa, nor is it an anaconda, as its body is much too large.

O'Dell, who has had a vast experience with snakes of all varieties, does not believe the snake is a native of Montana, but thinks it has drifted here from the Sierra Nevada mountains. The Indians claim the snake has been seen in the Little Pryor mountains for more than twenty years and have associated its doings with the actions of the "evil one." O'Dell does not believe another snake of its size could be found in the state and will present the huge reptile to the Society for the Preservation of Natural History of Montana.

ANOTHER MONSTER.
The Times and Democrat – June 13, 1911 – South Carolina

TALES ABOUT SERPENTS THAT SWIM THE SALT SEAS.

Steward of the Celtic Tells of the Strange Thing He Saw Skipping Over the Deck.

The White Star Liner Celtic, from Liverpool to New York, lately passed the very latest sea serpents. This fact, it should be stated, is not entered in the log. It was confided to the ultramarine reports by a steward, who was perfectly willing to furnish a description. Robert Hillard, the actor, was willing under duress to provide corroboration.

This sea serpent – witnesses differ as to its length – was sighted holding a whiskered, calflike head 10 feet above water. Behind, where the ear ought to have been, were two wings extending outward about ten feet, thus giving the saurian monster the appearance of an aeroplane skimming over the sea. The steward, in fact, described it as a monoplane sea serpent.

Anyway, it was seen off the Celtic's starboard bow in the early morning, and the early rising steward, who spotted it, instead of carrying the news forward to the bridge, ran to the rooms under his care and begged those within to come on deck and see it. He says he caught Mr. Hillard, who does not deny it, but begs that it be not printed, because he dislikes notoriety.

The serpent, according to both, was either pursuing a school of whales or keeping company with the school to keep from being lonesome. This last theory is the stewards who said moreover, that it turned a pair of large mournful green eyes upon those on the vessel's deck in a way to "touch your heart, sir." Then it passed on its monoplanic way, dipping up and down, just like that, but otherwise holding its head erect. Behind it appeared at intervals a dark green body moving through the water with a wiggly motion.

The report of the steward, with its accompanying corroboration by Mr. Hillard, moved the veteran, Samuel A. Wood, dean of the ultramarines to some enthusiasm. Sea serpent stories, said Mr. Wood, are rare at this port nowadays, but in the old days the men on sailing vessels saw many of them.

"Forty years ago," began Mr. Wood, "I wrote many of those stories but as steam has replaced sail and romance departed from the seas, the sea serpents have evidently moved away from the steamship tracks.

"It is now, I think, ten years ago since the Great Tabasco serpent was reported in the Bay of Campeche by the truthful mate of a schooner. This one was dark brown and made a noise like a Gatling gun. It is about the same length of time ago since the captain of the steamship American coming from Antwerp, reported one fifty feet long that swam like an eel. It had green whiskers.

"A strange looking monster ten fathoms long was reported by the skipper of the blue nose bark Howard D. Copp. The most authentic sea serpent sighting was made by the French liner Lorraine about three years ago. Her skipper gave the latitude and longitude where the monster was sighted, and the pursuer wrote a description of it for the French newspapers. This one was a drab color, and appeared to be accompanied by a water spout. As the vessel approached the spout was seen to be a mass of water thrown up by the serpent's fore fins.

Mr. Wood recalled that this last serpent was seen early in the morning. Searching his memory still further he remarked that from his experience, sea serpents had usually made their appearance early in the morning; in fact, usually the morning after, in which respect they had something in common with the pink elephant.

NICE HAS A DRAGON.

The Sea Coast Echo – July 13, 1912 – Mississippi

Strange Sea Monster Causes Panic in Italian City.

Residents of La Turbie Are Badly Frightened and No One Dares to Venture on Highways Without an Armed Escort.

Nice. – They say it is about two metres long and at least thirty-five centimeters broad, with enormous jaws well furnished with dentistry, but what kind of an animal it is no one knows. For the past several days the residents of La Turbie have been living in deadly terror of it. A search was organized, but as of yet only two persons have met the "thing" face to face.

About 11 o'clock in the morning recently a boy was passing through the quarter known as "Les Routes," carrying dejeuner to his father, who is employed in a quarry. Suddenly an animal, stranger than any he had ever seen, appeared in his path.

The boy ran, but so did the animal. Just as he was about to be caught the boy climbed on to a block of stone. The animal managed to get on its hind feet and was about to grasp the boy in its terrible jaws when the automobile which runs between La Turbie station and the Mont-Agel golf course approached.

Frightened at the noise, the "wild beast" took fright and fled. The boy shows marks on his breast which he says were made by the animal when it was reaching for him. He also declares the animal was covered with huge scales.

A posse was organized immediately and started in pursuit, but not even a trace of the animal was seen. Yesterday a laborer at the quarry says he found the strange thing stretched across the Mont-Agel road. The man was on his way to work, and upon seeing the animal he ran all the way back to the village. He swore he would never go to the quarry again.

La Turbie residents who do not believe in material manifestations of the supernatural say that the animal is a crocodile which has perhaps escaped from a menagerie. And why not, they declare, "Marseilles had its tiger!"

AN IMMENSE WILD MAN KILLED IN THE HILLS.

Albuquerque Evening Herald – February 3, 1913 – New Mexico

Hideous Monster Is Reported Slain Near Navajo Mine; News Brought to Gallup by Albuquerque Man.

Gallup, N.M., Feb. 3. – A vicious, grotesque, and hideous looking wild man was killed in the hills back of Navajo mine last Saturday morning by a young Indian boy. The object, beast or man which ever it may be termed had been menacing the natives in their daily work for the past five months. The man was entirely without clothing, his entire body being covered with a coat of thick, coarse dark hair four inches long. The only part of him which was normally human was his feet, which would perhaps have required a No. 10 or 11 shoe. The face was chinless and only one lip was visible; the forehead sloped directly backward of the head, something after the fashion of the Pin Headed Cannibal. Small beadlike pink eyes were concealed, set deep in the sockets behind long and grimy eyelashes. The arms of the man were four feet long, and long sharp cat-claws adorned the finger tips. The man measured full seven feet in height.

For five months the natives had been telling of this menacing object which had been seen by hundreds, prowling about the rocks both day and night, and it would always make a rapid escape over the rocks and disappear in a certain canyon, traveling with great speed. A young Indian boy was traveling across the country with a Winchester, and evidently must have cut the monster off from his retreat. He came straight towards the boy who raised his rifle and fired twelve shots at his body, eight of which took effect, but only one of them did any serious damage. The body was taken into camp at Navajo and the company physician prepared a glass coffin in which the body will be preserved in alcohol.

The Gallup Independent after telling this tale explains it as follows:

D.T. Brown, an itinerant photographer from Albuquerque brought the story back from a trip to the mines Sunday. What had the man been drinking, or what ailed him we are unable to say.

BIG SEA MONSTER WITH FOUR LEGS.
The Detroit Times – August 23, 1913 – Michigan

Dog-Sized Head, Finless, Fur-coated and a Good Bounder.

NEW YORK, Aug. 22. – No one is asked to believe this yarn. The author of it himself says so, for it is about a new and altogether astonishing sea monster seen on the west coast of Tasmania – a four-legged thing with a dog-sized head, a well-groomed fur coat and a lively bounding habit of traveling. It disappeared in the sea. But to begin –

The story is told by Mr. Hartwell Conder, the Tasmanian state mining engineer, and printed in Australian papers just received in this country. Mr. Conder, who is engaged in official prospecting in the little know country between Macquarie harbor and Port Davey, was so impressed by the thing, as vividly described to him by two of his companions, that he hurried the news along to headquarters over the telegraph wires. The monster he confesses at the very start, was so strange that "the men who saw it and I myself anticipate quite cheerfully the smiles and incredulity of those who read this account." He adds, philosophically, "No one is asked to believe it."

"The animal," he proceeds to relate, "was seen by Oscar Davies, foreman prospector, and his mate, W. Harris, who are working under myself. I have known both of them for a considerable number of years, and can guarantee absolutely their sobriety, intelligence and accuracy. They were walking along the coast April 20, just before sundown on a calm day, with small waves rolling in and breaking on the shore, when at a distance of about half a mile they noticed a dark object under the dunes which surprised them by showing signs of movement.

"They advanced toward it, and finally came within gunshot. When about 40 yards off it rose suddenly and rushed down into the sea. After getting out about 30 yards it stopped and turned around, showing only the head about five seconds, and then withdrew under the water and disappeared.

"The characteristics are summarized as follows:

It was 15 feet long.

It had a very small head, only about the size of the head of a kangaroo dog.

It had a thick, arched neck, passing gradually into the barrel of the body.

It had no definite tail and no fins.

It was furred, the coat in appearance resembling that of a horse of chestnut color, well groomed and shining.

It had four distinct legs.

It traveled by bounding – i.e., by arching its back and gathering up its body, so that the footprints of those fore feet were level and also those of the hind feet.

It made definite footprints. These showed circular impressions, with a diameter (measured) of nine inches.

"There was no evidence for or against webbing.... The creature traveled very fast. A kangaroo dog followed it hard in its course to the water, a distance of about 70 yards, and in that distance gained about 30 feet. When first disturbed it reared up and turned on its hind legs. Its height, standing on the four legs, would be from three feet six inches to four feet.

"Both men are quite familiar with seals and so-called sea leopards that occur on this coast. They had also seen before and subsequently pictures of sea lions and other marine animals and can find no resemblance to the animal they saw.

"Such are the details," concludes Mr. Conder. "When the humorists have enjoyed themselves at our expense the men of science may be able to connect this account with others which have come forward from time to time of strange beasts in our oceans. That no imprint was taken of the footprints and no marking out made of the form in the sand no one regrets more than we do. The next tide swept over them, and they were gone."

MAKES DRAWING OF A MARINE MONSTER.

Fort Mill Times – November 6, 1913 – South Carolina

Second Officer of the Steamship Corinthian Describes Fifty-Foot Sea Serpent.

IT CRIED LIKE A BABY.

Declares He Located Creature Off the Grand Banks, Near Where Titanic Sank – Had Bonny Blue Eyes and Neck Twenty Feet Long.

London. – Surely it would have been a mistake for the "silly" season to pass without its sea serpent. Down at the Surrey Docks is a man who has not only seen a fearful and wonderful marine monster but has even sketched it from life.

It is not exactly the sea serpent of hoary tradition, but a sort of sea giraffe – an extraordinary looking amphibious animal which is puzzling the zoologists who have heard of it and seen the drawing.

Some idea of this weird freak may be gathered from this first hand description of it: "Has bonny blue eyes; cries like a baby; neck twenty feet long; body fifty feet; big head with long ears and snout; three horned fins adorn its bony head; two big flapping fins; skin like a seal; brownish yellow in color, with pretty dark spots."

A plain, commonsense seaman, who tells his story bluntly, without any frills or trimmings, Second Officer G. Bachelor of the steamship Corinthian, describing his strange adventure with the sea giraffe, said:

"We were bound from London to Montreal, and it was my turn on watch on the bridge in the early morning of August 30. It was cold and the gray dawn was just breaking, when, as I was keeping my eye straight ahead on our course, I picked up a queer-looking object about a mile ahead. It disappeared, and as quickly it shot up again no more than 200 feet away from the ship.

"I distinctly saw it rise out of the water. First, there was a big head, with long ears and long snout, and bulging blue eyes that were mild and liquid. Then there was a neck – no end of a neck – and it swayed with the wash of the waves. What it was I couldn't guess, for in twenty years of sea-going, including trips in tropical waters, I've never seen anything like this sea giraffe that was staring right at the Corinthian.

"As this thing seemed to eye me it lashed the water with its big front fins. Then it suddenly dived and disappeared, at the same time giving an odd little wail like a baby's cry. You wouldn't think such a huge animal could have such a small voice.

"As soon as I went off duty I went below and made a sketch of the monster in India ink. When the Corinthian reached Montreal, my sketch was shown to Prof. F.E. Lloyd of McGill university, an expert in zoology. The professor said that whatever it was, it wasn't a serpent, but a sea mammal. It was certainly built on high speed lines, and its finlike protuberance was well adopted for running things up.

"I located this sea giraffe in latitude 47 degrees and 51 minutes north and longitude 48 degrees 32 minutes west, off the Grand Banks, and not many miles distant from the spot where the Titanic went down. I am inclined to think myself that the wreck of the Titanic has something to do with the presence of this strange creature in water where nothing of the kind has ever been noticed before. Is it making food of the dead bodies below?"

Mr. Bachelor made the gruesome suggestion in all seriousness. He was evidently impressed with the absolute accuracy of his observations.

Mr. Bachelor, it may be added, is a canny Scot, and his view is that there may still be more survivors of an almost extinct race of sea beasts. Anyway, zoologists are not unacquainted with an "amphibious or aquatic reptile" called sauraptergia, which curiously resembles the description of what Mr. Bachelor saw.

WINGED MONSTER TERRIFIES WELSH.

New-York Tribune – April 19, 1914 – New York

Weird Bird Snatches Up Lambs, Poultry, and Even Pups, According to Villagers.

[From the Tribune Correspondent.]

London, April 11. – Wales, like Ireland, is the home of traditions and superstitions, and the weirdest sort of creatures constantly appear and disappear in its mountain fastness. The latest story comes from West Denbighshire, where "a huge bird of prey, supposed to be an eagle," seems to possess a particular liking for the poultry and smaller livestock.

This, however, is not all the "eagle" has done by any means. Its habits of devouring lambs and attempting to kidnap more diminutive members of the canine world are bad enough, but the practice of frightening pedestrians who plod the lonely way late at night is especially to be condemned. There is reported, for instance, the nerve trying case of a Llanrwst resident who was walking along a deserted street after midnight.

He noticed a large bird of a gray color standing, ghostlike, in the roadway. The pale rays of the moonlight in which it stood blinking forbiddingly added to its sinister appearance. The man gave chase and the bird, "screaming fiercely," to quote the intrepid pursuer's words, ran swiftly down the street. The strenuous race continued along several streets, and when the bird found the man was slowly gaining upon him it extended its wings and flew toward the mountains.

This midnight adventure is only a sample of what the bird can do. At the farmsteads and countryside hamlets awestruck folk tell you that recently the winged terror darted from the blue and gobbled up a whole brood of chickens from a farm in Gwytherm; and after tickling its hunger with this dainty meal it flew off with the mother hen. The loss of a number of lambs is also attributed to its greed and temerity.

Even these plunderings do not satisfy it. The latest sensational act was at Trefriw. A Mr. Howell, of the Geirronydd Hotel, was sitting in the hotel grounds when this thief from the skies swooped down and snatched up a pup which was resting within a few yards of Mr. Howell. He immediately threw his stick at the abductor as the litter was on its way heavenward, and so startled it that its hold on the pup relaxed and the animal fell to the ground badly wounded.

CLEAR LAKE MYSTERY.

Evening Times-Republican – June 29, 1914 – Iowa

STRANGE INHABITANT OF SHORE WATERS STEALING FOOD NIGHTLY.

CAN'T EXPLAIN PRESENCE OF HUMAN APPEARING FISH.

Appears from Waters of Lake and Steals Food from Wharves – May Be Demented Man Who Prefers to Hide and Swim in Lake – Night Vigil of Resorters Fails to Solve Mystery.

Clear Lake, June 29. – What has been termed by the summer colony as the "Human Fish" has been discovered on the north shore of Clear lake and is causing more excitement than has prevailed at this summer resort for a number of years. The discovery of the strange phenomenon was brought about by cottagers who had food taken off their piers which run into the lake and the statement of a number who declare they have seen the strange creature. Several parties have gone out in an effort to catch the mysterious visitor, but each effort has been, up to date, without result.

A few nights ago, a party of guests at the Oaks Hotel went down to the lake beach and started in an all-night vigil in an effort to capture it. Just at midnight when the lights went out about the pier, a ripple in the water was seen and a human arm was extended out of the water. It grabbed some food which had been placed on the end of the pier and was again withdrawn into the water. The watchers rushed to the pier end, but they saw nothing. However, a dark spot a ways out in the lake near 100 yards away was seen hurrying thru the water and a weird laugh was heard rippling over the water.

Some fishermen who were out in a boat last Thursday claim to have seen what they took to be a man swimming with fish-like speed thru the water. They gave chase in their boat but as they neared the man or animal, it dove, and a similar laughter was heard from the rushes which were about fifty yards away.

Sea Monster or Man?

It is believed that the strange inhabitant of the lake, is either a sea monster which has by some method found a home in the lake or else it is a demented man whose love for swimming has caused him to spend most of his time in the water, getting his food from the piers and cottages and sleeping like Moses of old, in the bull rushes along the lake's shore. The proximity of the county home between Clear Lake and Mason City where a number of unfortunates are housed, let to an investigation and it was found that there are none of the inmates missing. Instead of solving the mystery the solutions seemed farther away.

Hunting the human fish has become a pastime with the colonists. The description given by those who claimed to have seen it describe it as a small sized man about 50 years of age and whose body seems to be covered with scales like a fish, caused perhaps by the roughening of his skin by constant staying in the water. Others claim it is impossible for the creature to be a man because of the long time it stays under water. However, every effort is being made to solve the mystery and motor launch loads of people can be seen daily skirting the lake looking for the strange creature whose mysterious visits have so aroused the summer colony.

A STRANGE CREATURE FOUND IN LOUISIANA.

The Hartford Herald – December 30, 1914 – Kentucky

New Orleans, Dec. 24. – With the head of an elephant, tusks measuring eighteen inches where they enter the mouth, and a body resembling nothing else ever seen to come out of the sea, an eighty-foot monster has been discovered off the southern coast of Louisiana.

The strange creature is dead and lying, partly embedded in sand, off Isle Dernier, a famous resort of the fifties and the scene of Lafcadio Hearn's novel "Chita."

The following telegram was sent to-night by G.J. Labarre and A.M. Dupont, planters of Terrebone Parish, to President Wilson, Congressman Broussard, the Smithsonian Institution and the Louisiana Conservation Commission:

"It is our pleasure to announce as your Christmas greeting that the State of Louisiana has furnished history and science the most wonderful discovery of centuries – the Leviathan of Anthology, eighty feet long, sixteen feet wide, approximately ninety tons weight.

"Description: The head of an elephant, eyes and jaws of the crocodile, the tongue is of a jellylike construction, porous with suckers and shaped like the trunk of an elephant; the tusks protrude in a straight line five feet and are eighteen inches wide at the jaw, and it is apparently a vegetarian."

REV. C. F. AKED'S BIG FISH STORY.

Charlevoix County Herald – January 2, 1915 – Michigan

The Strange Monster He Encountered in the Chilly Waters of Red Eagle Lake.

HE SAYS IT TRULY TERRIFED HIM.
Had a Head Like St. Bernard Dog's, and Got Away with About $60 Worth of His Fishing Tackle.

NEW YORK. – Rev. C.F. Aked, formerly pastor of the Rockefeller Baptist Church in New York City, is responsible for the following fish story:

What follows is fact – unadorned, unexaggerated fact. I could not have dreamed it. I cannot even now that I have begun to put pen to paper hope to tell it in such a way as to bring the scene with realizing earnestness before the eyes of my brother anglers.

It was evening. I was on Red Eagle lake, in the Glacier National Park, alone in my little canvas boat. The fishing had been good. I was returning to camp satisfied. The sack of fish, my fishing kit, discarded tackle, the net, etc., lying at the bottom of the boat, it seemed safer to leave the rod to poke out over the stern, the flies trailing the water – out of mischief, as I thought, where they could not get tangled with any of the truck.

So, I rowed along gently, happy in the slaughter I had accomplished and wishing my friends had been with me to do their share. And the rod shot over the stern of the boat before my very eyes!

I had the presence of mind not to make a forward dart and grab for it as it disappeared. Such a violent movement would undoubtedly have collapsed my collapsible boat. I sat in speechless amazement, too startled for thought.

And then close by a mighty splashing and plunging. I turned and saw on the top of the water something swimming, a red brown head and shoulders. I was frightened. It was so huge.

I thought of a bear, of a shark, and thoughts of sea monsters flashed through my mind. The thing was swimming slowly. What I could see of it looked for all the world like the head of a magnificent St. Bernard dog I used to own.

Then I came to myself. I realized that this was the fish of a species not known to me and of an incredible, unheard of size. He had taken my fly, had hooked himself on to the rod which he had dragged overboard and was swimming slowly because he was drawing it along the bottom of the lake.

I chased him. He dived, came up again with a splashing like that of an elephant in a pond and smashed down again. Almost I could keep up with him, so slowly did he swim and so much time did he waste in his frantic efforts to get free.

If I had been able to row properly, facing in a direction opposite to the one in which I was moving, I believe I could have overtaken him. But I needed to keep my eyes on him, and so had to backwater with the oars, losing power at every stroke I was thinking slowly. I was still too stunned to think normally. I was puzzled by the fact that such a monster did not break my frail tackle in a moment. There was no resistance so long as the 40 rods of line continued to unwind or the rod to move easily through the water.

As often as he swung over and dropped down on the six-foot leader it simply yielded beneath him. Five times he rose, and the fifth time I was quite near him. He seemed to be anything from four feet to six feet long. I have at home a muskallonge which I caught five years ago in the St. Lawrence river. He weighed 32 pounds and measured 47 inches. This fellow was much bigger and more terrifying. And I have no other means of guessing as to his size and weight.

Then with the sixth leap and dive something gave, and the monster was seen no more. I rowed slowly back to camp actually unnerved by the adventure. Literally – I felt afraid to be alone in the failing evening light, alone on such a piece of water inhabited by such creatures as the one who had pursued me and whom I had pursued.

AWFUL MONSTER; NO IT AIN'T, YES'TIS.

Webster City Freeman – May 11, 1915 – Iowa

Whatever-it-is Causes Much Worry and the Division of Opinion in Peaceful Town.

CAUSES CELLARS TO BE FLOODED.
Roots, Says Sewer Inspector General – Escaped Zippotherantheus, Says Circus Scientist.

Geneva, Ohio. – Barnum had his Whit-is-it, his successors had their Human and Animal Enigmas and museums have mystified the world and made money with their Thinking Automatons – grim, iron-visaged figures that beat all comers at checkers or chess or for the small expenditure of a dime handed the investor his or her fortune neatly printed and enclosed in neat and sealed envelope. It remained for Geneva, however, to produce the whatever-it-is, a fierce looking, awful monster that has been taken from the darkest precincts of our village sewer, and which has divided our generally peaceful residents into two armies of wildly excited verbal contenders.

At the head of one army is General Edward Towne, sewer inspector extraordinary – that is, extraordinary inasmuch as he's some more sewer inspector. At the head of the other array – faction, if this term suits anti-war readers better – is Gen. Tom J. Forde, inventor and circus man even before Walter Main dreamed of building his winter quarters here.

Let's call what's been said a prelude and begin the real story here. The curtain rises on the main action. The scene shows scores of cellars in Geneva filling with water which has backed up from Geneva's sewer lines.

A hurry call is sent for Gen. Edward Towne, sewer inspector extraordinary. The sewer at a certain place is undiscovered and there before the very eyes of a crowd of terrified onlookers is a monster with so many tentacles, or whatever you call them, that even a senior in a first-grade high school couldn't count 'em. Anyway, Gen. Tom J. Forde, circus man, calls it a monster.

Here's where the trouble comes in. Everybody in Geneva doesn't agree with Gen. Tom J. Forde, inventor and circus man. There's division of opinion in Geneva and citizens take the difference seriously.

While scores of honest-to-goodnessly brave men argued the Wat-ever-it-is in the sewer wasn't a real for sure monster, there was only one man in all Geneva who carried life insurance enough to warrant him to attempt removal from the sewer of the aforesaid What-ever-it-is. That man was Gen. Tom J. Forde, inventory and circus man. Everybody agreed to that.

Well, to stretch out a long story, Gen. Tom J. Forde, inventor and circus man, was notified. Would he attempt the capture or removal of the Whatever-it-is from the sewer of our fair Geneva? Would he? Would he?

He would.

It was dark down there in the sewer, but Gen. Tom J. Forde, inventory and circus man, braved the terrors while Geneva gasped, prayed, laughed or mentally applauded.

Zip! Just like that, and the Whatever-it-is was captured. A shout of triumph came from the sewer. Block and tackle quickly were obtained, and the Whatever-it-is as quickly was hoisted to the surface.

Aha! Gen. Tom J. Forde, inventor and circus man, took one look and was convinced that the Whatever-it-is (let's remain neutral) is the petrified corpse of a monster zippotherantheus that escaped from his menagerie 20 years ago when it was in winter quarters in Geneva. Gen. Tom J. Forde, inventor and circus man, says the Whatever-it-is, or zippothe-the- (see what we wrote above) is of priceless value.

Gen. Edward Towne, sewer inspector extraordinary, contend the Whatever-it-is – zippolococus – or what Gen. Tom J. Forde calls it – is an abnormal growth of poplar roots.

And here's where the Geneva mix-up comes in, where all Geneva is divided into two parts; one supporting Gen. Tom J. Forde, inventory and circus man even before Walter Main dreamed of building his winter quarters here; the other backing Gen. Edward Towne, sewer inspector extraordinary – and then some.

"BLUE MAN" RETURNS TO HIS OZARK HAUNTS.

The Washington Times – July 9, 1915 – Washington D.C.

Searching Parties in Mississippi Unsuccessfully Trail Wild Creature.

SPRINGFIELD, Mo., July 7. – News comes to this city that after an absence of four years the mysterious "Blue Man of Spring Creek" has again appeared in his old haunts and is causing great excitement in the wild and hilly country along the Big North Fork, Indian and Spring creeks, in the eastern end of Douglas county.

It was in the beginning of 1865 that a noted Ozark rifleman and tapper, "Blue Sol" Collins, came across strange tracks in the snow along Spring Creek. He had trailed many a bear, and these tracks resembled a bear's, but this bear must surely be the largest bear in all Missouri. The imprints in the snow were longer and broader than any bear tracks Collins had seen, and along the tracks were queer markings, seemingly made by great claws.

Collins was fearless and followed the footprints, determined to slap the greatest bear in history of the region. Hour after hour he followed the trail. He was toiling up the slope of Twin mountain when he heard a noise on the hill above him. Looking up, he was just in time to leap to one side as a huge bowlder swept past him down into the valley. Another and then another bowlder swiftly followed. When Collins had time to look closely and see what was causing the avalanche of rocks, he was terrified.

SAW GIGANTIC FIGURE.

On the steep hillside above him stood a gigantic figure. An enormous man, stark naked except for a breech cloth and a shoulder piece of some animal's skin. The huge body was covered with long hair almost black in color, and as thick as that of any wild animal. On this man's feet were rude moccasins of deerskin tied with thongs of leather. The ends of these thongs had made the claw like marks in the snow.

The terrifying figure was armed with a club six or eight feet long. This he had laid aside in order that he might more readily tear the bowlders from the frozen soil. Collins was no coward, but he never denied that after one look at that fearsome figure on the hill he turned and fled.

The Ozarks were a thinly settled region fifty years ago, but several of the scattered families among the hills missed calves, sheep and hogs, and after long searches found discarded hides and clean picked bones in remote crannies among the hills. Some of them, too, saw the fearsome figure slipping among the woods.

After 1865 the "wild man" disappeared and became no more than a tradition in the remote region. In 1874 he reappeared, was seen by probably a score of men, and was systematically tracked by men skilled in trailing wild animals. But all efforts to capture him were in vain.

During the next sixteen years the "Blue Man" made several trips to his original haunts and on each trip the farmers lost some of their smaller animals. Every incursion was marked by energetic efforts to capture the strange creature now universally known as the "Blue Man of Spring Creek." Why "Blue" no one knows unless the name was given because it was "Blue Sol" Collins who first saw him.

In 1880 it was rumored a party of searchers had captured the quarry so long sought, but this proved false. Evidently, however, they made it too hot for the "Wild Man," for again he disappeared. It was not until 1911 that he again appeared. This time his den was found, but he disappeared.

NOT SO FAT NOWADAYS.

Six weeks ago, an Ozark farmer noticed two of his lambs did not come home with the rest of the flock. He searched the hills and at last found their bloody pelts in a hollow in a remote part of the woods. The next day he saw the "Blue Man" running down a hog in the woods and since then several other farmers have seen the creature. The wild man is said to be less robust than formerly. His blue-black coat of hair now is iron gray and his limbs are not as well muscled as formerly. Nevertheless, it may be safely wagered that there is not a man among the sturdy Ozark mountaineers who would like to risk combat singlehanded with the fearsome creature.

Before the Revolution, while this region was yet under the flag of France, it is said that a French Indian trader came into the Ozarks, bringing with him a beautiful Spanish woman, a native of Florida. Somewhere in the region the trader abandoned the woman or sold her to the Indians. From this poor outcast descended a race of Indian-Spanish half breeds. One of these in the third or fourth generation may be the "Blue Man of Spring Creek." This was the theory of "Uncle Jerry" Hildebrand, who settled in what is now Douglas county in 1820 and lived there until 1885.

In the course of nature, the "Blue Man" cannot be expected to live much longer. Whether he ever will be caught or whether the secret of his long absences and mysterious returns will ever be solved is doubtful.

BATTLE WITH GIANT EAGLES.

The Mukwonago Chief – November 24, 1916 – Wisconsin

California Deer Hunters Had Fierce Fight Before Overcoming Two Monarchs of The Air.

Attacked by two monster eagles while deer hunting in the Malibu district, Doctor Kingsbury of Ocean Park, G.M. Wilson, a rancher, and Policeman Harry Wright of Santa Monica, fought two hours before they were able to kill the birds, writes a Los Angeles correspondent.

Shrieking and screaming, the eagles tore at the men with their claws, tearing Wright's clothing in many places and inflicting a flesh wound on Kingsbury's right shoulder.

The fight began with only one of the birds. The men were hunting on the Williams ranch with two dogs. Suddenly a huge eagle swooped down and grabbed one of the dogs. It circled 20 feet in the air with the dog in its talons before the men could fire. The first shot missed, but the second shot from Kingsbury's gun brought the bird down.

As the three men rushed forward, the eagle dropped the dog and struck out at Wright, screaming all the while. Its screams brought its mate, the latter making an attack on Kingsbury and sinking its talons into his shoulder.

Williams shot and killed the bird that was fighting with Wright and then the two rushed the remaining eagle. It started to fly away and then came back. The men began shooting at it, driving it a little further away with each shot. For four miles they chased the bird before finally killing it.

BELGIAN HUNTER RUSHED BY PRIMEVAL MONSTER.

The Mena Weekly Star – December 11, 1919 – Arkansas

Animal Later Demolishes Native Village – Appeared About 24 Feet Long – Hind Feet Cloven.

Port Elizabeth, Dec. 5. – The head of the local museum here has received information from a Mr. Lepage who was in charge of railway construction in the Belgian Congo of an exciting adventure last month. While Lepage was hunting one day in October he came upon an extraordinary monster which charged at him. Lepage fired but was forced to flee, with the monster in chase. The animal before long gave up the chase, and Lepage was able to examine it through his binoculars. The animal, he says, was about twenty-four feet in length, with a long-pointed snout adorned with tusks like horns and a short horn above the nostrils. The front feet were like those of a horse and the hind hoofs were cloven. There was a scaly hump on the monster's shoulders.

The animal charged through the native village of Fungurume, destroying the huts and killing some of the native dwellers. A hunt was at once organized, but the Government has forbidden the molestation of the animal on the ground that it is probably a relic of antiquity. There is a wild trackless region in the neighborhood which contains many swamps and marshes where, says the head of the museum, it is possible that a few primeval monsters may survive.

STORIES FROM THE:

1920's

WHATEVER THE ANIMAL IS THE DOGS DON'T LIKE IT.

Marble Hill Press – January 1, 1920 – Missouri

WINONA, MINN. – Roaming in the wooded land where it evidently has a hidden place in which to hibernate is a large, strange animal, so ferocious that it has caused men ordinarily frightened at nothing to flee in great fear at the sight of the beast, according to advices from Pickwick, in the lower end of Winona county.

So aroused over the reports have the residents there become that the woods three miles south of Pickwick at the upper end of Big Trout valley are likely to be invaded by a force of armed men determined to rid the community of the invader.

Reports of seeing the beast have persisted for several weeks. What it is none who has seen it can say. The most reliable information thus far is said to have been gained from Carl Nelson, a farmer residing on the edge of the infested woods. Nelson swears he saw the beast plainly and that it was light gray in color, striped and about as large as a yearling calf.

David Huffors, a retired merchant, went into the woods with two good hunting dogs and a high-powered rifle. Several miles below Pickwick his dogs picked up a trail. They followed it to a heavily wooded place which backs into a rocky draw.

The dogs began to bay, then suddenly broke and fled to their master, tails between their legs. Huffors turned around and went home. He said he didn't see the animal – didn't even have a desire to see it. The fear of the dogs satisfied him, he said.

Others who have sent dogs on the trail of the beast declare that they become greatly excited when the trail is first picked up, but after following it for some distance break for home, displaying unusual fear.

Farmers around Pickwick believe the animal escaped from a circus, has worked its way to the Mississippi river and is unable to cross it.

MYSTERIOUS MARINE MONSTER CAPTURED BY FISHING CREW.

The Punta Gorda Herald – April 1, 1920 – Florida

Strange Creature Found Tangled in Fish Nets – Capture Attended by Much Excitement.

LANDED ON CITY DOCK AND MAY BE SEEN THERE TODAY.

Not Even Captain Jack McCann Can Name Species to Which it Belongs – Will be Preserved.

The large yacht, the P.W. McAdow, owned by the West Coast Fish Company and commanded by Captain Fred Quednau, arrived here from the fishing waters last night and, in addition to a big cargo of mullet, brought up one of the strangest and most horrid-looking marine creatures ever seen. This nondescript was landed on the outer end of the municipal dock, because this dock affords more room for that note expert taxidermist, Thos. Hartigan, to do the work of mounting the monster, for which purpose he has been engaged by T.C. Crosland, the enterprising manager of the fish company.

It is difficult to describe the monster properly, but it may be said that it is eight feet long and is estimated to weigh 500 pounds. Its back and sides are of a green-black color, while its breast and belly are of lighter shades. Its head and mouth resemble a huge catfish, but the teeth are like those of a royal Bengal tiger. There are no pectoral or ventral fins, but there is a fringe, like that of an eel, running along the back from the base of the head to the tail, and the tail is shaped like that of a porpoise. The fish, or whatever it may be called, has a short neck, which, while alive, enabled it to move its head from side to side without moving its body.

But possibly the strangest things about this remarkable creature are a horn about two feet long extending from the base of the head and curving over the back, and four big webbed feet armed with talons over two inches long. The horn, in shape, curve and material, resembles an elephant's tusk, while the feet are not unlike those of an alligator, but are much larger.

The capture of this unknown monster was attended with considerable excitement. It was affected Tuesday evening at Taxahatchee, a short distance from Chokoloskee, by Captain J.P. Daniels and his fishing crew of twelve men. Going to their gill-nets that afternoon, about six o'clock, they found them torn to pieces and this monster tangled and helpless in the wreck it had made. When the men approached, however, it made desperate struggles, not to get away, but to attack the men. It was simply furious, according to the men who assisted in its capture, but the nets in which it was entangled balked its efforts to get at them, and they dared not approach very near the creature.

After a brief consultation, a member of the fishing crew was sent to camp for a Winchester rifle, which was kept in a lighter, otherwise their house-boat. He soon returned and opened fire on the leviathan. The shots served to enrage the creature and provoke it to renewed efforts to get at the men. Finally, a well-directed shot struck the monster fairly in the forehead, and its struggles soon began to weaken. It was almost, if not fully, an hour before its struggles ceased and it was seen to be dead; and then the men towed it to their camp and applied themselves to the task of stripping off the entangling nets. They moored the monster beside the lighter and went to bed; and, yesterday morning, when the McAdow came along for a load of fish, the only fish she found at this camp was this marine monster.

Captain Quednau decided to bring it to Punta Gorda and accordingly took it aboard and brought it to the town dock where it was landed. On seeing it, Mr. Crosland decided that it was an extraordinary creature that it ought to be preserved. Thos. Hartigan was engaged to mount it and will begin the work today. After it is mounted, Mr. Crosland will ship it to the Museum of Natural History in New York.

Many people have gone down to the dock to see this strange, repulsive monster, but not one of them, not even Jack McCann, can name the species to which it belongs.

ROOSEVELT BELIEVED TALES REPORTING ANCIENT MONSTER FOUND IN PATAGONIA JUNGLE.

The Morning Tulsa Daily World – April 2, 1922 – Oklahoma

The Then President Took Enthusiastic Interest in Reports of American Prospector that He Had Seen and Tracked Amphibian Monster and Secretly Nourished Hope to Search for Beast, but Chose River of Doubt Trip Instead.

WASHINGTON – Theodore Roosevelt believed there might be some huge surviving amphibian in the jungles of the Southern Andes, such as recently have been described in cable dispatches from South America, and when the former president went on his expedition which discovered the River of Doubt, he had some idea of looking for it.

John Barrett, late director of the Pan-American union and minister to Argentina during President Roosevelt's administration has just disclosed that part of Colonel Roosevelt's expeditionary plans which hitherto are said to have been untold.

PROSPECTOR SAW THE BEAST.

"On reading the first cabled report," said Mr. Barrett, "that Martin Sheffield, an American of whom I have personal knowledge, had reported that he had seen what appeared to be a plesiosaurian monster, or huge amphibian swimming in the waters of a southern Andean jungle lake, I recalled that nearly twenty years ago, in November, 1903, when I was minister to Argentina, a clear-headed typical American prospector and explorer, whose name I have forgotten, came to the legation and in a convincing way, proceeded to relate to me a story almost identical with that now reported as told recently by Sheffield, to the effect that he had seen swimming in a lake a huge lizard-like monster with a curved neck. His expert discussion of the mineral and timber resources of the Andean plateaus and plains convinced me of his sincerity and responsibility. He urged me to help him raise money in either Argentina or the United States, preferably the latter, to outfit and conduct an expedition to locate and capture the extraordinary animal and begged me to write to President Roosevelt about it and mention his name because he had been associated in some way with Roosevelt in the Cuban campaign.

"Although I gave him no promises, he said he would call again. Shortly afterward I wrote President Roosevelt a personal and unofficial letter referring to this incident. In about a month and a half there came in the legation pouch a personal letter from the president written in his own handwriting and expressing real interest in the story of this American whom he said he well remembered and asking me to get without fail into touch with him at once and ask him to write all about what he had seen.

"The man meanwhile sent word that he was off again on a mineral and timber prospecting tour in southern Argentina and Chile but giving no address and no name of those he might represent.

FOUND BEAST'S TRAIL.

"In April, five months later, just before I went to Panama as first American minister, I received a letter from the prospector written from some faraway place in Chubut, or so-called Patagonia. He was almost enthusiastic in his story of how he had again found a fresh trail of a strange animal leading to the waters of a lake, although he had not actually again seen the beast as in his first experience. This letter I at once forwarded to President Roosevelt and I am wondering if it is still in his archives which may have been preserved. Since then I have never received any further word from or about this American prospector. Possibly he may be alive and read this and give the world some further information.

"When I returned to the United States the first salutation President Roosevelt gave me as I entered his office in the White House was; "Well, Old Pan-America, where is your Argentine amphibian and what has happened to -----, calling the man's name. It is my impression that Representative Cannon and several other congressmen were in the room at the time and they may recall this salutation because everybody seemed amused by it.

"After the departure of the others the president for half an hour discussed, as an enthusiastic naturalist and scientist the possibility of there being some huge surviving amphibian descended from the ancient plesiosaurians, and actually took stock, so to speak, in the story of the American prospector whom he said he well remembered. I mentioned the incident to Secretary Loeb as I left the president's office and he may possibly recall my conversation.

TEDDY WANTED TO FIND THE MONSTER.

"Years later when Colonel Roosevelt made his famous trip to South America, he told me confidentially just before sailing that, although he had never heard anything further from this American prospector, I should not be surprised if, after his arrival in Argentina, he decided to make a special trip of exploration to southern Argentina and Chile, in the hope of ascertaining whether there was any truth in these stories of this monster amphibian, which strongly appealed to him. He wanted nothing said about it lest there should be ridicule if he did not succeed.

"Shortly before he left Buenos Aires, Argentina, for his notable and possibly fatal trip up the Panama and Paraguay rivers in the heart of Brazil, he sent me word through a mutual Argentine friend that he had finally decided on the Brazilian instead of Argentine exploring expedition.

"After his return to America and when he was recovering from the poison and fever contracted in the wild hot tropical jungle of Brazil I saw him for a long talk, when he said: "Well, while I am game and glad that I discovered this unknown river in Brazil, I would probably be far better physically if I had gone to the cooler region of southern Argentina and Chile and I might have found that mysterious amphibian which would have aroused far more human interest throughout the world than an unmapped river."

"When later he passed away suddenly, undoubtedly as a result of the poison contracted in hi Brazilian jungle travels, I could not help thinking that if had gone after the unknown beast of Argentina instead of the unknown river of Brazil, all history might have been changed. Anyway, I hope the relation of this incident may be inspiration to Jose Cinagi, superintendent of the Buenos Aires zoological garden, and Emilio Frey, the distinguished Argentine engineer, who are on an expedition to ascertain the facts about this extraordinary plesiosaurian or surviving amphibian whose ancestors go back through untold ages."

WILD MAN LIVES ALONE IN CAVE.

Worcester Democrat and the Ledger-Enterprise –
April 29, 1922 – Maryland

Makes Night Raids on Neighboring Farms and Carries Away Animals.

FIGHTS WITH HUNTERS.
Won Hand-to-Hand Encounter with Man Who Battled Him in His Cave in Effort to Win Reward.

Mt. Sterling, Ill. – A wild man, living in a cave near here, is thwarting all efforts of police and armed citizens to capture him and is keeping the countryside in terror with his raids on outlying farms. A price has been set on his head, but desperate attempts to capture him in his lair have proved vain.

The wild man recently made a series of bold robberies near Mt. Pleasant, carrying off calves and sheep to a deserted mine where he stays hidden in the daytime. Ambrose Smith, a dead shot and a tireless hunter, was seriously wounded in a terrific hand-to-hand encounter with the mysterious man-monster.

Is Huge Creature with Bony Hands.

"The wild man has long, wiry hair that bristles about his savage-looking face," Smith said in his home, where he is recovering from the adventure. "In the uncertain light of the cavern, I made him out to be a great towering creature. His hands are thin, and the flesh is stretched over the bones like leather."

People feared black damp in the long empty galleries of the mine so much that even a reward of $500 for the wild man, dead or alive, failed to result in his apprehension. At last Smith, accompanied by J.M. Blair and others from Mt. Pleasant, all quick with a gun, went to the cave. It was late in the afternoon. Smith had the others stand back 200 yards from the mouth of the cave and entered alone, armed only with his large hunting knife. His dog followed him.

Fought for Hour in Damp Cave.

Night fell and the watchers waited in vain for Smith's return. Then there was a great noise and the dog ran out whimpering. The men went into the cavern in search of Smith. They groped along through the twisting passageways in the darkness but were unable to find any trace of him. At midnight Smith crawled from the cave on his hands and knees and fell faint and exhausted at the feet of his friends.

"I did not get more than 50 feet into the cave boys," he said, as they carried him to the doctors, "when I saw the wild man glaring at me a few feet away. Then he sprang at me and held me in his steel-like grip. I tried to knife him, but he held my wrist. For more than an hour we fought together on the wet floor of the cave.

"I weakened and he slipped from my grip. I felt his hot breath on my face and then a heavy blow on my head knocked me unconscious. I don't know what happened after that. When I get well, I'll make another attempt, and next time I'll get him."

GREAT, ACTIVE HORNED ALLIGATOR SAYS HUNTER OF LAKE MONSTER.

Evening Star – July 25, 1923 – Washington D.C.

By the Associated Press.

OMAHA, Neb., July 25. – By far the most vivid picture of actions and appearance of the monster which for about three years has terrified tourists, fishermen, farmers and others in the vicinity of Big Alkali Lake, near Hay Springs, Neb., was received by the Omaha World-Herald today from J.A. Johnson, who signed his residence as Hay Springs:

"I saw the monster myself while with two friends last fall," Johnson's communication stated in describing the monster, "I could name forty other persons who have also seen the brute. But owing to its apparent preference to nights, and apparently dark nights, few have had as good a view as I."

In telling of his experiences, the communication declared:

SEEN IN EARLY MORNING.

"We had camped a short distance from the lake on the night before and all three of us arose early to be ready for the early duck flight. We started to walk around the lake close to the shore, in order to jump any birds, when suddenly, coming around a slight rise in the ground, we came upon this animal, nearly three-fourths out of the shallow water near the shore. We were less than twenty yards from him, and he saw us at the same time we came upon him: It lifted its head and made a peculiar hissing noise and disappeared.

"The animal was probably forty feet long, including the tail and the head, when raised in alarm, as when he saw us. In general appearance the animal was not unlike an alligator, except that the head was stubbier, and there seemed to be a projection that was like a horn between the eyes and nostrils. The animal was built much more heavily throughout than an alligator and was not at all sluggish in its actions. Its color seemed a dull gray or brown, although it was hardly light enough to distinguish color well.

LEFT BAD SMELL.

"There was, however, a very distinctive and somewhat unpleasant odor noticeable for several moments after the beast itself had vanished into the water. We stood for several minutes after the animal had gone, hardly knowing what to do or say, when we noticed, several hundred feet out from the shore, a considerable commotion in the water, like a school of fish sometimes make.

"Sure enough, the animal came to the surface, floated there a moment and then lashed the water with its tail, suddenly dived and we saw no more of him.

"My theory is that there is a subterranean passage from that lake to other underground lakes, and that the beast, and probably others, live underground, coming up only occasionally: Such geological formations are not rare. Many are known to exist in Kentucky and Virginia, where blind fish and other creatures have been frequently found. I can explain nothing more."

The Antler's Club, at Alliance, near Hay Springs, yesterday authorized its president to order a whale harpoon, line and whaling gun from a Boston concern, a World-Herald special dispatch stated. A large posse will be formed, and the lake will be thoroughly searched in an effort to find the animal.

GREAT SEA MONSTER INFESTS INLAND LAKE.

The L'Anse Sentinel – August 31, 1923 – Michigan

Omaha. – An order to a Boston firm for a whale harpoon, line and whaling gun was mailed from the town of Alliance, Neb. With it went the interest of thousands of Nebraskans, whose curiosity for years has been piqued by the mysterious freak of Alkali lake, near the village of Hay Springs, Neb.

For two years reports have been originating from farmers that a huge amphibious monster resembling a prehistoric dinosaur has made the alkali water its habitat, coming out at various intervals to prey upon livestock and in some instances terrorizing swimmers, fishermen and autoists who camped nearby.

All doubt in Hay Springs as to the truth of the animal's existence was destroyed two weeks ago, when three tourists appealed to the Hay Springs chamber of commerce to rid the lake of the antediluvian monster, because they had been chased for several yards by the animal.

Two of the tourists were from Texas and the other was a Nebraskan. One of the trio sent in a signed communication to an Omaha paper asking for aid in capturing the freak.

By unanimous vote the Alliance Anglers' club took the first step in ordering weapons. A large posse will be formed, the members announced, and the lake will be searched with the aid of a large drag net. Men with boats will watch the marshy sections with guns and hooks.

WHAT, THE DEVIL? LOOKS LIKE HIM.

New Britain Herald– July 3, 1924 – Connecticut

West Orange, N.J., Reports Strange Monster.

New York, July 3. – The lieutenant in charge of the West Orange, N.J., police station answered the telephone yesterday afternoon and found that Patrolman George Deckenback and a lot of excitement were on the wire,

"Say!" said the policeman. "Say, I just seen something!"

The lieutenant immediately motioned to the three policemen on reserve, and they piled into the station house automobile and went roaring away to Patrolman Deckenback's post, while the policeman continued:

"I just seen an animal that has a head like a deer, that runs like a rabbit and has fiery eyes What do you think it is?"

The lieutenant talked as soothingly as possible, meanwhile writing a note to another policeman to bring Chief Patrick Donough. By the time the chief arrived the three reserves came back with Patrolman Deckenback sitting with them in their automobile. Deckenback launched into a description of the strange animal he had seen, while the others patted him on the back and told him not to worry. Deckenback was beginning to think they weren't believing him, when Mrs. Clyde Vincent, of Pleasant Valley, came breathlessly into the station with her two children.

"Lieutenant," she said finally, "we were picnicking on the road a while ago when an animal that had a head like a deer, ran like a rabbit and had fiery eyes came along and jumped over us."

Latter Patrolman Deckenback received further vindication when Chief James Ashby, of the Livingston police, telephoned that a farmer there had reported seeing the "devil" jumping about his fields. Several policemen and fifty boys passed the rest of the afternoon searching for the creature, but unsuccessfully.

The West Orange police think the animal is a kangaroo that escaped from a circus or zoo, though they are stumped by the fiery eyes.

STORIES FROM THE:

1930's

CARCASS OF LIZARDLIKE ANIMAL, 42 FEET LONG, FOUND IN ALASKA.

Evening Star – November 25, 1930 – Washington D.C.

Strange Creature, With Fur in Perfect Condition, Incased in Ice of Columbia Glacier.

By the Associated Press.

CORDOVA, Alaska, November 25. – Reports received from Valdez today said the carcass of a giant lizardlike creature, with fur in perfect condition, had been found on Glacier Island, near here.

The strange creature reported to be 42 feet long, including a tail measuring 16 feet, was believed to have been preserved since prehistoric times by being incased in ice in the upper reaches of the Columbia Glacier. The ice was believed to have worked its way gradually to the sea. The head was reported to be 6 feet long and the body 20 feet in length.

NEW YORK, November 25 (AP). – Bernard Brown, curator of the American Museum of Natural History, has requested Dr. Charles E. Bunnell, president of Alaska College at Fairbanks, to investigate the carcass of the strange creature found on Glacier Island.

The museum was informed of the supposed find 10 days ago.

"So far as we know," said Mr. Brown, "there was no prehistoric creature of the dimensions given in the dispatch from Alaska.

"If the creature was incased in ice it must have lived when the ice was formed. The prehistoric animals of Alaska of which we know were the mammoth and the buffalo and many small creatures, none of which would reach the dimensions of the lizardlike animal.

"The description suggests a reptile something like a dinosaur, but dinosaurs died out millions of years before the ice age. The only other possibility is that it is some sort of a marine creature like a whale."

Mr. Brown does not expect a report from Dr. Bunnell for some time because of the difficulty of making a Winter journey from Fairbanks to Glacier Island.

SKETCH MADE OF QUEER MONSTER CAUGHT AT FOWEY ROCKS LIGHT.

The Key West Citizen – May 23, 1934 – Florida

Detailed Description Is Sent to Bureau of Fisheries by Superintendent Demeritt.

One of the queerest fish caught off the Florida coast was taken several days ago by H.S. Perry, keeper at Fowey Rocks lighthouse. It was such an odd-looking specimen the keeper drew a sketch of it and sent it with a detailed description to the bureau of fisheries, through Superintendent W.W. Demeritt's office.

The fish was 8 feet 6 inches long and weighed 275 pounds. It was 36 inches around the body, back of the head, which was shaped like that of an alligator. In the head were funny little eyes of yellowish grey about the size of a shirt button.

In the mouth, which was 8 inches wide and 12 inches long, were three rows of teeth, long, sharp and double edged set in gums that could be so manipulated as to completely cover them.

The back of the oddity was green, brown and white. The sides of the bright green tint of the lizard and the belly as white and so smooth as to resemble enamel.

Stripes of pale green were on the head and sides and the formation of these were such as to appear as though vulcanized to the hide. The odor of the fish, writes Keeper Perry, was that of the large black grouper and not anything like that of a shark.

That it was of a savage nature was indicated by the several attempts made to bite the line with which it was being raised to the platform of the light where it expired about 10 minutes later.

CLAIM CANADA HAS RACE OF MONSTER MEN.

The Times News – October 9, 1935 – North Carolina

SETTLERS NEAR VANCOUVER DESCRIBE HAIRY GIANTS ROAMING THERE.

VANCOUVER, B.C., Oct. 9. (UP) – Sasquatch men, remnants of a lost race of "wild men" who inhabited the rocky regions of British Columbia centuries ago, are reported roaming the province again.

After an absence of several months from the district of Harrison Mills, 50 miles east of Vancouver, the long, weird, wolf-like howls of the "wild men" are being heard again and two of the hairy monsters were reported seen in the Morris Valley on the Harrison river.

Residents in the district tell of seeing the two giants leaping and bounding out of the forest and striding across the duck-feeding ground, wallowing now and again the bog and mire and long, waving, swamp grasses.

REPORTED AGILE AS GOATS

The strange men, it was reported, after emerging from the woods, came leaping down the jagged rocky hillside with the agility and lightness of mountain goats. Snatches of their weird language floated on the breeze across the lake to the pioneer settlement at the foot of the hills.

The giants walked with an easy gait across the swamp flats and at the Morris creek, in the shadow of Little Mystery mountain, straddled a floating log, which they propelled with their long, hairy hands and huge feet across the sluggish glacial stream to the opposite side. There they abandoned the log and climbed hand over hand up the almost perpendicular cliff at a point known as Gibraltar and disappeared into the wooded wilderness at the top of the ridge. They carried two large clubs and walked round a herd of cattle directly in their path.

INDIAN'S STORY RETOLD

The return of the giants to the legendary stronghold of the Sasquatch monsters recalls the narrow escape of an Indian at the same spot last March. A huge rock narrowly missed his canoe while he was fishing and looking up, he said he saw a huge hairy monster stamping his feet and gesticulating wildly. The Indian escaped by cutting his fishing tackle and paddling away. The same Indian declares the Sasquatch twice have stolen salmon which he tied in a tree outside his house out of reach of dogs.

The latest appearance of the monsters was peaceful. They avoided the trails usually used by the people of the valley and molested neither cattle nor human beings.

People who have reported seeing the giants on their rare appearances described them as "ferocious looking wild men, nine feet tall and covered from head to toes with thick black hair."

STORIES FROM THE:

1940's

SCOTCHMEN CHASE HUGE SEA MONSTER.

The Wilmington Morning Star – July 20, 1945 – North Carolina

Strange Aquatic Animal Had Five-Foot Head Two Sailors Report.

NEWCASTLLE ON TYNE, England, July 19 – (U.P.) – A sea monster the like of which has not been seen since pre-war days was spotted Tuesday in the sea off the mouth of the Tyne.

Two Scots operating a salvage steamer through binoculars saw the monster moving against the tide at a fast clip. It was huge – with a head and neck of five to six feet and a back almost 10 feet broad.

Salvage Officer John Hamilton of Edinburgh was the first to spot something bobbing six feet out of the water about a quarter of a mile away. He called Skipper Lownie of Kincardine, who immediately put off in a motor launch with two of the crew in a pursuit of this strange new creature.

"We chased the monster for five or 10 minutes, but it kept well ahead of us," said Lownie. "What we took to be its head and neck was five or six feet above the surface of the water and its back was eight to ten feet across."

But try as they could the pursuers could not get closer to the monster and soon it disappeared completely.

"We never saw it again, but we are all of the opinion it was a sea monster of some kind," said Lownie.

THREE SWEDES REPORT SEEING TWO MONSTERS

STOCKHOLM, July 19 – (U.P.) – A parson's wife and a local policeman saw two "sea monsters" near the seaport of Umae yesterday, only a fortnight after an amphibious monster with three huge bumps on its back was spotted at a lake outside Storsjoe.

The witnesses said they saw two "heads" which they first believed to be those of swimmers. When the heads suddenly disappeared and a tail and fin emerged a few seconds later they decided they had seen a sea monster, last seen in 1943, when a group of amateur anglers tried to catch it. One member of the same party has already left for Umae to try his luck again.

The monster at Storsjoe, which reportedly crawled onto the bank and disappeared into the underbrush, made its appearance about 10 years ago.

REWARD POSTED FOR SEA MYTH.

The Wilmington Morning Star – March 9, 1947 – North Carolina

Fishermen Claim Monster of Deep Has A Fin 30 Feet Long.

SEATTLE, March 9 – (U.P.) – They put a price on the head of the Puget Sound's sea serpent today. But it wasn't likely to be collected.

"$5,000 – dead or alive" was the reward posted by aquarium owner Ivar Haglund for the sea beast called the Madrona sea monster that was sighted for the fourth time in two weeks today in state of Washington waters.

When spotted today, Madrona was fleeing Puget Sound. With fishermen and boatmen alerted by the "wanted notices; he was "blowing the country," the waters "too hot" for him.

Photographer A.L. Thompson saw the monster early this morning moving through Puan De Fuca Straits one-half mile off Ediz hook today and Arelene Ray, wife of the manager of the local salmon club, spotted it through binoculars from her home on the Ediz Hook Spit.

Thompson's two-cylinder outboard motorboat was no match for the speed of the jumped, three-finned "thing" that is estimated to be more than 30 feet long – possibly 60 feet.

Madrona submerged before Thompson could get within camera range.

"I watched Thompson take chase, but he never gained," said Mrs. Ray.

Nobody has a complete conception of what Madrona looked like because all they have ever seen of him is his black humped back – 30 feet of it.

Nobody knows whether he has claws, teeth or breaths fire in the best tradition of the monsters depicted on the "unknown seas" of Christopher Columbus' navigation charts.

SKIPPER TELLS OF 'SEA MONSTER' STRUCK BY U.S. LINER AT SEA.

Evening Star – December 31, 1947 – Washington D.C.

(Editor's note – The following story was written by the captain of the Santa Clara, Grace Line vessel, at the request of the Associated Press and radioed to New York after the ship's report to the Coast Guard that it had struck a "sea monster" in the Atlantic off the North Carolina coast.)

By J. Fordan,
Master of the S.S. Santa Clara

ABOARD THE S.S. SANTA CLARA, Dec. 31 (AP) (By Radio). – On December 30, 1947, the Grace Line steamer, Santa Clara, was cleaving through sunlit calm blue seas 118 miles due east of Cape Lookout, en route from New York to Cartagena.

The Santa Clara had just crossed the Gulf stream when William Humphreys, chief mate; John Rigney, navigating officer, and John Alexson, third mate, assembled on the starboard wing of the bridge to take the noon sight at 11:55 a.m.

Suddenly John Alexson saw a snake-like head rear out of the sea about 30 feet off the starboard bow of the vessel. His exclamation of amazement directed the attention of the other two mates to the sea monster, and the three watched it unbelievingly as, in a moment's time, it came abeam of the bridge where they stood, and was then left astern.

The creature's head appeared to be about 2 ½ feet across, 2 feet thick and 5 feet long. The cylindrically shaped body was about 3 feet thick and the neck about 1 ½ feet in diameter.

As the monster came abeam of the bridge it was observed that the water around the monster, over an area of 30 or 40 feet square, was stained red. The visible part of the body was about 35 feet long.

It was assumed that the color of the water was due to the creature's blood and that the stem of the ship had cut the monster in two, but as there was no observer on the other side of the vessel there was no way of estimating what length of body might have been left on the other side.

From the time the monster was first sighted until it disappeared in the distance astern, it was thrashing about as though in agony. The monster's skin was dark brown, slick and smooth. There were no fins, hair or protuberances on the head, neck or visible parts of the body.

BONUS:

MYSTERY
AIRSHIPS

THAT MYSTERIOUS LIGHT.

Sacramento Daily Record-Union – November 19, 1896 – California

Was It an Air-Ship or a Will-o'-the-Wisp?

Stories That are Floating Around Concerning the Supposed Floating Visitor.

Regarding the aerial visitor that passed over Sacramento Tuesday evening, and which was described at the time as being a pure white light of about double the power of an electric arc light, many queer stories are told.

Whether the light was a meteor, or attached to a balloon, or whether it was a genuine flying machine, is not positively known, though ninety-nine out of 100 men in the city regard the matter in the light of a huge hoax. The stories told by some of the parties who saw the light follow, and the reader can pay his money and take his choice:

R.L. Lowry, who was formerly in the employ of the street railway company in this city, but who has been absent for some time and only recently returned, says he was near East Park and saw the apparatus when it was not more than fifty feet from the ground. He declared that the machine was cigar-shaped and was operated by four men who sat aside the cigar and moved as though they were working their passage on a bicycle. He stated that the machine was fitted with wing-like propellers after the fashion of those of an ocean steamer.

T.P. De Long, whose residence is not mentioned in the city directory, said he saw the light and heard voices, but couldn't hear what was said.

Daniel Curl, a horse-trainer, is authority for the statement that he not only saw the light but heard someone suggest that "they go up higher."

F.E. Briggs, a motorman on a G-street car, said he saw the light and called attention to it. His passengers requested him to stop, which he did. He heard singing which appeared to come from the direction of the light and seemed to be wafted down in gusts.

M.F. Shelley, a motorman on a J-street car, saw the light and heard a voice shouting orders.

C.H. Lusk, Secretary of the street-car company, noticed the light. He said it had an up-and-down and side-to-side motion.

G.C. Snider, foreman of the street-car barn, saw the light, and gave it as his opinion that it was an aerial machine of some kind.

Frank A. Ross, Assistant Manager of the street railway company, said he had talked with many persons concerning the matter, and, having seen the light, is fully assured that it was some kind of a flying machine.

Thomas Allen stated very seriously that a flying machine, the invention of a citizen of Sacramento, actually did ascend from the vicinity of Oak Park, and that four men, among whom was Nat Liebling, ascended with it. The machine, he related, was fastened to the earth with a cable, which broke and let the aerial wonder float away. It would not, owing to a defect in the steering apparatus, be guided, and sailed around at random. First it made for Suisun, but after having accomplished half the journey veered around, once more passed over the city, and is now at a point near Arcade Station, ten miles northeast of this city.

It puzzles one to understand how the machine could have started from Oak Park, which is southeast of the city, and passed over from the northeast to the southwest, and it is also puzzling to know how Nat Liebling could have taken such a wild, wild ride, when he was seen near the Post office only two hours later.

There are other puzzling things also, but the average citizen will choose what he wishes, and the burning question still is, "What was it?"

IT FLIES AT NIGHT.

Kansas City Journal – March 28, 1897 – Missouri

MYSTERIOUS AIRSHIP SEEN BY SCORES OF KANSANS.

IS UNDER PERFECT CONTROL.

PLOWS THE AERIAL MAIN AT THE WILL OF THE NAVIGATOR.

Has Passed Over Belleville Several Times Within a Week – Generally Believed That It Is the Machine First Seen in California.

Belleville, Kas., March 27. – (Special.) The mysterious airship which has been sighted at various points in Kansas and Southern Nebraska during the past month has been seen on numerous occasions within a week by a number of Belleville people. More than fifty persons had a plain view of it as it passed over the other night about 10 o'clock, going south, and three or more saw it the next morning at 5 o'clock returing north. It has been seen on at least four successive nights, and so plainly that there can be no possible mistake about the reality of the mysterious contrivance.

The airship seems to be under perfect control of the navigator, raising, lowering and changing direction and speed in prompt obedience to the steering gear and motive power. The ship has a brilliant electric headlight which appears in the sky larger than the headlight of a locomotive, and by which the movements of the airship may be watched long after the ship itself has been lost in darkness. The speed of the ship is estimated by those who have seen it to be from sixty to seventy-five miles an hour.

On one occasion this week, when it passed over Belleville, it moved so close to the ground that the electric headlight made the city almost as light as day. The ship seemed to stop a few miles northeast of the city, remaining almost stationary for twenty or thirty minutes. Then it sailed up and down, north, south, east and west, now rapidly, now slowly, as if the navigator were testing the possibilities of his aerial steed. It rose at one time far above some scattering clouds, and then sailed away to the north, and was lost to view. At 2 o'clock in the morning it was seen going south again, and three hours later was again seen on its way north.

It is generally believed that the ship is the same one which created such a sensation in California a few months ago, and that the men who are experimenting with it have brought it to this part of the country to bring it to perfection, the furor that it stirred up on the coast having made secret experimentation there out of the question. It is probably that, unless the machine soon reaches the point where its inventor or inventors are ready to initiate the public into its mysteries, there will have to be another move, for it has been seen so many times in this vicinity that its resting place during the day will soon be discovered and secrecy will no longer be possible.

When the story was first told in California that an airship had been seen flying about mysteriously at night, it was received with little credence, but it was not long until a reputable lawyer, when pinned down, admitted that the inventor was his client and that it was a fact that the problem of aerial navigation had been solved. He stated that all that remained to be done before bringing the wonderful discovery to the full attention of the public was the perfection of small details, and that the mysterious nightly journeys were taken for the purpose of discovering and correcting weaknesses. After this admission the stories of the marvelous machine received more respectful attention, which the developments of the past week in Kansas have demonstrated they were entitled to.

THAT ELUSIVE AIRSHIP.

The Indianapolis Journal – April 5, 1897 – Indiana

The Mysterious Wanderer of the Heavens Last Seen in Illinois.

CHICAGO, April 4. – The Herald says: It was not to be supposed that the people of Nebraska and Kansas were long to have the monopoly of gazing on mysterious airships that soared into the heavens after dark and dazzled the wondering and awestruck spectators with their brilliant searchlights. But it was the general understanding that Indiana would next be chosen for the visitation because of the national reputation of the Chicago correspondents at Winamac, Anderson and Pink Mink Marsh. And now comes sober, cultured and conservative Evanston and gravely deposes that on the 3d day of April, A.D. 1897, at 8:40 p.m., a mysterious light, evidently that of an air ship, was seen passing rapidly over the city, going west-northwest. The light was very bright, more like an electric light than anything else, and gave out a curious sort of flash at intervals. It seemed to be about a quarter of a mile above the earth. At 8:55 it mounted high in the heavens and was rapidly lost to sight. The story is probably true, for the Evanstonian who reported it was afraid of being laughed at and declined to give his name.

SEEN BY KANSANS.

INDEPENDENCE, Kan., April 4. – The mysterious airship that has been seen at various points over Kansas and Nebraska and has recently caused so much comment, beyond a doubt paid southern Kansas a visit last night. It passed over the city at an early hour last night and was seen by many people whose veracity is beyond question. The strange ship appeared in the southeast about 8 o'clock. At first the persons who saw it thought it was a star, but it gradually came nearer and increased in brilliancy as it approached. It could be observed that it did not travel in a straight line, but darted first this way, then that, but always keeping in the same course. Suddenly it veered to the south, then turned and passed directly over the city, in a northerly direction.

When first observed it appeared very low, but as it approached it rose higher and higher and passed over this place at a considerable height and was traveling at a high rate of speed. After it had passed it again descended and for five minutes appeared perfectly stationary. Then it was set in motion, darting back and forth, up and down, and after a short interval continued on its journey and disappeared gradually in the northwest. It was about half an hour from the time it was first seen until it disappeared.

THE AIR SHIP.

The Manitowoc Pilot – April 15, 1897 – Wisconsin

If there is an airship it is ubiquitous or else the air is full of 'em. On Saturday night it was seen everywhere. It was in Green Bay, Manitowoc and Minneapolis. The people of Minneapolis viewed the thing from the tops of buildings having previously been notified by telegraph that it was headed that way. The lights are the same in each case, one white and one green. The outlines of the aerial navigator can be seen by some. Marshfield was particularly favored. The airship spent Saturday in the woods at that place. It rose after sundown "like a meteor," after having been kept in chains all day, no doubt. After good people had retired for the night the airship began to manifest itself at many places. It was seen in Manitowoc, moving in an erratic fashion. Though its appearance was simultaneous in various places, the direction of its movement was always different. It started for Minnesota but seems to have reached that place before it had got fairly under headway from the lake coast.

An amateur photographer photographed the thing near Chicago. The proof that he did so is that three "persons saw him do it." That, of course, puts that matter beyond dispute, just as the man who descended from the moon proved his claim by showing the rope by which he descended. The photograph is a good one, but experts say the negative was monkeyed with.

Several people in this city saw this denizen of the air on Saturday night. It must have failed to reach its destination, or else made a trip round the world in 24 hours, because it put in an appearance again on Sunday night. C.W. Giffey made some careful observations on Sunday night and is satisfied it was something else than a balloon or a star. He was skeptical to begin with but is now open to conviction.

SIGNS OF AN AIRSHIP EXPLOSION.

Dakota Farmers' Leader – April 23, 1897 – Minnesota

Citizens of Pavilion, Mich., Hear a Mysterious Noise.

Since the airship was seen by residents of Chicago reports from a large number of other points indicating that it has been seen by great numbers of persons have been received. The most startling report comes from Pavilion, Mich., where it is claimed that an airship, while passing over the town, exploded. Not only was the flash of an explosion seen, but the noise resulting was heard by a large number of reputable citizens.

The airship was traveling at a rapid rate, when there was a loud report, and the lights that had been visible at each end were extinguished. The machine disappeared, and, it is expected, was blown into atoms. Carpenters engaged in shingling a house beneath the point at which the ship was seen to explode assert that when they resumed work the following morning the roof was covered with innumerable particles that looked as though they had fallen from above during the night.

Telegrams from Madison, Wis., assert that several railroad men who have been at Baraboo recently are sure the airship was simply a circus advertising scheme. They believe it was controlled by cables and that it was in reality nothing more than something on the order of the stationary balloon that was seen at the World's Fair.

Reports from Macoupin County, Ill., however, say an airship has been seen at several points in the county, alighting at two places and resuming its journey when delegations started in the direction of the points where it alighted in order to inspect it. These reports say the ship traveled at the rate of thirty miles an hour at least, and that it seemed to be under complete control of those in charge of it. Other points at which an airship has been seen are Emporia, Kan., Wabash and Muncie, Ind., Perry, Okla., and Palmyra and Ripon, Wis.

THE LATEST.

Griggs Courier – April 30, 1897 – North Dakota

The mysterious airship came to earth last Sunday afternoon shortly before 6 o'clock and struck the shore of Lake Osakis near Buck point. The saloons here were of course closed all day and a large number of sober citizens witnessed the landing, and through their field glasses plainly discerned the mammoth air-boat which appeared to be shaped like a sugar beet or a Nonpareil cigar. The decks were alive with people who were busying themselves taking on tons of ice that had been blown up on the shore. It is conjectured that the ice was either for ballast or ice cream. The air ship was floating a peculiarly designed flag from the mast head, thought to be the national ensign of the Planet Mars. The men were of immense stature, probably 20 feet in height and wore ulsters. The women were extremely handsome and were attired in red bloomers. They appeared anxious to stop here. No lights were displayed. The air ship remained on earth less than 20 minutes when it started in a north-easterly direction traveling very rapidly and at least a quarter of a mile high.

– Osakis Review.

MYSTERY OF NIGHT FLIGHT OF AIRSHIP.

The San Francisco Call – September 27, 1908 – California

Berkley's Residents Are Puzzled by a Nocturnal Visitor in the Sky.

BERKELEY, Sept. 26. – Whether airship, balloon or what not, many residents of the college town were mystified last night by the appearance in the heavens of a dark, gliding object, at the end of which dangled a light. The mysterious visitor moved apparently 500 to 1,000 feet overhead and in a southerly direction.

In the darkness the form of the moving object could not be distinctly made out. If it was a balloon and carried occupants, it disappeared so rapidly that there was no way of ascertaining definitely. Many persons saw the moving light and speculated upon its appearance. There was a suggestion of mysterious airship experiments, but nothing was certain as to that theory. Rumor had it that L.H. Lane, a South Berkeley delver into the secrets of airship construction, was trying out a machine, but this was exploded upon inquiry. Lane declared that his model was in pieces, and besides was of the aeroplane type.

SAW A MYSTERIOUS AIRSHIP.

Abilene Weekly Reflector – August 19, 1909 – Kansas

A Train Crew Reports a Race of 12 Miles with One Near Peoria, Illinois.

Peoria, Ill., Aug. 12. – Conductor Watkins in charge of a work train on the Rock Island railroad and members of his crew report an exciting race with a mysterious airship from Chillicothe, Ill., to the city limits of Peoria, a distance of 12 miles. The ship appeared to be about 200 feet up in the air, bore lights on the front and rear and for several miles gave the train a lively race. Near Peoria, the ship took flight westward and disappeared over the bluffs. No one could be discerned on the craft, it being too dark, but the huge black body of the ship, which was described as cigar shaped, was plainly visible. It was apparently under perfect control.

AIRSHIP FLIGHT A DEEP MYSTERY.

Ottumwa Tri-Weekly Courier – December 25, 1909 – Iowa

AEROPLANE HOVERS OVER CITY OF WORCESTER THROWING POWERFUL SEARCHLIGHT.

Worcester, Mass., Dec. 23. – Flying at a speed of thirty to forty miles an hour, a mysterious airship last night appeared over Worcester, hovered over the city a few minutes, disappeared for about two hours and then returned, to cut four circles above the gaping city, meanwhile using a searchlight of unusual power.

Thousands of persons thronged the streets to watch the mysterious visitor. The airship remained over the city for about fifteen minutes, all the time at a height that most of the observers set at about 2,000 feet, too far to enable even its precise shape to be seen.

The glaring raps of its great searchlight, however, were sharply defined by reflection against the light snowfall which was covering the city at the time. The dark mass of the ship could be dimly seen behind the light.

After a time, it disappeared in the direction of Marlborough, only to return later.

At the time of the airship's visit, Wallace E. Tillinghast, the Worcester man who recently claimed to have invented a marvelous aeroplane, in which he said he journeyed to New York and returned by way of Boston, was absent from his home and could not be located.

MYSTERY AND SPECULATION OVER SMETHPORT, PA., AIRSHIP.

The West Virginian – July 20, 1915 – West Virginia

SMETHPORT, Pa., July 20. – That some inventor has chosen the sparsely settled section of Norther Pennsylvania to try out a dirigible not unlike the Zeppelin is the only explanation given of the unusual appearance in this vicinity of a cigar shaped airship which has hovered over this vicinity in the small hours of the morning for several days. The ship was seen by a large number of persons last night.

At first it was thought that agents of the German government had induced someone to make an attack on the Emporium Explosives Company plant and that the ship was kept in hiding in the hills near here awaiting an opportune time of attack when the big mills were completed.

In all its flights, however, though Emporiumites have been alarmed and have been watching, the airship has not appeared over that village or the power works nearby.

For several days past the guard about the Emporium mill has been particularly active but all denied any fear of an attack.

Campers who have selected a site outside Smethport, about eight miles over Bush Hill, where the dirigible was first seen by Smethport people, say that the searchlight of the giant ship has repeatedly been thrown on their tents. In the party were Mr. and Mrs. Bernard Garlick, who both say they saw the airship. Scott Walker, a well-known glass blower, says he has seen the dirigible plainly toward dawn, the whirring of the motors on one occasion being perceptible as the machine flew about 1,000 feet high. Hiram Bockus, another Smethport man, has seen it and heard it.

INDEX

SOURCE NEWSPAPERS BY LOCATION

ABOUT THE RESEARCHER

Adam Benedict, a native Wisconsinite, is a designer by trade and a researcher by choice. Drawn to the weird at a young age thanks to the likes of Robert Stack and Leonard Nimoy, Benedict has spent a good portion of his life studying up on the weirder parts of history. Realizing that the knowledge he had gained might be of some interest to others, Benedict founded The Pine Barrens Institute in 2015. Since its creation, The PBI has become a well-received online gathering point for general Midwest Strangeness.

When not spending countless hours reading through old folk tales and yellowed newspapers in hopes of finding that next weird story to write about, Benedict spends his time with his wife, their four kids, and the family dogs. Sometimes though, this family time also ends up swaying towards the weirder side of things. Every so often, lazy family day trips end up inside old forgotten cemeteries, on stretches of road thought to be the stomping ground of a monster or driving around searching for lakes said to be the dwelling place of horrible creatures.

CRYPTIDS - FOLKLORE - SIGHTINGS
PINEBARRENSINSTITUTE.COM

OTHER AVAILABLE TITLES IN THIS SERIES:

Ghosts In Print: An Assemblage of Spirits, Spooks, & Specters From Newspapers of Old

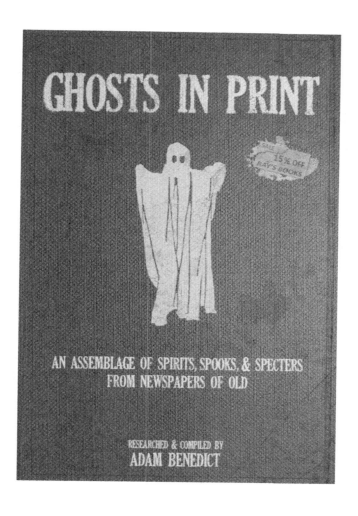

Made in the USA
Monee, IL
08 November 2020

47034481R00246